Springer Education Innovation Book Series

For further volumes:
http://www.springer.com/series/10092

Springer Education Innovation Book Series

Education holds the key to unlock human resources that a society needs to survive and flourish. This is particularly salient in a borderless knowledge economy. For the past decades, the sterling performance of economies such as Hong Kong, Finland, Japan, Singapore and Taiwan in international studies (e.g. TIMSS, PIRLS and PISA) has channeled much attention away from the traditional centers of education research in America and Western Europe. Researchers, policy makers and practitioners all over the world wish to understand how education innovations propel the emerging systems from good to great to excellent, and how different their trajectories were compared to the systems in America and Western Europe.

The Education Innovation Book Series, published by Springer, will delve into education innovations enacted by the Singapore education system and situate them in both the local and the boarder international contexts. Primary focus will be given to pedagogy and classroom practices; education policy formulation and implementation; school and instructional leadership; and the context and interface between education research, policy and practice. We believe that the latter is critical in making education innovations come to bear. Each volume will document insights and lessons learned based on empirical research (both quantitative and qualitative) and theoretical analyses. Implications to research, policy and professional practice will be surfaced through comparing and synthesizing Singapore's experience with those of successful systems around the world.

The audience of the edited volumes and monographs published in this series includes researchers, policy makers, practitioners and students in the fields of education and teacher education, and public policies related to learning and human resources.

Sing Kong Lee • Wing On Lee • Ee Ling Low
Editors

Educational Policy Innovations

Levelling Up and Sustaining Educational Achievement

Springer

Editors
Sing Kong Lee
National Institute of Education
Nanyang Technological University
Singapore, Singapore

Wing On Lee
National Institute of Education
Nanyang Technological University
Singapore, Singapore

Ee Ling Low
National Institute of Education
Nanyang Technological University
Singapore, Singapore

ISSN 2211-4874 ISSN 2211-4882 (electronic)
ISBN 978-981-4560-07-8 ISBN 978-981-4560-08-5 (eBook)
DOI 10.1007/978-981-4560-08-5
Springer Singapore Heidelberg New York Dordrecht London

Printed on acid-free paper

Springer is part of Springer Science+Business Media (www.springer.com)

Series Editors' Foreword

We are very pleased to present you this pioneer volume of the *Springer Education Innovation* (SEI) Book Series – *Educational Policy Innovations: Levelling up and Sustaining Educational Achievement*, edited by Sing Kong Lee, Wing On Lee and Ee Ling Low.

This Series aims to record the educational innovations that have taken place in the Singapore education system over the last 40 years. The Series will provide a wide spectrum of analyses on pedagogy and classroom practices; education policy formulation and implementation; school and instructional leadership; and the context and interface between education research, policy and practice which make these innovations possible. Complementary notions of teacher education are also analysed and interpreted in the context of the educational system.

Changes in education policy, education and organisational structure, teacher education, school management, curriculum, instruction and assessment over the last 30 years have contributed to the sharp rise in the quality of education since the 1980s. While Singapore's successes are notable, the process, reasons and factors that have contributed to the process towards success have, as yet, not been systematically captured in a comprehensive manner. The book series aims to fill the gap by analysing various aspects of education innovations in Singapore, drawing on knowledge and research done both internationally and locally, highlighting how Singapore has successfully mobilised resources and efforts to improve learning and teaching across the various subject disciplines and education sectors. The Series will compare and synthesise the Singapore experience with the wider international experience.

True to this spirit, this first volume will kick-start the Series and is a rich resource for policymakers, educators and teacher educators who wish to gain a greater insight of high performing education systems (HPES) – defined as those systems that have gained international attention for their successful implementation of innovative educational policies that have both raised and sustained educational achievement. This is also one of the pioneering books that have approached this topic from an introspective insiders' approach. This volume begins with a discussion of educational policy and planning and teacher education that aims to strengthen the education system, and goes on to provide a discussion on the equity and quality issues in HPES. The volume will then include a series of country case chapters authored by renowned scholars and educators from HPES. The volume will be concluded by a comparative analysis of a common feature in these HPES where the teacher, teaching and teacher education are taken very seriously in these systems.

The volume is designed as a platform for dialogue between policymakers and scholars, thus including authors who are both from within HPES and outside them. Andreas Schleicher's and A. Lin Goodwin's chapters have offered their valuable insights, looking at the various significant issues such as education and economics and employment, the issues of equity and quality, and the significance of teachers. Goodwin particularly cautions that we should not look at teachers' workload just from the perspective of working hours, particularly implying that working longer hours need not be a critical factor for success. Interestingly, instead of celebrating success, HPES are generally critical about their own systems, choosing instead to use a self-reflective lens to interpret the successes but also to identify the potential challenges that lie ahead. The book provides a valuable perspective in that while many countries are somewhat alarmed by the success of HPES, those from within are keenly aware of their own weaknesses and quick to identify potential challenges that lie ahead in the continued sustainability of their success. Perhaps it is such self-reflection and constructive criticism that is behind the ability not just to achieve success in the first place, but to ensure that the success attained, thus far, is sustainable in the longer run.

National Institute of Education
Nanyang Technological University, Singapore

Wing On Lee
David Wei Loong Hung
Laik Woon Teh

Foreword

Why is it that Finland, Canada and Singapore do so well on international tests on student achievement in schools while Australia, the United States and the United Kingdom do not? Why is it that Denmark, Norway and Sweden, which invest more heavily in schools and have very similar social policies, rank considerably lower than a country like Finland, which traditionally has been looked upon as more economically backward and culturally isolated than its Nordic neighbours? Why has Singapore skyrocketed past its contiguous neighbours on international tests while other nations in its region have had far greater natural resources to boost their economies and their schools?

Some educators (Hopmann, Brinek, & Retzel, 2007; Spring, 2011; Zhao, 2009) are sceptical of international comparisons such as the Programme for International Student Assessment (PISA) of the Organisation for Economic Co-operation and Development (OECD). These scholars argue that cultural and linguistic differences among peoples are too large to develop objective measures of learning. Others (Braun, 2013; Solano-Flores, Contreras-Niño, & Backhoff, 2013) value the information that the tests can provide, but worry that they are misinterpreted by policymakers and the public, who tend to focus on the relatively crude postings in the rankings rather than corresponding score differences and who are not aware of other distortions in results. Finally, still others (Carnoy & Rothstein, 2013; Levin, 2013) contend that the tests are subject to sampling errors and they overemphasise cognitive skills at the expense of non-cognitive orientations.

All of these concerns are important. But even if they are imperfect instruments – all human artefacts, alas, are tainted with imperfection – we can learn much from the findings of various international assessments generated by PISA, the Trends in International Math and Science Studies (TIMSS), and the Programme in International Reading and Literacy Survey (PIRLS). Likewise, we can also learn from the interpretations of the data provided by international consultancies such as McKinsey & Company (Barber & Mourshed, 2007; Mourshed, Chijoke, Barber, & McKinsey & Company, 2010) and think-tanks like the National Center on Education and the Economy (Tucker, 2011) in the USA. These have taken the necessary first steps to aggregate nations into sectors and to establish criteria for lifting schools from one sector to the next. Finally, interpretations by independent scholars (Darling-Hammond, 2010; Hargreaves & Shirley, 2009, 2012; Wagner, 2008) who raise questions about the strengths and weakness of the tests also enrich our on-going journey in policy learning across provinces, states and nations.

However, as the editors of this outstanding new anthology indicate, up to the present moment one perhaps paradoxical phenomenon of international educational change has been that high-achieving jurisdictions have been collectively quiet on the reasons for their achievement. It may be the case that a certain shared culture of modesty and reluctance to grandstand contributes to a focus on what needs to be learnt next rather than the vices of boasting and bragging. In general, the sources of much of the testing data have been located geographically outside of high-achieving regions – for example, with OECD in Paris, McKinsey & Company in London, and NCEE in Washington, DC.

This anthology offers an important contrast to the prevailing orthodoxy. Scholars based predominantly in Singapore, Hong Kong, Shanghai and South Korea have examined their own school systems to investigate the riddle of their top-level achievement on international assessments. Simultaneously, they have solicited contributions from other top scholars for commentaries. Andreas Schleicher of the OECD, Ben Levin of Ontario, Canada, Hannele Niemi from Finland, and A. Lin Goodwin from the USA provide additional lenses for understanding the preconditions and supports needed for optimal student learning. The net effect is to acquire a kaleidoscope of rich and variegated interpretations that reinforce the message that a common set of policies and values promote high achievement. Educators, political leaders and the public should be sure to read through the chapters carefully and repeatedly and consider deeply the implications on their own students and schools.

The overall message is bracing and perhaps shocking for many contemporary school reformers. Systems such as Singapore have paid exquisite attention to the development and sustainability of an educational profession that is anchored systemically in the Ministry of Education, in the National Institute of Education at Nanyang Technological University, and in the schools themselves. Educators move within and across these three sectors of the system continuously, promoting incessant communication among all components of the profession and ensuring that research enriches practice. Innovation is valued, but not fetishised; there is a stubborn persistence in focusing on building a strong system first and foremost. While marketplace values saturate Singaporean society, there is abundant space within and across schools for continual collaboration, so that what competition does exist is supplemented with a collective professional ethic of learning and sharing across schools.

The authors of this volume do not pretend that Singapore or other high-achieving systems have achieved all of the answers in the international quest for optimal and persistent learning. The political discourse on education in Singapore is officially one that is moving into a 'student-centric, values-driven' phase in its educational development. However, like other East Asian school systems, there still appears to be a strong and perhaps excessive emphasis on test score results, though clear initiatives are in place to explore other forms of assessment. These should inform and enhance the teaching and learning processes in order to promote a more holistic consideration of student learning outcomes through a discourse of '21st century competencies' as described in the chapter by Sing Kong Lee and Ee Ling Low of the National Institute of Education. While increasing work is undertaken in regard to teacher inquiry and research, it is not clear that teachers have, or know how to occupy, a cultural space in which they could have informed and spirited professional arguments with one another. On the other hand, the system has had considerable success in recent years in expanding extracurricular offerings and encouraging schools to develop themed identities that can work against systemic uniformity and consequent anonymity.

All of this fits into a broader analysis of the Singapore 'miracle'. Like Hong Kong and Finland, Singapore has shown us that high achievement is entirely compatible with a small population and few natural resources. Still, understanding the myriad of factors that support that high achievement requires careful investigation and skilful critique lest one isolates contingent rather than essential phenomena and misapplies their lessons in other settings. For this reason alone, the present volume represents a superlative new contribution to the international literature on high achievement. Read on, for a richly rewarding experience awaits you!

Lynch School of Education, Dennis Shirley
Boston College, Chestnut Hill, MA, USA

References

Barber, M., & Mourshed, M. (2007). *How the world's best-performing school systems come out on top*. New York: McKinsey & Company.

Braun, H. (2013). Prospects for the future: A framework and discussion of directions for the next generation of international large-scale assessments. In M. von Davier, E. Gonzalez, I. Kirsch, & K. Yamamoto (Eds.), *The role of international large-scale assessments: Perspectives from technology, economy, and educational research* (pp. 149–160). Dordrecht, The Netherlands: Springer.

Carnoy, M., & Rothstein, R. (2013). *What do international tests really show about U.S. student performance?* Washington, DC: Economic Policy Institute.

Darling-Hammond, L. (2010). *The flat world and education: How America's commitment to equality will determine our future*. New York: Teachers College Press.

Hargreaves, A., & Shirley, D. (2009). *The fourth way: The inspiring future for educational change*. Thousand Islands, CA: Corwin.

Hargreaves, A., & Shirley, D. (2012). *The global fourth way: The quest for educational excellence*. Thousand Islands, CA: Corwin.

Hopmann, S. T., Brinek, G., & Retzl, M. (2007). *PISA zufolge PISA (PISA According to PISA)*. Vienna: LIT.

Levin, H. M. (2013). The utility and need for incorporating noncognitive skills into large-scale educational assessments. In M. von Davier, E. Gonzalez, I. Kirsch, & K. Yamamoto (Eds.), *The role of international large-scale assessments: Perspectives from technology, economy, and educational research* (pp. 67–86). Dordrecht, The Netherlands: Springer.

Mourshed, M., Chijioke, C., Barber, M., & McKinsey & Company. (2010). *How the world's best-performing school systems keep getting better*. New York: McKinsey & Company.

Solano-Flores, G., Conreras-Niño, L. A., & Backhoff, E. (2013). The measurement of translation error in PISA-2006 items: An application of the theory of test translation error. In M. Prenzel, M. Kobarg, K. Schöps, & S. Rönnebeck (Eds.), *Research on PISA: Research outcomes of the PISA research conference 2009* (pp. 71–36). Dordrecht, The Netherlands: Springer.

Spring, J. (2011). *The politics of American education*. New York: Routledge.

Tucker, M. S. (2011). *Surpassing Shanghai: An agenda for American education built on the world's leading systems*. Cambridge: Harvard Education Press.

Wagner, T. (2008). *The global achievement gap*. New York: Basic Books.

Zhao, Y. (2009). *Catching up or leading the way: American education in the age of globalization*. Alexandria, VA: ASCD.

Contents

Chapter 1
Introduction: Levelling Up and Sustaining Educational Achievement

Sing Kong Lee, Wing On Lee, Ee Ling Low, and Jocelyn Shi Yah Tan

Introduction

With the emergence of university ranking exercises such as the Quacquarelli Symonds (QS) University World University Rankings, Shanghai Jiaotong Academic Ranking of World Universities, Times Higher Education's World University Ranking, and Ranking Web of World Universities (Webometrics), there is an undeniable contest and competition amongst universities to outperform each other in the various dimensions measured by these ranking indices. This ranking 'syndrome' is not limited to the higher education sector. Recent internationally benchmarked tests of student achievement, such as the Organisation for Economic Co-operation and Development (OECD), Programme for International Student Assessment (PISA), the Trends in International Mathematics and Science Study (TIMSS), and the Progress in International Reading and Literacy (PIRLS) have attracted worldwide scrutiny as diverse student performance scores of the same age cohorts call into question the notion of what contributes or hinders student achievement scores across different education systems. Educational policy issues related to equity, quality, effectiveness and efficiency in educational budget as a proportion of the country's Gross Domestic Product (GDP) are examples of factors raised to account for the varied educational performance across participating countries in these tests.

S.K. Lee
Director's Office, National Institute of Education, 1 Nanyang Walk,
Singapore 637616, Singapore
e-mail: singkong.lee@nie.edu.sg

W.O. Lee • J.S.Y. Tan
National Institute of Education, 1 Nanyang Walk, Singapore 637616, Singapore
e-mail: wingon.lee@nie.edu.sg; jocelyn.tan@nie.edu.sg

E.L. Low
Office of Teacher Education, National Institute of Education, 1 Nanyang Walk,
Singapore 637616, Singapore
e-mail: eeling.low@nie.edu.sg

S.K. Lee et al. (eds.), *Educational Policy Innovations: Levelling Up and Sustaining Educational Achievement*, Springer Education Innovation Book Series 1,
DOI 10.1007/978-981-4560-08-5_1, © Springer Science+Business Media Singapore 2014

The countries that consistently emerged top of the ranking league across these numerous internationally benchmarked tests were Finland, Singapore, Hong Kong SAR, South Korea, Japan, Chinese Taipei and recently Shanghai, China. The fact that an overwhelming number of high performing systems are geographically in East Asia has prompted governments and their policymakers to flock to these countries to find out exactly what the 'secret' formula or formulae are that help these nations to achieve educational success as measured by high student achievement scores. The triumph that these East Asian systems have forged in the educational arena may be analogised by the economic miracle of the 1980s created by Asia's 'Four Tigers', that is, Chinese Taipei, Hong Kong SAR, Singapore and South Korea. These successful jurisdictions has been variously described as 'top performing', 'high performing' and 'best performing' education systems (Low, 2012; Mourshed, Chijioke, & Barber, 2010), strong performers and successful performers (Organisation for Economic Co-operation and Development [OECD], 2011), and/or the world's leading education systems (Tucker, 2011). In this volume, we have decided to use the term *high performing education systems* (HPES) because we feel that it veers away from the concept that there is a 'top' performing education system as the latter begs the further question of what really counts as a top performing system vis-à-vis its ranking. An important aim of this volume is not just to tease out the success factors of the countries selected to be featured in it but the more important consideration of how educational achievement is sustained. Higher educational performance that is sustained is under focus here and equally important is the question of how high performing systems help to level up performance of their low performers, that is, how they level out the performance of the so-called 'tail'. Issues of equity, equality, efficiency and quality come into the interplay in the quest for not just educational success and ultimately, in ensuring its sustainability.

Success Factors

The United States first commissioned a meta-analysis for identifying 'factors for success' from the high performing countries. The result of this analysis is the OECD (2011) report entitled *Strong Performers and Successful Performers in Education: Lessons from the PISA for the United States*. Several common themes emerged from the analysis of high performing education systems:

- Developing a commitment to education and a conviction that all students can achieve at high levels
- Establishing ambitious, focused and coherent education standards that are shared across the system and aligned with high-stakes gateways and instructional systems
- Developing more capacity at the point of delivery
- Providing a work organisation in which teachers can use their potential: management, accountability and knowledge management
- Institutionalising improved instructional practice
- Aligning incentive structures and engaging stakeholders

- Complementing accountability to agents outside schools with accountability professional colleagues and parents
- Investing resources where they can make the most difference
- Balancing local responsibility with a capable centre with authority and legitimacy to act
- The importance of workplace training to facilitate school-to-work transitions
- Ensuring coherence of policies and practices, aligning policies across all aspects of the system, establishing coherence of policies over sustained periods of time and securing consistency of implementation
- Ensuring an outwards orientation of the system to keep the system evolving, and to recognise challenges and potential future threats to current success

Another report by Marc Tucker (2011) has drawn out almost the same observation in terms of the success factors for high performing education systems:

- Aggressive international benchmarking
- A quality teaching force
- Use of aligned instructional systems and external examinations that measure complex thinking skills
- Deciding to get all students to those standards
- Use of professional systems of work organisation instead of blue-collar models
- Funding systems that put the most funds behind the students who are hardest to educate
- Coherence in the design of the overall education system itself

In 2012, the Grattan Institute published a report entitled *Catching Up: Learning from the Best School Systems in East Asia* (Jensen, 2012). The report identified some success factors for HPES, such as:

- High equity
- Effective learning and teaching
- Connecting policy to classroom learning
- Focus on best practices
- Focus on initial teacher education
- Emphasis on induction and mentoring
- Emphasis on school principal education
- Developing teacher groups for research and classroom observation
- Having career structures for teachers

The vision for developing this volume was built upon our observation that many efforts have recently been made to look into the success factors of high performing systems. However, interestingly, all these reports and treatise are authored mainly by those outside the high performing systems being discussed and analysed. The high performing systems have been staying relatively quiet and rather modest and cautious about, first of all, being labelled as a high performing system, and next, about what are the secrets to this so-called success. In fact, if one has the opportunity to attend international summits or symposia where some of these high performing nations are represented, what you tend to hear is more about self-reflection and self-critique about what else needs to be done, rather than a spirit of self-applause or celebration. Perhaps then one of the driving factors for the high performing systems is this high degree of self-reflection and self-critique that drives these systems to keep on improving themselves, leading to not just sustaining but even achieving newer peaks of educational attainment.

Insider–Outsider Dialogue on Education Success: Emergent and Emerging Themes

Being one of the 'insiders' among the high performing systems, the National Institute of Education (NIE), NTU in Singapore wished to break the ice and called for a roundtable symposium. This was in hope that a frank discussion could take place between Finland and the other high performing countries in East Asia with the key goals of answering questions of what contributed to their performance and what other lessons needed to be learnt if these systems wanted to sustain and even scale new peaks of performance. The call was responded to very favourably, and a symposium took place in April 2012, attended by Hannele Niemi from Finland, Youngdal Cho from South Korea, Esther Ho from Hong Kong SAR, and Laik Woon Teh from Singapore. In addition, A. Lin Goodwin from Teachers College, Columbia kindly accepted our invitation to participate and present her views about the lessons that the United States had for and from these systems. Ruth Hayhoe from Canada, as an expert in comparative education, also kindly agreed to participate and moderate the discussion. This forum was first published in NIE's *CJ Koh Professorial Lecture Series*, entitled *Portraits of Top-Performing Education Systems* (Low, 2012). The feedback for this special issue has been more than overwhelming, leading us to think that we have to further expand this work to be published with a more academic focus as a monograph. Once again, we have received warm and enthusiastic support from our authors. Andreas Schleicher from OECD, Ben Levin from the University of Toronto, Minxuan Zhang, Jinjie Xu and Chuangyuan Sun from Shanghai Normal University accepted our invitation to contribute to this volume, so that the volume can cover broader perspectives from even more systems and will, we hope, become a seminal reference for international dialogue on issues related to educational success and sustainability.

The reflection from the various insiders who have authored this volume is telling, indeed. As mentioned, none of the authors from the high performing systems really reported about how they became so-called successful. Conversely, they talked about the major issues confronting their education systems, and perhaps from this perspective, if there is a lesson to be drawn from them, a high performing education system is one that actually continuously critiques its own system, and continuously seeks creative solutions to solve anticipated challenges ahead. Nonetheless, certain common themes emerged from the chapters and we have delineated them into five major themes which we hope can offer a useful insight into what contributes to and sustains educational success and performance.

Taking Teachers and Teacher Education Seriously

First, all high performing countries take the issue of ensuring and sustaining a high quality teaching workforce and the preparation of pre-service teachers via teacher education and teacher professional development very seriously. Chapter 13 by Wing On Lee later in this volume covers this issue in great depth but this introductory chapter will highlight key features across the systems covered in this volume.

The Teacher Factor

Schleicher (Chap. 3 in this volume) in his chapter 'Developing Educational Policies in a Holistic Skills Framework' raises the macro issue of skills development within a society and how people need to continually possess relevant skills and continually learn to ensure that they possess skills that are valuable. To ensure that education and developmental programmes, even till adulthood, are of high quality and relevant in preparing people for the workforce, he emphasises the importance of the teacher factor and the quality of the teaching profession:

> Teaching must be valued as a profession so that the best are recruited and the most effective teachers are retained.

The importance of teachers is further emphasised in the contribution from the United States where Goodwin (Chap. 11 in this volume) singles out three major lessons that "have universal application and sit at the heart of meaningful education reform and excellent teaching". Out of the three 'lessons' that Goodwin highlights, two are centred around teachers and teacher education:

- Lesson One: Teaching as a high quality profession – Attracting, retaining and sustaining quality
- Lesson Two: Teachers as professionals at the centre of educational reform, Improvement and accountability

In reflecting on the link between Singapore's language policy and its educational success, Low (Chap. 6 in this volume) detailed how teacher selection from the point of view of language competence is viewed as an important gateway in the selection process. From upholding a strict language competency entry criteria to a comprehensive English language teacher preparation programme to English language teacher professional development, Low provides us with a glimpse into how Singapore has intentionally selects, trains and develops her teachers to be not just proficient users of the English language but also be able to teach and pass on this competency and proficiency to their students. In the Shanghai and Singapore chapters, the authors have also detailed how the teacher education programme, career progression and continual professional development within their systems have provided them with high quality teaching workforce.

In the case of Shanghai, the Teacher Qualification Certificate System (TQCS) which was introduced in October 2001 stipulates that all teacher candidates must undergo basic pre-service professional training and must pass three tests in the areas of pedagogy, educational psychology and teaching methods. Basic educational levels of teachers at different levels of the school system are also carefully stipulated in order to ensure quality as far as teachers' academic backgrounds are concerned. For example, teachers teaching in junior secondary schools and upwards must possess at least a Bachelor's degree. The purpose of the TQCS is not just to ensure quality in selection and preparation, but also a means to raise the social status of teachers. Since the introduction of TQCS, the percentage of teachers with at least a Bachelor's degree or above in the Shanghai workforce has been steadily and rapidly on the rise, and it is fair to state that the new bar for entering teaching has been raised to candidates who have at least a Bachelor's degree and who have undergone some form of pre-service teacher education programme or professional training.

Levin (Chap. 12 in this volume) in his chapter describes how the Ontario government carries out its sustainable, large-scale educational reform and singles out increasing the salary for its staff as the largest proportion of its funds allocation "so that it can attract and retain good people". The Ontario government has also prioritised its spending in areas of expanding staffing in various critical areas including employing specialist teachers in primary schools to heighten preparation time, and has enhanced specific professional development for its teachers. Consequently, surveys reported that fewer teachers are choosing early retirement and leaving the profession and these are also indicators of improved teacher morale.

High quality teaching and learning outcomes were built on the foundation of a coherent system, professional practice and high quality training. Top talents aspire to teach in South Korea with high prestige, respect and job security associated with the teaching profession (see Cho, Chap. 8 in this volume). South Koreans believe that good outcomes derive from good teaching practices, which are conducted by good teachers, and therefore teachers are the cornerstone of their education system.

Teacher Education

Rigorous and carefully thought through pre-service teacher education programmes also feature strongly in the higher performing systems. W. O. Lee (Chap. 13 in this volume) has devoted his entire chapter on the discussion of teachers, teaching and teacher education, evaluating the self-analysis of various HPES which surfaced a common emphasis on teachers and teacher education. Teacher education in these countries is a highly rigorous and systematically conceptualised endeavour. In the case of Shanghai, teacher education in the 1980s were delivered mainly through normal universities and colleges for the preparation of senior and junior secondary school teachers and through normal secondary school for primary and kindergarten teachers. However, since 1995, as a result of a regulation implemented by the Shanghai municipal government, students who used to undergo training in normal secondary schools were transferred to normal colleges and universities instead. Teacher education for pre-school teachers took place within the faculty of pre-school and special education in East China University and later on the Faculty of Education within Shanghai Normal University while primary school teacher education took place within Shanghai Normal University. Significantly, today, pre-service teacher education in Shanghai has been successfully upgraded to university-based programmes for teachers of all levels. Additionally, tuition fees are waived via student grants for 200 student teachers at Shanghai Normal University and for 150 student teachers at East China Normal University.

The Finnish teacher education programme described by Niemi (Chap. 7 in this volume) stands out worldwide because by the time teachers step into the profession, they each have a Master's degree. The Finnish teacher education programmes have also a strong research focus which exposes student teachers to both qualitative and quantitative research methods. The research-based focus aims to allow student teachers to be able to reflect and analyse the problems they might encounter when they enter the profession through doing their own research. The thesis component within the pre-service programmes requires student teachers to formulate their own research questions in an educational context, to collect, analyse and write up their findings and implications of their research coherently in the form of a thesis. The underpinning goals of the research-intensive, inquiry-based teacher education programme is documented by Niemi. To summarise, the belief is that teachers require knowledge of the latest research in the discipline that they are to teach and about teaching and learning. Interdisciplinary research in both subject and pedagogical content knowledge helps provide the firm foundation required to innovate teaching methods for differentiated instruction. Teacher education itself is seen to be worthy of being the subject of much research since we should find out how effective and high quality teacher education can be implemented in different cultural settings.

Teacher Professional Development

In several of the chapters, teacher professional development is mentioned and is certainly not left to grow organically in an ad-hoc manner but is planned, conceptualised and implemented at a systemic level. Low (Chap. 6 in this volume) talked about the three career pathways that have been developed by the Ministry of Education in Singapore, namely the teaching, leadership and specialist tracks. These pathways ensure that teachers can develop according to their strengths as identified by themselves in consultation with their reporting officers. Paid professional development of 100 h per year is given as an entitlement to each teacher while paid higher degree opportunities tenable locally or abroad are made possible via the Professional Development Continuum Model (PDCM).

In Shanghai, Zhang et al. (Chap. 9 in this volume) state that school-based teacher professional development is important and has several different foci and formats of delivery, such as mentoring for new teachers, teaching and research groups, lesson preparation groups, grade groups, classroom observation and evaluation, task-driven training and vacation training, and school visits. The aim of all these activities is to allow teachers to grow together in groups to form professional learning communities and to provide opportunities for peer collaboration and mentorship. The Teaching Research Groups have been talked about in the OECD report (2011), and its main aim is to allow new teachers to improve their teaching skills through mentorship and guidance from their more experienced colleagues. Classroom observations and peer reviews are used as common tools for discussion and mentoring. Occasionally, new teachers are even asked to deliver public demonstration lessons for other teachers to observe and comment on their performance. These activities are held on a bi-monthly basis and it is important to note the structure and organisation of such professional development activities in Shanghai. As a result of the success of such professional development platforms, teaching and research are now regarded by teachers in Shanghai as part of their professional routine of activities. Gang (2010, as cited in Chap. 9 in this volume) documented that at least 87.6 % of teachers surveyed participated in teaching and research activities at least once a week and only 2.3 % reported that they did not participate in such activities at all.

In Hong Kong, teacher's autonomy over school-based problems and subsequently solutions in a shared approach (in discussion with the school-leadership) are stated to be the reasons that instruction and assessment continually impact learning outcomes positively (see Chap. 10 in this volume).

In Finland, "the core of the teaching profession relies on teachers' research ability" (Niemi, Chap. 7 in this volume). The influence that Finnish teachers have on their country's performance is their contribution to research. This has helped to continually shape and improve their education system over time.

This section has underscored the importance of the teacher factor, a strong and deeply conceptualised and contextualised teacher education programme, and a systematic and highly organised professional development at the systemic level to be key drivers for success in the high performing education systems surveyed in this volume.

Bottom-Line, Tail-End Performance Matters

The next theme that emerged about HPES is that they are all focus on the performers not just at the top of their performing spectrum, but also those who are struggling at the bottom, sometimes called the 'tail'.

Schleicher (Chap. 3 in this volume) paints the picture of a society that aggregates its limited resources to prioritise the skill-sets of its citizens across governmental bodies, combining short-term and long-term goals, and inculcating the importance of lifelong learning that is inclusive across all strata of society. Schleicher contrasts it to the current situation where many people do not possess the required skills for the economy. These individuals with the lowest level of foundational skills are reported to be 1.8 times more likely to face unemployment, 1.4 times more likely to be facing health problems and 1.5 times more likely to have low levels of trust compared to those who possess the highest of foundational skills (see footnote 2 of Chap. 3 for the definition of foundational skills). With such realistic circumstances at hand, HPES are very concerned with those who struggle – the bottom-liners or tail-end performers – and have been very intentional in their efforts to level them up.

Teh (Chap. 5 in this volume) provides us with an insightful perspective as he dissects the PISA trends and accounted for Singapore's long tail of 'under-performing' students. He clearly typifies the introspective nature that one takes when accounting for reasons to account for 'failure'. Upon closer examination of the data collated in PISA 2009, he made a keen observation that Singapore ranked relatively lower in 5th percentile scores and higher in mean minus lower-5th percentile scores consistently in the three domains of reading, mathematics and science, implying that under-performers in Singapore perform better than under-performers from other systems. He also observed that close to 60 % of students who took the test do not speak the language of assessment at home, suggesting that 'diverse home language patterns among Singaporean students' may have contributed to the longer 'tail'. Being an insider, he recounts Singapore's turbulent historical and political past, and struggle with the language policy in its initial years to explain the phenomenon in Singapore. Teh devotes a section of his chapter to describe the efforts of the government to level up academically low-achieving students. From delivering a lower primary curriculum that focuses on literacy, to providing a differentiated curriculum that caters to academically low-achieving students, and to implementing early intervention programmes and setting up specialised schools for academically weaker students, the Singapore government has spared no efforts to level up the 'under-performing' students, ensuring that these students are definitely not left behind.

Finland builds its education system upon the pillars of uniformity, to provide free education, free school meals and special needs education. Inclusion has been a guiding principle for all students within the Finnish education systems, setting the same goals while maintaining realistic expectations for individuals to attain various levels of success, "providing extra support for the weakest students" to raise the overall performance of the cohort (Niemi, Chap. 7 in this volume). It is mandatory that all students with learning difficulties or challenges are provided with extra help or support to overcome their challenges. This may come in the form of extra lessons, special needs instruction within their classes, or temporary or permanent aids in special classes. In 2011, a decree was passed that every teacher is responsible for identifying students with learning difficulties as early as possible. This has deepened the responsibility of teachers to solve the problems faced by these students collectively, and has raised the importance of helping those who struggle academically.

Efforts has also been made in Ontario to ensure that additional funding has gone to small and isolated schools to expand their assistance plans towards students. Under Ontario's Literacy and Numeracy Strategy, sustainable and meaningful change in teaching and learning practices in Ontario's primary schools target key under-performing groups of students including "minority students, English as a second language (ESL) students, students in special education, aboriginal students and boys" (Levin, Chap. 12 in this volume). In areas of greatest need in high school, class sizes were reduced for students who need extra help. The Ontario government is committed to provide resources to support better outcomes for all students through its funding programme.

South Korea faces a very different set of problems when it comes to deal with low performers. In the South Korean society, parents strive to provide their children with the 'advantage' over their peers. This phenomenon, known as the 'shadow education', is widespread across the nation, and students from families who cannot afford (the best) private tutoring are academically disadvantaged. This problem is so severe that the government has to intervene at various levels including the prohibition of illegal private tutoring practices, and the equalisation of school resources to prevent inequality among schools.

Equity and Quality

In the discussion about ensuring and sustaining educational attainment in HPES, undeniably, the issues of equity and quality for all have become a focal point for discussion. Only when a high quality education has been provided for all can equity within the system be said to have been reached. The real challenge to each system, then, is how to strike a balance between the two and to achieve both quality and equity at the same time.

Niemi (Chap. 7 in this volume) describes how equity and quality are connected in the Finnish educational system. Her chapter describes a brief history of the Finnish comprehensive school and how equity has become the most important value throughout the system. The Finnish system aims to support learners to become active agents in their daily lives and in the society as a whole. Values related to lifelong learning are important at all levels of the educational system. In order to connect equity and lifelong learning the educational system needs to be very flexible and learners must be able to continue schooling at any stage of their lives. The chapter also introduces the major tools for keeping up the quality in the system. The national decision has been to use all evaluations for improvements, not ranking. This enhancement-led principle is connected with local responsibility to design school-based curricula and implementation of the national core curricula. There is no national achievement testing. Local educational providers are responsible for the quality of teaching. The key issue is the high quality teachers whose teacher education prepares them to work as reflective professionals. As mentioned by Niemi (this volume),

> the main objective of the Finnish education policy is to offer all citizens equal opportunities to receive education, regardless of age, domicile, financial situation, sex or mother tongue. Education is considered to be one of the fundamental rights of all citizens.

One defining characteristic of the Finnish system which breeds equity is one that does away with 'dead-ends.' Although compulsory education is for only 9 years, the national goal is to keep children within the school system for at least 12 years and thereafter, to provide them with routes for continual lifelong learning. In order to ensure that equity is upheld across the system, special requirements are set for teachers, the teacher profession and the teacher education programmes offered by the universities.

In upholding equity, quality is by no means underplayed in the Finnish system. In fact, evaluation is based on the principle of enhancement and the assessment of outcomes is seen as an important tool to improve the education system. However, there is no central inspectorate system as documented by Jakku-Sihvonen and Niemi (2007, as cited in Chap. 7 in this volume) and Sahlberg (2011, as cited in Chap. 7 in this volume). In order to ascertain whether schools have reached the national goals in terms of learning outcomes for their students, national sample-based assessments are used. Upper secondary schools design their own statute-based final examination. It is important to point out that the national assessments are meant to provide checks and balances against learning outcomes spelt out in the national core curricula and they include only a sampling, not the entire cohort. The results are used to inform further improvements within the education system. As Niemi points out,

> the aim of the national evaluation system is to support the local/municipal education administration and the development of schools as goal-oriented and open units, and to produce and provide up-to-date and reliable information on the context, functioning, results and the effects of the education system. (Niemi & Lavonen, 2012, as cited in Chap. 7 in this volume)

As Niemi (Chap. 7 in this volume) rightly notes, connecting equity and quality requires both purpose and persistence. Without strong political will, it is impossible to achieve. Feedback and evaluations to further develop a system is needed in the light of the changing educational needs for a changing global workplace and society.

In the case of Hong Kong, School-Based Management (SBM) is a major avenue for the decentralisation of the education system. Typically, SBM entails the setting up of a school governing board that comprises teachers, parents and community representatives who are empowered to make decisions in terms of school organisation, budgeting, staffing, curriculum design and instructional plans. The main objective of the School Management Initiative (SMI) as stated by Ho (Chap. 10 in this volume) is "to improve the system of accountability and to provide better school services by a comprehensive programme of managerial and financial changes which is consistent with the basic principal of the Public Sector Reform".

In the climate of decentralisation, to ensure quality, the Quality Assurance Inspection (QAI), renamed 'the External School Review (ESR)', gives a mandate for external quality assurance to outline key strengths and weaknesses of each school and to provide a direction for school improvement.

Shanghai's education system is built up on the quality and equity in their learning outcomes (see Zhang et al., Chap. 9 in this volume). The achievement gaps between the 95th percentile and the 5th percentile is relatively narrow, and even the performance of the 5th percentile is higher than the OECD average. The PISA 2009 results reveal the teacher–student relationship is highly positive and students generally felt 'listened to', 90 % of students reported that teachers are readily available when they needed extra help. Throughout the entire chapter, one will note the level of details that the Shanghai government has placed in the importance of learning in the classroom. Instead of reducing class-size, they focus on placing the best teacher in the classroom (OECD, 2011). Effective teachers are promoted to more classrooms instead of leadership position that take them away from the students. There is also a greater focus on levelling up underperforming schools through partnership and sharing of resources with another higher performing school (2011).

In S. K. Lee's chapter (Chap. 4 in this volume), he documents the setting up of the Office of Academic Quality Management (OAQM) within Singapore's sole teacher preparation institute (i.e., NIE) as a self-regulating quality assurance measure that tracks graduands' perceptions of their preparedness for the teaching workforce and also stakeholders' perceptions about the competencies and preparedness of the beginning teachers coming into their schools. The self-regulating measure ensures that even though pre-service teacher education currently takes place through the institute, quality is not sacrificed in the absence of competition from other teacher education providers.

Systemic Coherence

In many of the systems featured in this volume, the importance of systemic coherence is clearly highlighted as a factor for success. This is especially clear in the Singapore chapter by S. K. Lee (Chap. 4 in this volume), who states unequivocally that the tripartite partnership between the nation's teacher education institute, the Ministry of Education and the 360 schools is at the heart of Singapore's educational success. In the case of Singapore, governmental policies define what the desired outcomes of education should be. The policies have to be translated into the right practices in the schools in order to achieve the desired learning outcomes. To ensure that the right practices are to be implemented at NIE that prepares all teachers for the entire system, NIE needs to translate the policies into the preparation of teachers who can deliver such educational outcomes. It is the tight alignment and coherence within the Singapore system that contributes to its high performing status.

In the case of Finland, Niemi (Chap. 7 in this volume) mentions that the concept of equity leads Finnish education policy, which permeates throughout the entire education system from pre-school to higher and even adult education. Niemi references the MEC document (2011, as cited in Chap. 7 in this volume), stating that "everyone needs sufficient learning skills and opportunities to educate and develop themselves in different learning environments throughout their lifespan."

Such a policy of equity also entails inclusion for all sectors of the population such as those requiring special needs and both these policies of equity and inclusion cannot be achieved if systemic coherence is not present in the Finnish education system. Policy can only be implemented if there is cooperation between all involved in the education of the Finnish.

The Shanghai chapter (Chap. 9 in this volume) outlines massive and rapid reforms in the past 30 years which have helped raised the overall quality of the teaching force via the upgrading of academic qualifications and pre-service teacher education provided for all teacher candidates, the standardisation of teacher induction programmes, the presence of a systemic teacher professional development scheme that is financed and funded by the municipal government and the careful and rigorous preparation of school leaders and principals which are also publicly financed. All of these reforms could not have taken place without the political will of the local government and the systemic coherence ensuring their careful implementation.

In the case of Hong Kong, school decentralisation and teacher participation are highlighted by Ho (Chap. 10 in this volume) as being the essential contributors to high performance. However, the management of the decentralised schooling is exactly where systemic coherence may be exemplified to have taken place since the government has to centralise learning outcomes by establishing a rigorous accountability system of multiple levels that includes both students' performance assessment and standardised public examinations and the conducting of both internal and external evaluation of schools. What is noteworthy is that the reason for the government introducing the decentralisation policy was to increase school accountability and also to tighten the control over the aided-school section by devolving authority to key stakeholders such as parents, teachers and community members. The case of Hong Kong, therefore, clearly typifies a successful case study in systemic coherence accounting for high performance in student achievement outcomes.

Danger of Over-Emphasis of the International Benchmarking Exercises

A fifth theme emerging from the chapters in this volume is the caution of not overly emphasising the importance of international benchmarking exercises. There is a danger of creating and education 'fever' and driving each system to become externally assessed for international benchmarking. This will turn education from being an end itself to become a means to an end instead – a means for international competition and consequentially internal competition. Education as a means for competition will disempower teachers and teaching will become so achievement-oriented that it will become 'de-pedagogised' as Cho (Chap. 8 in this volume) strongly argues.

Goodwin (Chap. 11 in this volume) provided us with the case study of the Global Education Reform Movement (GERM) and its set of strategies that has been exchanged internationally that advocates competition, benchmarking, top–down curriculum, and results-driven accountability. Its strategies have been accepted and adopted in many parts of United States as a quick fix, causing the phenomenon of chasing after results instead of focusing on learning. The ends have been substituted by its means. This industrialised form of educational reform in Goodwin's opinion is a collection of international benchmarking strategies that the United States needs to unlearn. Practices that "emphasise teachers as professionals and decision-makers, all learners as diverse but capable of success, accountability as a professional responsibility and reform as a process done with and not on, teacher and schools" reflect that educators, learners, parents as the focal of education, and not education as a tool merely for international competitiveness and economic growth.

Ho (Chap. 10 in this volume) insightfully points out that

> whether Hong Kong and other East Asian societies such as Shanghai, Singapore, South Korea and Japan should be claimed as strong performers depends on how we define success and how we access success. In fact, students from these East Asian societies share similar strengths in terms of the high achievement, high aspiration, and orderly disciplinary climate in school. Yet they also share common weaknesses of low self-concept, high test anxiety and disengaged learning climate.

Her comments underpin the caution that we need to exercise when relying on internationally benchmarked tests of student achievement that may lead to unintended consequences of anxiety caused by such high levels of competition. She further warns that allowing national assessment practices to be dictated by the design of internationally benchmarked tests is dangerous as one might lose the local context that is necessary for the development of assessment that can truly improve the learning outcomes for our students.

Conclusion

We began this chapter with the consideration that this volume is interested not just about teasing out success factors in each of HPES being covered, but also about the ways in which educational attainment can be sustained. We started as a collective voice from within HPES rather than cases to be studied from the outside looking in. In the end, we have found a collective trait of self-reflection and analysis across the systems. A trait that is about the need to underplay the so-called secrets of success and to continually engage in a critical and constructive analysis of the challenges that lie ahead for each system in order to not just level up and sustain high performance levels, but also to reach new heights. The five major themes that emerged from the outstanding scholars that have contributed to this volume may be distilled into the following main learning points:

- Developing and sustaining a high quality teaching workforce. This entails stringent selection, recruitment, a highly rigorous teacher education programme and a highly systematised teacher professional development plan.

- Ensuring that 'no learner is left behind'. All of these systems are careful to ensure their bottom-line, tail-end performers are helped systemically as early as possible and in as sustained a way as possible.
- Balancing between equity and quality. A key concern in all of these systems is that equity and quality must not be achieved at the expense of each other, and that equity must never be sacrificed at the expense of quality.
- Ensuring that there is systemic coherence in order to translate policy initiatives with fidelity of implementation into practice across key stakeholders in the education system.
- Not over-relying on performance in internationally benchmarked tests. Over-relying on analysing and meta-analysing rankings and student performance may lead to undesired consequences of competition and a narrowly focused view of student achievement as being measured by performance in internationally benchmarked test scores.

Central to all of these systems is the deep belief that the learner is at the centre of all our educational endeavours and that the goal of education must be to help every individual to fully realise their life's potential. With such an altruistic goal, the future of these highly performing education systems can only look more promising.

References

Jensen, B. (2012). *Catching up: Learning from the best school systems in East Asia: Summary report*. Melbourne, Australia: Grattan Institute.

Low, E. L. (Ed.). (2012). *Portraits of top-performing education systems* (CJ Koh professorial lecture series). Singapore: Office of Education Research, National Institute of Education, NTU.

Mourshed, M., Chijioke, C., & Barber, M. (2010). *How the world's most improved school systems keep getting better*. London: McKinsey & Company.

Organisation for Economic Co-operation and Development (OECD). (2011). *Strong performers and successful performers in education: Lessons from PISA for the United States*. Paris: Author.

Tucker, M. (2011). *Surpassing Shanghai: An agenda for American education built on the world's leading systems*. Cambridge, MA: Harvard Education Press.

Chapter 2
How Useful Are the Experiences of the High Performing Education Systems?

Wing On Lee, Ee Ling Low, and Sing Kong Lee

Introduction

The last chapter mentioned about the emergence of quite a number of international meetings and publications awakening in the world the emergence of the 'high performing education systems' (HPES) phenomenon. The pattern of alarm and reaction is quite compatible with the 'Nation at Risk' phenomenon in America in 1983, during which a series of education reform reports, or excellence reports (Lee, 1991), were published within 1 year, namely, *A Nation at Risk: The Imperative for Educational Reform* (National Commission on Excellence in Education, 1983), *Action for Excellence* (National Commission of the States Task Force on Education for Growth, 1983), *Educating Americans for the 21st Century* (National Science Board Commission on Pre-college Education in Mathematics, Science and Technology, 1983), *High School: The Need for a National Response* (Boyer, 1983), among others. These reports were echoed by a series of other publications in the late 1970s and throughout the 1980s, including Vogel's (1979) *Japan as Number One: Lessons for America*, Duke's (1985) *The Japanese Schools: Lessons for Industrial America*, and Lynn's (1988) *Educational Achievement in Japan: Lessons for the West*. Early in the 1990s, Stevenson and Stigler's (1992) famous *The Learning Gap* was published, with a subtitle "Why our schools are failing and what we can learn

W.O. Lee (✉)
National Institute of Education, 1 Nanyang Walk, Singapore 637616, Singapore
e-mail: wingon.lee@nie.edu.sg

E.L. Low
Office of Teacher Education, National Institute of Education, 1 Nanyang Walk, Singapore 637616, Singapore
e-mail: eeling.low@nie.edu.sg

S.K. Lee
Director's Office, National Institute of Education, 1 Nanyang Walk, Singapore 637616, Singapore
e-mail: singkong.lee@nie.edu.sg

S.K. Lee et al. (eds.), *Educational Policy Innovations: Levelling Up and Sustaining Educational Achievement*, Springer Education Innovation Book Series 1,
DOI 10.1007/978-981-4560-08-5_2, © Springer Science+Business Media Singapore 2014

from Japanese and Chinese education?" In 1997, Cummings and Altbach (1997) published *The Challenge of East Asian Education: Implications for America*. All these publications ring a bell, as the sentiments and emergence of the reactions to the education crisis was similar to that of the 'PISA Shock' today. The OECD commissioned report entitled *Lessons from PISA for the United States: Strong Performers and Successful Reformers in Education* (2011) sounds almost exactly the same as the excellence reports published 10–20 years ago. However, the warning bell was accompanied by a strong learning spirit, showing the effectiveness of America's self-alarm system and its enthusiasm of learning from successful examples. Indeed, America has a strong crisis awareness or self-alarm, for example, the Sputnik crisis in the 1960s, A Nation At Risk in the 1980s, and now the PISA shock in the twenty-first century. The question 'Is America still at risk?' has been penetrating the last few decades, and there is no sign of stopping (Khadaroo, 2013; Lee & Lee, 2011). What we can learn from America is that once the Americans learn someone else has done better, they will immediately be alarmed and start to learn from the best practices they have identified from elsewhere.

The Emergence of High Performing Education Systems

HPES, or sometimes 'top performing education systems' (TPES), is a term emerging in the last few years to describe education systems that have excelled in the Programme for International Student Assessment (PISA) 'league tables'. PISA is an international assessment of 15-year-old students across the world, commissioned by the Organisation for Economic Co-operation Development (OECD). It aims to compare education systems across the world on their participation, quality, equity and efficiency in delivering a robust education (OECD, 2011). Similar terms such as 'world-class education systems' (Stewart, 2012), 'international models' (Stewart), 'high-performing education systems' (OECD), 'high-performing systems' (Tucker, 2011), 'top performers' (OECD), amongst others, often refer to the similar list of countries. However, the list of HPES is not cast in stone, and evolves with the PISA that occurs every 3 years. These systems are identified as those with "high participation, high performance, high equity and high efficiency" (Tucker, p. 15). Different scholars and education experts have different views of what defines the top but there are a few nations that have frequently been cited. The two countries in Asia that have been featured in all recent publications are Shanghai and Singapore. Shanghai has topped the table on all three areas of testing and therefore, there is an immense study by the Americans and Australians of how Shanghai has managed to build an efficient, equitable and high quality education system (Jensen, 2012; OECD, 2011). Singapore, on the other hand, has been featured in all publications due to its short burst to success, with a strong focus on its teacher and leadership education programme and its career management system for its teachers. Hong Kong, SAR, another HPES, has been associated with Shanghai when featured in certain books probably due to its governance by China. There appears to be a significant representation of East Asian countries, with much of the literature associated with the 'Asian Tigers/Dragons' – a term that was used to describe the booming economies of Chinese Taipei, Hong Kong SAR, Singapore and South Korea in the 1980s.

Education and Economics

Reviewing the literature on HPES, an outstanding theme or concern emerges, that is, economic strength. A common theme in the recent publications concerning PISA is the strong correlation between educational outcomes and a nation's economic development (OECD, 2011; Stewart, 2012; Tucker, 2011). The economics dimension is one of the strongest arguments why HPES experiences cannot be ignored as education systems have to develop high-skilled people that will demand higher wages for the competitive world economy due to globalisation and technological advances (OECD). The argument that the ramification of automation has resulted in declining the demand for low-skilled jobs and low-skilled workers face pending unemployment; that every job that could be automated, outsourced or digitised will be done so, rendering the skills of these low-skilled workers practically obsolete. The threat of potential higher unemployment rates and declining GDP figures compel governments to act in the interest of their economy to provide an education system that will be robust enough to develop every citizen to be a 'knowledge worker', equipped with twenty-first century skills (OECD).

This immense need to raise education standards raised by the OECD has led to the proliferation of 'best practices' utilised by HPES that has been linked to their predicted economic growth. The literature in recent years point to a paradigm shift from using national standards to international standards of HPES in the way nations should evaluate their education systems to secure a competitive edge in the world economy. Perhaps, as a result of these reported linkages, and the highlighting of these results in the media, there has been a stronger incentive and pressure for policymakers around the world to focus on improving educational outcomes for stronger future economic growth. There has also been a greater attention on the application of the principles of economics in education; with a greater awareness of working within limited resources and the opportunity costs associated with it, the need to regulate the education sector and the workings of micro-economics of individuals' decision making in the wider landscape of the education sector.

The alarm caused by the educational achievements of HPES is in many respects coupled with their economic performance and human development indexes. Figure 2.1 shows the correlation between the mean reading scores and GDP per capita from the 2009 PISA results. Obviously, HPES are at the top performance corners of the figure, well above and beyond the OECD average. In addition, they have notably higher GDP per capita, well above the OECD average, with the exception of Shanghai and South Korea.

Table 2.1 shows the GDP per capita growth of the HPES from 2008 to 2011. Notably they generally suffered from the economic backlash in 2008–2009, but from 2010 onwards, they all performed reasonably well.

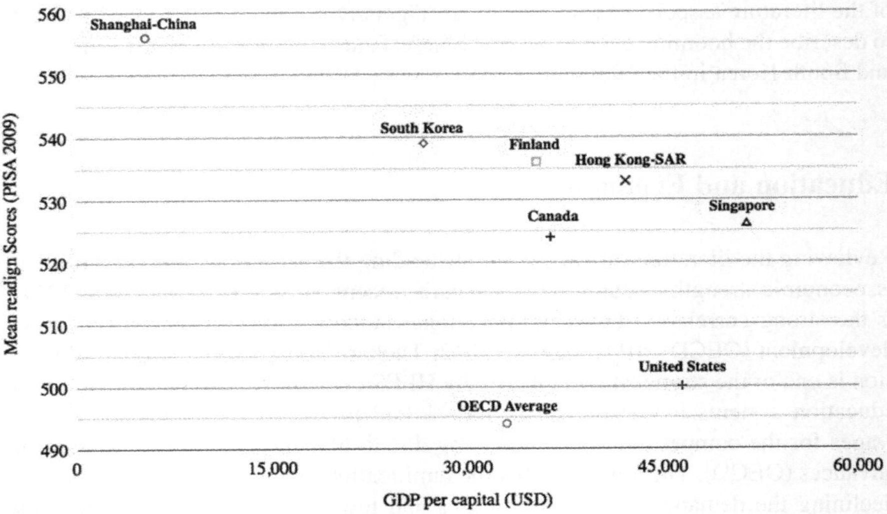

Fig. 2.1 Correlation between the mean reading scores and GDP per capital (USD) (OECD, 2010, p. 34, 2011, p. 16)

Table 2.1 GDP per capita growth (annual %) in HPES, 2008–2011 (World Bank, 2013)

Countries	2008	2009	2010	2011
Canada	−0.5	−3.9	2.0	1.4
Shanghai-China	9.0	8.7	9.9	8.8
Finland	−0.2	−9.0	2.9	2.3
Hong Kong SAR	2.4	−2.8	5.8	4.8
Singapore	−3.6	−3.9	12.7	2.7
South Korea	1.6	−0.2	5.8	2.9
USA	−1.3	−4.4	2.2	1.0

HPES are also notably highly ranked in the Human Development Reports, being placed in the 'very high human development' category. According to the Human Development Report 2013, the Human Development Index (HDI) ranking of the HPES and their respective HDI values are very high and their index rankings are quite close to one another, as shown in Table 2.2. The Human Development Index, developed by the United Nations Development Programme (UNDP, 2013), is a composite measure of indicators along three dimensions: life expectancy, educational attainment and command over the resources needed for a decent living. The high index values show the success of these jurisdictions in levelling up the well-being of their populace, including education attainment, in association with economic growth.

The OECD Report (2011) in its analysis of the impact of achievement gaps reported that economies are incurring significant recurring economic loss for the citizens that are unable to perform to their optimum capacity. Utilising economic modelling to correlate cognitive skills to economic growth reveals (with certain caveats) that minor improvements in the skills of a nation's work force can have a major impact on that country's future progress. Although there are uncertainties

Table 2.2 Human development index (ranking and values) of HPES (UNDP, 2013, p. 25 & p. 144)

Countries	HDI ranking	HDI value
Japan	10	0.912
Canada	11	0.911
South Korea	12	0.909
Hong Kong, SAR	13	0.906
Singapore	18	0.895
Finland	21	0.892
Shanghai	N/A	0.910

linked with the estimates, it is evident that gains from improved learning outcomes will be translated towards significant economic output.

In recent publications, educators and policymakers appear to have taken on a more realistic approach, recognising that within a limited timeframe and resources, they have to prioritise education reform to make it effective. Although, it is no secret that educators work with limited resources, it appears that HPES have been more deliberate to report how they have calculated their cost, and found ways to maximise their resources more efficiently by prioritising teacher quality and development amongst other fundamental and important agendas in education. It has also been suggested that the glass-ceiling and limitations of current education system and frameworks can only be broken with high-quality educators and policymakers who have the willingness and ability to drive change for the betterment of their nation. The literature also focuses largely on how HPES spend their money, the distribution of teachers in classes, the socioeconomic status of students, parental involvement in education and immigrant population support (OECD, 2011; Stewart, 2012; Tucker, 2011).

Equity and Quality in Education

The traditional debate on educational policy is one of ‘equity or excellence’. Given that resources are limited, how should resources be distributed among the populace such that it would benefit the country in terms of its overall competitiveness? Policymakers often face such a dilemma. The debate on ‘equity or excellence’ implies that if educational resources are given to all equally and spread thin, it is at the expense of excellence that requires the purposeful concentration of particular resources to achieve certain levels or aspects of excellence, knowing that excellence cannot be achieved without additional and targeted investment. This is what Evetts (1973) referred to as “more means worse”, implicating that if the talents are not given additional resources and supports, and without proper and purposeful nurturing, talents will not be able to develop optimally. This is eventually the society’s loss for not having these talents becoming top of the world. However, the notion of equity versus excellence has been challenged from the start of the debate, and is regarded as a wrong assumption. Not only that, it assumes a zero-sum game both in terms of the distribution of talents in a society and the distribution of resources. More importantly, making the two concepts mutually exclusive and dichotomised has been regarded as unnecessary and unproductive.

Astin (1985) criticises the traditional views of excellence, in terms of reputation, resources and outcome, as inadequate. Excellence in terms of reputation and resources is not consistent with education's primary purpose to develop talents; nor does it contribute to the expansion of educational opportunities. According to Astin, the concept of excellence should be emphasised on the intellectual and personal development of individual students as a fundamental educational purpose. In addition, Robbins (2007) argues that equity and excellence should not be dichotomised – they can co-exist. Equity and excellence is still a lively issue of debate today, but the tendency of the debate is towards how to achieve both, rather than a selection between the two.

'Equity and quality' is an emerging terminology or concept that focuses on the quality of education, instead of 'excellence', and it seems levelling up the quality for all is a more acceptable concept and a more worthwhile goal to achieve. Schleicher (Chap. 3 in this volume) points out that PISA findings show that equity and quality in education are not mutually exclusive concepts. Investing in high-quality childhood education and initial schooling, particularly for children from socioeconomically disadvantaged backgrounds, is an efficient strategy to ensure that children start strong in their education careers so that first skills beget future skills. OECD published a report in 2012 entitled *Equity and Quality in Education: Supporting Disadvantaged Students and Schools* (2012).

The Report firmly states:

> The evidence is **conclusive**: equity in education pays off. The highest performing education systems across OECD countries are those that combine high quality and equity. In such education systems, the vast majority of students can attain high level skills and knowledge that depend on their ability and drive, more than on their socio-economic background (p. 14).

The PISA 2009 Report also states that:

> PISA suggests that maximising overall performance and securing similar levels of performance among students from different socio-economic backgrounds can be achieved simultaneously. These results suggest that quality and equity need not be considered as competing policy objectives.... These [HPES] countries display high student performance and, at the same time, a below-average impact of economic, social and cultural status on student performance (as cited in OECD, 2010, p. 57).

In Fig. 2.2, Shanghai, South Korea, Canada and Japan are located at the top right quadrant, which shows these countries achieve the highest scores in reading and at the same time least affected by their home background, as compared to the OECD average.

Niemi (Chap. 7 in this volume) points out that equity is the fundamental principle of education policy, whereby the whole system is built upon it and teacher education is guided by it:

> Equity has been a leading principle of Finnish education policy and it covers the whole educational system from early education to higher education as well as adult education....

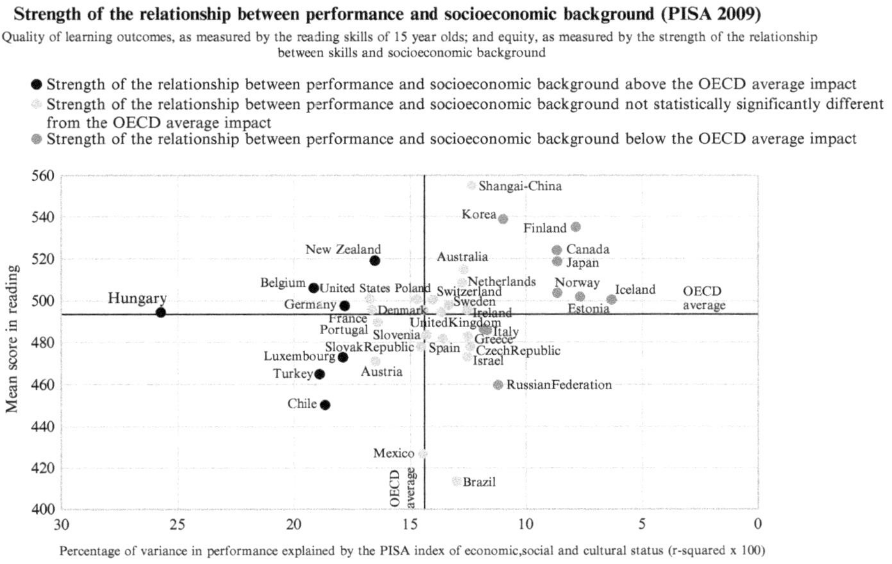

Fig. 2.2 High performing education systems combined with equity and quality (OECD, 2011, p. 15)

The aims related to equity and the enablement of all people's development through learning and education set special requirements on teachers, the teaching profession and teacher studies at universities.

It is to be noted that, as shown in Table 2.3, the HPES's Gini indexes show considerable disparities in terms of the gap between the rich and the poor. With the exception of Finland, the East Asian HPES seems to have similarly high Gini indexes.

However, despite a notable gap between the rich and the poor, the average high scores in PISA 2009 illustrate that the average quality of education in the HPES are among the highest in the world. On this issue, the Human Development Report 2013 interprets that these education systems have provided very high quality of education that benefits the whole population regardless of the socioeconomic conditions of the students:

> In the most recent PISA, conducted in 63 countries and territories in 2009, many countries showed impressive strides in **quality of learning** outcomes. Students from Shanghai, China, outperformed students from 62 countries in Reading, Mathematics and Science skills. They were followed by students from the Republic of Korea, Finland and Hong Kong (SAR) in reading; Singapore, Hong Kong, China (SAR) and the Republic of Korea in mathematics; and Finland, Hong Kong, China (SAR) and Singapore in science.... Investments by some countries in **education quality** will likely bring future payoffs in a more knowledge-driven globalised world (emphasis added, UNDP, 2013, p. 33).

Table 2.3 Gini index of HPES, 2007

HDI rank (2007)	Country	Richest 10 % to poorest 10 %	Gini index
4	Canada	9.4	32.6
12	Finland	5.6	26.9
23	Singapore	17.7	42.5
24	Hong Kong SAR	17.8	43.4
26	South Korea	7.8	31.6
92	China	13.2	41.5

Note: The Gini index lies between 0 and 100. A value of 0 represents absolute equality and 100 absolute inequality

In the IEA International Civic and Citizenship Study (ICCS) 2009 Report (Schulz, Ainley, Fraillon, Kerr, & Losito, 2009), It was reported that Hong Kong's achievements in student performance was not influenced by:

- On average, across ICCS countries, parental occupational status accounted for 10 % of the variance in scores on the civic knowledge scale. However, there were considerable differences in this percentage across countries. For Hong Kong SAR, it ranged from 0.5 % to 20 % (p. 81).
- Although the size of the difference between students with or without an immigrant background varied across countries, in every system except Hong Kong SAR, the pattern was for students without such a background to score higher than students from immigrant families (p. 76).

Analysing the student performance in the various PISA studies in relation to their Economic, Social and Cultural Status (ESCS), Ho's (2013) conclusion about Hong Kong is strikingly similar to the findings of the ICCS 2009:

> Hong Kong being in the top three on the graph with a gentle gradient indicates that Hong Kong's 15-year-olds perform well in reading, mathematics and science, and the impact of ESCS is modest. We can argue tentatively that Hong Kong is providing education opportunity with relatively high quality and high equity regardless of their ESCS (p. 34).

On the issue of equity and quality in education, the Grattan Report (Jensen, 2012) makes the following observation:

- High performing education systems in East Asia have successfully increased performance while maintaining, and often increasing, equity. Compared to Australia and most OECD countries, a child from a poorer background in these systems is less likely to drop out or fall behind.
- There is less of a gap between high and low performing students in South Korea, Shanghai and Hong Kong compared to many other OECD education systems.
- Low performing students are also better prepared for their future. The bottom 10 % of math students in Shanghai perform at a level that is 21 months ahead of the bottom 10 % of students in Australia. This gap rises to 24 months in the UK, 25 across the average of the OECD, and 28 months in the USA.

- Increasing performance and equity has been achieved with high and increasing participation. For example, 30 years ago about 40 % of young South Koreans (aged 25–34) finished secondary education. Now the figure is 98 %, 10 percentage points above the OECD average (p. 10).

What's more, the Grattan Report argues that the high quality in student learning outcomes overall shows the equity of the system. The HPES case shows an interesting dimension towards the equity–quality debate. Does equity lead to quality in education, or would quality enhance equity? The HPES performances seem to show that education quality can offset economic inequalities, or can become an equaliser that would enhance equity. There is a strong culture and belief in East Asia that education is considered a crucial key to achieve social mobility, and the higher the quality of education, the higher the opportunity for social mobility, that is, the higher the equity. This is actually a classic view of functionalist sociologists, like Talcott Parsons, that with universal standards, for example, open examinations, everyone in the society will have an equal chance to climb the social ladder based on the open standards available for competition. The major weakness of functionalist sociology is only that the social ladder is a given if one has to climb the social ladder. Critics of functionalist sociology argue that this given assumes and accepts social inequality in the first place. The purpose of our book is not to trigger sociological debates, but it seems that the HPES performances in international assessment projects show that the opportunity to overcome socioeconomic inequalities can be demonstrated in the average top performances that would require every child to perform, including those from the lower socioeconomic sector.

In sum, in a recent report, the Asia Society (2012) defines HPES as systems that can achieve both equity and quality:

> The Highest Performing Education Systems are those that combine quality with equity. Equity in education means that personal or social circumstances such as gender, ethnic origin or family background, are not obstacles to achieving educational potential (definition of fairness) and that all individuals reach at least a basic minimum level of skills (definition of inclusion). In these education systems, the vast majority of students have the opportunity to attain high-level skills, regardless of their own personal and socio-economic circumstances. Within the Asia-Pacific region, for example, South Korea, Shanghai-China, and Japan are examples of Asian education systems that have climbed the ladder to the top in both quality and equity indicators. In North America, Canada is among such countries as well. The United States is above the OECD mean in reading performance but below the mean with regard to equity (p. 6).

Conclusion

How useful are the HPES experiences? There are differing perspectives of how the use of PISA results can enlighten policies and practice. While there are many who advocate the importance of learning from HPES, there are contesting voices to caution negative implications that may arise, citing examples of how policymakers or educators may misinterpret findings and implement policies that may backfire or be counter-productive if they are unable to anticipate and prepare for change. Both arguments direct to a prudent approach towards understanding and learning from HPES, not just how successful they are, but more critically to understand the rationale behind their policies and practices, to envisage their challenges, how they proposed to overcome it and if there was any way one could avoid the pitfalls they have experienced. Instead of taking a fast route to education reform, those who argue for taking cautious views suggest that it will be advisable to understand and take time to investigate the achievements and challenges of HPES, and how they manage change in an ever-changing global landscape. Perhaps the strongest lesson is not what to change, but how they cope with change and find ways out.

For those who advocate for learning from HPES, their concerns mainly come from three perspectives. First, as mentioned above, there is a strong concern about economic consequences related to education performance. Second, there is a call for admitting the outcomes of the international benchmarking exercise. Third, more objectively admitting that HPES were successfully improving systems as compared to their previous international performance.

Social, economic and cultural inequalities have always been a problem of public concern. Browsing through the sociological literature in particular, there exists countless research and analyses to show that inequalities perpetuate, and economic growth brings about wider differences between the rich and the poor, instead of bring their gaps closer. With the growth of the middle class, economic capitals are transformed into cultural capitals that would further perpetuate and even enhance their advantages over the lower socioeconomic and cultural groups. The Gini indexes of many countries with high economic growths are discouraging, indicating the powerlessness of the free market economy to close the income gaps between the rich and poor. However, the above studies on the HPES phenomenon seem to provide a hope. If a country invests in education, levelling up the bottom line and achieving quality education for all that would lead to a high average performance, the quality of education will bring about, and even enhance, equity in the system. The equity–quality conundrum can be resolved from the perspective that quality brings equity. The previous equity versus excellence debate is now replaced by equity and quality, and the move towards quality is the key to unlock the barriers for achieving equity.

Acknowledgements The authors will like to thank Ms Jocelyn Shi Yah Tan for her assistance in the drafting process, and for gathering data for this chapter.

References

Asia Society. (2012). *Equity and quality in education: Supporting disadvantaged students and schools*. Retrieved from http://asiasociety.org/education/learning-world/equity-and-quality-education

Astin, A. (1985). *Achieving educational excellence: A critical assessment of priorities and practices in higher education*. San Francisco: Jossey-Bass.

Boyer, E. L. (1983). *High school: A report on secondary education in America*. New York: Harper & Row.
Cummings, W. K., & Altbach, P. G. (Eds.). (1997). *The challenge of Eastern Asian education: Implications for America*. Albany, NY: State University of New York Press.
Duke, B. (1985). *The Japanese schools: Lessons for industrial America*. New York: Praeger.
Evetts, J. (1973). *The sociology of educational ideas*. London: Routledge & Kegan Paul.
Ho, E. S. C. (2013). Overall quality and equality of Hong Kong basic education system from PISA 2000+ to PISA 2006. In E. S. C. Ho (Ed.), *Multilevel analysis of the PISA data: Insights for policy and practice* (pp. 17–36). Hong Kong, China: Hong Kong Institute of Educational Research, The Chinese University of Hong Kong.
Jensen, B. (2012). *Catching up: Learning from the best schools systems in East Asia*. Melbourne, Australia: The Grattan Institute.
Khadaroo, S. T. (2013, April 26). 'A nation at risk': How much of 'apocalyptic' education report still applies? *The Christian Science Monitor*. Retrieved from http://www.csmonitor.com/USA/Education/2013/0426/A-Nation-at-Risk-How-much-of-apocalyptic-education-report-still-applies
Lee, W. O. (1991). The search for excellence and relevance in education: Lessons from Japan's fourth educational reform proposals. *British Journal of Educational Studies, 34*(1), 17–32.
Lee, W. O., & Lee, S. K. (2011). Learning from success. *International Alliance of Leading Education Institutes Newsletter, 2*, 1–4.
Lynn, R. (1988). *Educational achievement in Japan: Lessons for the West*. Hampshire, UK: Macmillan.
National Commission of the States Task Force on Education for Growth. (1983). *Action for excellence*. Denver, CO: Education Commission of the States.
National Commission on Excellence in Education. (1983). *A nation at risk: The imperative for educational reform*. Washington, DC: US Government Printing Office.
National Science Board Commission on Pre-college Education in Mathematics, Science and Technology. (1983). *Educating Americans for the 21st century: A Report to the American people and the National Science Board*. Washington, DC: U.S. Government Printing Office.
OECD. (2010). *PISA 2009 results: Overcoming social background – Equity in learning opportunities and outcomes* (Vol. 2). Paris: Author. doi:10.1787/9789264091504-en.
OECD. (2011). *Lessons from PISA for the United States: Strong performers and successful reformers in education*. Paris: Author. doi:10.1787/9789264096660-en.
OECD. (2012). *Equity and quality in education: Supporting disadvantaged students and schools*. Paris: Author. doi:10.1787/9789264177338-en.
Robbins, L. (2007). Equity v. excellence: Is education still a zero-sum game? *Peabody Reflector*. Retrieved from http://peabody.vanderbilt.edu/equity_vs_excellence.xml
Schulz, W., Ainley, J., Fraillon, J., Kerr, D., & Losito, B. (2009). *Initial findings from the IEA international civic and citizenship study*. Amsterdam: IEA.
Stevenson, H. W., & Stigler, J. W. (1992). *The learning gap: Why our schools are failing and what we can learn from Japanese and Chinese education*. New York: Touchstone.
Stewart, V. (2012). *A world-class education: Learning from international models of excellence and innovation*. Alexandria, VA: ASCD.
Tucker, M. S. (2011). *Surpassing Shanghai: An agenda for American education built on the world's leading systems*. Cambridge, MA: Harvard Education Press.
United Nations Development Programme (UNDP). (2013). *Human development report 2013. The rise of the South: Human progress in a diverse world*. New York: Author.
Vogel, E. F. (1979). *Japan as number one: Lessons for America*. New York: Harper & Row.
World Bank. (2013). *World development indicators*. Retrieved from http://databank.worldbank.org/data/home.as

Chapter 3
Developing Educational Policies in a Holistic Skills Framework

Andreas Schleicher

Introduction

What kinds of skills are needed in different economies? How can today's students and workers prepare themselves for a rapidly evolving labour market? How can countries ensure that available skills are used productively? While education policy is central to answering these questions, it can provide only part of the picture. If skills are to be developed effectively over a lifetime, then a broad range of policy fields are implicated, including education, science and technology, family, employment, industrial and economic development, migration and integration, social welfare, and public finance. A coordinated approach also allows policymakers to detect policy trade-offs, such as between spending on early education and investing in welfare programmes later on. Building on the OECD Skills Strategy, this chapter sets out a systematic and comprehensive approach that can help education policymakers to:

- **Prioritise investment of scarce resources**: Since education is costly, skills policies need to be designed so that these investments reap the greatest economic and social benefits.
- **Combine short- and long-term considerations**: Effective skills policies are needed to respond to structural and cyclical challenges, such as rising unemployment when economies contract or acute skills shortages when sectors boom, and to ensure longer-term strategic planning for the skills that are needed to foster a competitive edge and support requiring structural changes.
- **Build a case for lifelong learning**: By seeing skills as a tool to be honed over an individual's lifetime, a strategic approach is needed to assess the impact of different kinds of learning – from early childhood education through formal

A. Schleicher (✉)
OECD PISA, 2 rue André Pascal, 75775 Paris Cedex 16, France
e-mail: Andreas.SCHLEICHER@oecd.org

S.K. Lee et al. (eds.), *Educational Policy Innovations: Levelling Up and Sustaining Educational Achievement*, Springer Education Innovation Book Series 1,
DOI 10.1007/978-981-4560-08-5_3, © Springer Science+Business Media Singapore 2014

schooling to formal and informal learning later on – with the aim of balancing the allocation of resources to maximise economic and social outcomes.

- **Align the perspectives of different levels of government**: With often major geographical variations in the supply of and the demand for skills within countries, there is a strong rationale for considering skills policies at the local level. This will help countries to align national aspirations with local needs.
- **Include all relevant stakeholders**: Designing effective skills policies requires more than coordinating different sectors of public administration and aligning different levels of government – a broad range of non-governmental actors, including employers, professional and industry associations and chambers of commerce, trade unions, education and training institutions and, of course, individuals, must also be involved.

The Value Proposition of Effective Education Policy

Skills transform lives and drive economies, putting high quality education policies at the centre of the success of individuals and economies. Without adequate investment in skills, people languish on the margins of society, technological progress does not translate into economic growth, and countries can no longer compete in an increasingly knowledge-based global society. People with poor skills face a much greater risk of experiencing economic disadvantage, and a higher likelihood of unemployment and dependency on social benefits (see Fig. 3.1[1,2]). Conversely, according to one estimate, if student performance in the OECD area is raised by just half a school year, that would add USD115 trillion to the OECD economy over the working life of the generation born this year. Skills affect people's lives and the well-being of nations also in ways that go far beyond what can be measured by labour-market earnings and economic growth (see Fig. 3.1). For example, skills relate to civic and social behaviour as they affect democratic engagement and business relationships.

[1] How to read this graph: This figure shows that, for example, individuals with the lowest level of foundation skills are 1.8 times more likely to be unemployed, 1.4 times more likely to report health problems and 1.5 times more likely to have low levels of general trust as individuals with the highest level of foundation skills. Odds ratios reflect the relative likelihood of an event occurring for a particular group compared with a reference group. An odds ratio of 1 represents equal chances of an event occurring for a particular group vis-à-vis the reference group. Ratios with a value below 1 indicate that there is less of a chance of the event occurring; ratios with a value above 1 indicate that there is a greater chance.

[2] Foundation skills are defined here as problem solving in technology-rich environments (the ability to use technology to solve problems and accomplish complex tasks); literacy (the ability to understand and use information from written texts in a variety of contexts to achieve goals and further develop knowledge); and numeracy (the ability to use, apply, interpret and communicate mathematical information and ideas. Adjusted for age, gender, education, parents' education and immigrant status.

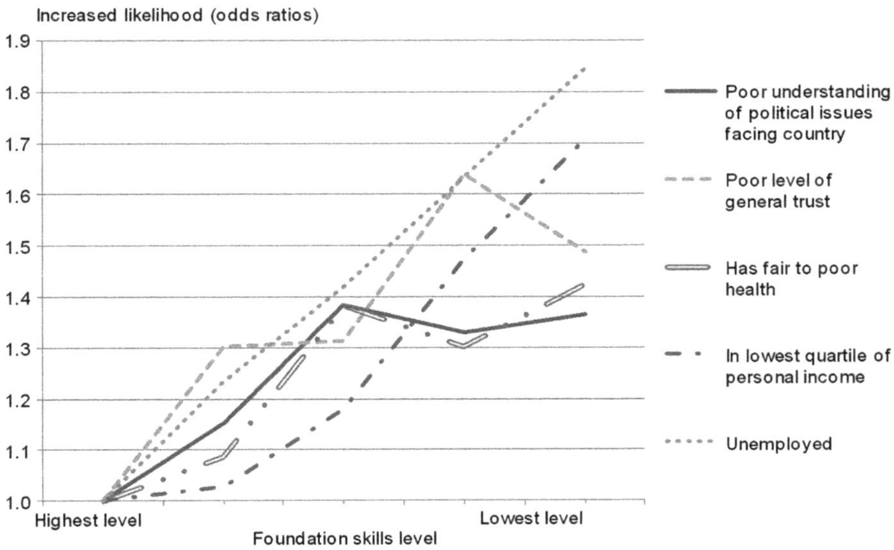

Fig. 3.1 Foundation skills and social and economic disadvantage (See footnote 1 and 2 for details) (Programme for the International Assessment of Adult Competencies [PIAAC], 2010. Note: The increased likelihood of experiencing social and economic disadvantage, by foundation skills level, adults aged 16–65. The figure uses preliminary data from the OECD Survey of Adult Skills, a product of the OECD's Programme for the International Assessment of Adult Competencies (PIAAC, see also Appendix 1). Although these data are not based on representative samples, they illustrate trends)

In short, skills have become the global currency of twenty-first century economies. But this 'currency' can depreciate as the requirements of labour markets evolve and individuals lose the skills they do not use. For skills to retain their value, they must be continuously developed throughout life. Getting the best returns on investment in skills requires the ability to assess the quality and quantity of the skills available in the population, determine and anticipate the skills required in the labour market, and develop and use those skills effectively in better jobs that lead to better lives. Working towards achieving this is everyone's business. Governments, employers, employees, parents and students need to establish effective and equitable arrangements as to who pays for what, when and how.

There is ample evidence that countries can do better in developing and using the skills that are available to them. Large proportions of young people do not reach even the lowest level of foundational skills by the end of compulsory education, and significant numbers of adults do not possess the most basic skills considered necessary to succeed in today's societies and economies. Even at the height of the economic crisis in 2010, more than 40 % of employers in Australia, Japan, Mexico and Switzerland reported difficulties in finding people with the appropriate skills (see Fig. 3.2). At the same time, unemployment rates in a number of countries are still at record high. In some countries, up to one-third of workers report that they have the skills to cope with more complex tasks at work, and another 13 % believe

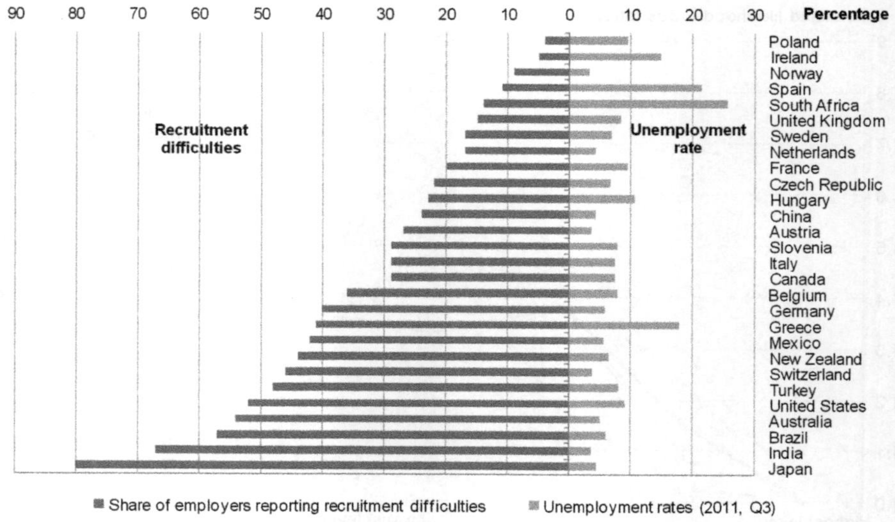

Fig. 3.2 Share of employers reporting recruitment difficulties and unemployment rates (ManpowerGroup, 2011; OECD, 2011a, 2011b. Note: Selected countries 2010 and 2011. Brazil: Urban areas only; China: Registered unemployment rate in rural areas in 2009; India: 2009/10; Indonesia: 2011Q1)

that they are not skilled enough. This means that many people do not have the required skills or are not using their skills productively for the economy at all.

How Can a Country Improve the Quality and Quantity of Its Skills?

Encouraging People to Learn

Gather and Use Evidence About the Changing Demand for Skills

Sound education policies with a lifetime perspective are at the heart of skills policies. During the past few decades, there have been major shifts in the economic underpinnings of OECD countries and, more recently, of many emerging and developing countries too. These changes imply a decline in the demand for craft skills and physical labour and a rise in the demand for cognitive and interpersonal skills, and for higher-level skills more generally. As economies continue to evolve, the types of skills demanded by the labour market will necessarily change too. Governments and businesses need to work together to gather evidence about present and future demand on skills, which can then be used to develop up-to-date curricula and inform education policies and training systems.

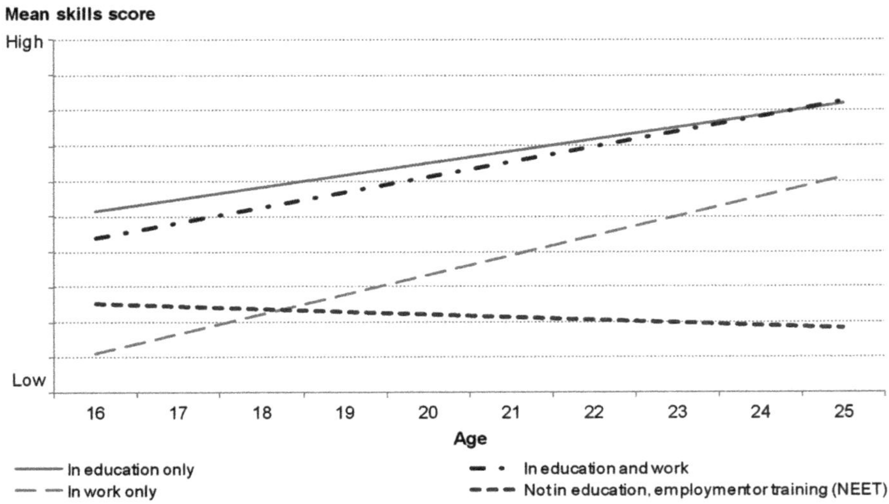

Fig. 3.3 Young people in their mid-20s who are in education and work have higher average levels of foundation skills, country average (PIAAC, 2010. Note: The figure uses preliminary data from the OECD Survey of Adult Skills, a product of the OECD's Programme for the International Assessment of Adult Competencies (PIAAC). Although these data are not based on representative samples, they illustrate trends)

Involve Social Partners in Designing and Delivering Education and Training Programmes

Skills development is more effective if the world of learning and the world of work are linked (see Fig. 3.3). Compared to purely government-designed curricula taught exclusively in schools, learning in the workplace offers several advantages: it allows young people to develop 'hard' skills on modern equipment, and 'soft' skills, such as teamwork, communication and negotiation, through real-world experience. Hands-on workplace training can also help to motivate disengaged youth to stay in or re-engage with the education system and to smoothen the transition from education into the labour market. Workplace training also facilitates recruitment by allowing employers and potential employees to get to know each other, while trainees contribute to the output of the training firm. Employers have an important role in training their own staff; but some, particularly small- and medium-sized enterprises, might need public assistance to provide such training. Trade unions can also help to shape education and training, protect the interests of existing workers, ensure that those in work use their skills adequately, and see that investments in training are reflected in better-quality jobs and higher salaries.

Remove Barriers to Investing in Further Learning

Preparing young people for their entry into the labour market with up-front education and training is only one facet of skills development; working-age adults also need to

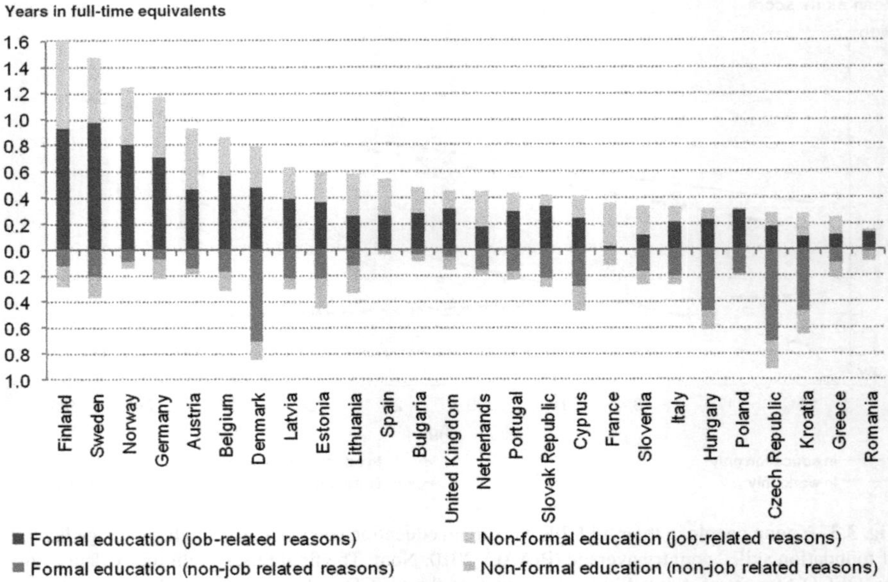

Fig. 3.4 Expected number of years of work-related formal and non-formal education and training over a working life (Eurostat, 2005–2008. Notes: Per adult between the ages of 25 and 64. Full-time equivalent (FTE) years indicates the length of time a person attends formal and non-formal education and training on a full-time basis)

develop their skills so that they can progress in their careers, meet the changing demands of the labour market, and do not lose the skills they have already acquired (Fig. 3.4). A wide spectrum of full- or part-time adult-learning activities needs to be available: from work-related employee training, formal education for adults, second-chance courses to obtain a minimum qualification or basic literacy and numeracy skills, language training for immigrants, and labour-market training programmes for job-seekers, to learning activities for self-improvement or leisure. The OECD Skills Strategy identifies a number of policy approaches that can help to dismantle barriers to participation in continued education and training. These include:

- **Greater transparency**: Making the returns on adult education and training more transparent help to increase the motivation of users to invest in adult education and training. Governments can provide better information about economic benefits (including wages net of taxes, employment and productivity) and non-economic benefits (including self-esteem and increased social interaction) of adult learning.
- **Information and guidance for potential learners**: Less-educated individuals tend to be less aware of education and training opportunities or may find the available information confusing. A combination of easily searchable, up-to-date online information and personal guidance and counselling services to help individuals define their own training needs and identify the appropriate programmes is needed, as is information about possible funding sources.

- **Recognising learning outcomes**: Clear certification of learning outcomes and recognition of non-formal learning are also incentives for training. Transparent standards, embedded in a framework of national qualifications, should be developed alongside reliable assessment procedures. Recognition of prior learning can also reduce the time needed to obtain a certain qualification and thus the cost of foregone earnings.
- **Flexible delivery of relevant programmes**: It is essential to ensure that programmes are relevant to users and are flexible enough, both in content and in how they are delivered (part-time, flexible hours) to adapt to adults' needs. A number of countries have recently introduced one-stop-shop arrangements, with different services offered in the same institution. This approach is particularly cost-effective as it consolidates infrastructure and teaching personnel and makes continuing education and training more convenient. Distance learning and the open educational resources approach have significantly improved users' ability to adapt their learning to their lives.

Ensure That Education and Training Programmes Are of High Quality

Spending time in education is one thing; learning is another. The OECD's Programme for International Student Assessment (PISA) shows that significant numbers of 15-year-olds in many countries do not acquire even a minimum level of skills through compulsory schooling. Governments can help to foster quality in education and training from early education through school and beyond. Education and training institutions need to be governed by a clear quality-assurance framework that serves both accountability and improvement purposes, and that combines internal and external evaluation without imposing an excessive administrative burden. Teaching must be valued as a profession so that the best candidates are recruited and the most effective teachers are retained. Workplace training should also be subject to quality control, in the form of contractual arrangements, inspections and self-evaluations.

Promote Equity by Ensuring Access to, and Success in, Quality Education for All

Individuals who have low levels of skills because they do not have access to good-quality education, because they fail to succeed in education or because they do not get a second chance to improve their skills later on are much more likely to have poor labour market and social outcomes. As Fig. 3.1 illustrates, people with poor foundational skills are at greater risk of economic disadvantage and a higher likelihood of unemployment and dependency on social benefits. They also are much more likely to report poor health and to lack trust in others. Yet findings from PISA show that equity and quality in education are not mutually exclusive

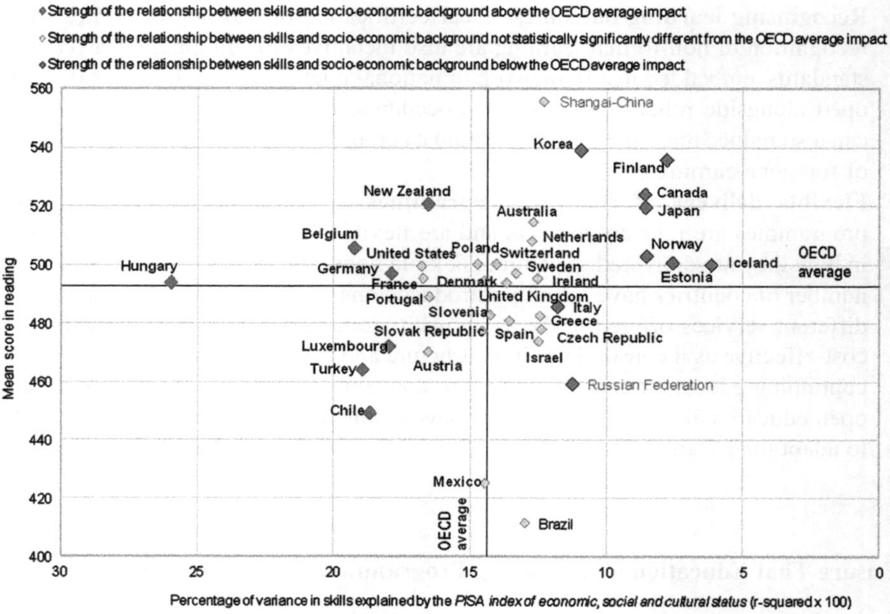

Fig. 3.5 High performing education systems combine equity with quality rates (OECD, 2011a. Note: Quality of learning outcomes, as measured by the reading skills of 15-year-olds, and equity, as measured by the strength of the relationship between skills and socioeconomic background (taken from 2009 PISA study))

(see Fig. 3.5). Investing in high-quality early childhood education and initial schooling, particularly for children from socioeconomically disadvantaged backgrounds, is an efficient strategy to ensure that children start strong in their education careers so that first skills beget future skills. Financial support targeted at disadvantaged students and schools can improve the development of skills. And since individuals with poor skills are unlikely to engage in education and training on their own initiatives and tend to receive less employer-sponsored training, second-chance options can offer them a way out of the low skills/low income trap.

Ensure That the Costs of Education and Training Are Shared

Employers have to create a climate that supports learning, and invest in learning; and individuals must be willing to develop their skills throughout their working life. Governments can design financial incentives and favourable tax policies that encourage individuals and employers to invest in post-compulsory education and training. For example, allowing taxpayers to deduct the cost of such education from their income taxes could help to offset the disincentives to invest in skills resulting from progressive personal income taxes. Some countries fear that, with rising enrolment rates and the increasing cost of tertiary education, they might not be able to sustain these investments. To make investing in tertiary education more cost effective, individuals can be encouraged to shoulder more of the financial burden, and funding can be linked more closely to graduation rates. At the same time, individuals need to have access to the necessary financing, which can be best assured through income-contingent loans and means-tested grants.

Maintain a Long-Term Perspective, Even During Economic Crises

In periods of depressed economic conditions and when public budgets are tight, governments tend to cut investments in human capital first. But cutting investment in skills at such times may be short-sighted, as a skilled workforce will play a crucial role in generating future jobs and growth. If cuts to public spending have to be made, they should be based on the long-term cost/benefit ratios of alternative public investments. On these grounds, there is usually a strong case to be made for maintaining public investment in skills.

Encouraging Skilled People to Enter the Country

Facilitate Entry for Skilled Migrants

Countries may not have an adequate supply of skills because they have booming emerging sectors, and not enough people trained in those fields because their societies are ageing and there are too few young people to replace retiring workers or because they want to move major parts of the economy to higher value-added production, which requires a well-trained workforce. Labour-migration policies can complement other measures to address these shortfalls. While all countries select labour migrants, they differ in the extent to which public authorities and employers intervene in the selection process. Many countries focus on the migration of highly skilled workers, but there is also a continuing demand for low-skilled work that many native-born people do not want to do. This demand is often met by low-skilled migrants, through both legal and illegal/irregular channels. Countries might want to consider making it easier for recent immigrants to participate in lifelong-learning activities to help them and their families integrate more fully into society.

Design Policies That Encourage International Students to Remain After Their Studies

International student mobility has increased dramatically over the past years. The advantage of international students for host-country employers is that they have a qualification that can be easily evaluated. Many of them also work part-time during their studies, allowing them to develop ties with the host-country society and labour market, which in turn facilitates their transition from learning to work. To make better use of this source of skills, several OECD countries have eased their immigration policies to encourage international students to stay on after their studies for employment. The overall stay rate varies, averaging 25 % in 2008–2009 among international students who did not renew their student permits. In Australia, Canada, the Czech Republic, France, Germany and the Netherlands, the stay rate is more than 25 %.

Make It Easier for Skilled Migrants to Return to Their Country of Origin

Migration flows can also have a positive impact on the stock of human capital in countries of origin: returning migrants bring back knowledge and experience that are of use to their home country. To recap these advantages, a number of countries have tried to eliminate disincentives to return and, indeed, to facilitate and encourage return migration. One approach can be to provide financial support to municipalities that invite returnees and provide them with housing; another option is to provide income tax concessions, particularly to highly skilled nationals returning to their home country. However, the track record of such measures is mixed. Cooperation on skills policies between source and destination countries can result in win-win outcomes. For example, some countries provide training to guest workers for as long as they participate in the host country's labour market – and the workers can then take this knowledge back to their home countries when they return.

Promoting Cross-Border Skills Policies

Invest in Skills Abroad and Encourage Cross-Border Higher Education

While skills policies are typically designed nationally, an increasing number of employers operate internationally and must derive their skills from both local sources and the global talent pool. Some countries have therefore started to consider skills policies beyond their national borders and have begun to invest in the skills of people in other countries. This has the double advantage of providing well-trained workers to branches of firms located abroad and reducing the incentives to emigrate, especially among highly skilled individuals. Another way to encourage skills development globally is to design policies that encourage cross-border tertiary education. This can help a country to expand its stock of skills more rapidly than if it had to rely on domestic resources alone. How can a country encourage people to supply their skills to the labour market?

Activating People

Identify Inactive Individuals and Why They Are Inactive

People may have skills, but for a variety of reasons they may not be willing or able to supply them to the labour market. In most countries, significant numbers of people are out of the labour force by choice, or because of their personal/family circumstances, or because there are financial disincentives to work.

Labour-force participation rates – the sum of people in employment and in unemployment as a percentage of the working-age population – range from close to 90 % in Iceland to below 60 % in Turkey. Some socio-demographic groups are more likely to be inactive than others, notably women and people with disabilities or chronic health problems, particularly if they are also low-skilled. Integrating under-represented groups into the labour force has a great potential to increase the skills base in an economy. Targeting activation policies efficiently requires identifying inactive individuals and their reasons for inactivity.

Unused human capital represents a waste of skills and of initial investment in those skills. As the demand for skills changes, unused skills can become obsolete; and skills that are unused during inactivity are bound to atrophy over time. Conversely, the more individuals use their skills and engage in complex and demanding tasks, both at work and elsewhere, the more likely skills decline due to inactivity can be prevented.

Create Financial Incentives That Make Work Pay

Costly childcare services, tax systems that make work economically unattractive, or benefit systems that offer better compensation compared with expected salaries can make it uneconomical to work. For people with disabilities, incentives to withdraw from the labour force largely depend on their access to full disability-benefit schemes. A number of countries have either abolished partial disability benefits or have made full disability schemes exclusive to people who can no longer work. In some countries, people who can still work are increasingly being counted as unemployed, and are thus subject to the so-called 'mutual obligation', whereby they have to comply with job-search and training requirements or risk losing part or all of their unemployment benefits. When examining beneficiary claims, countries need to shift the focus from assessing health status to assessing the remaining capacity to work.

Dismantle Non-financial Barriers to Participation in the Labour Force

Inflexible working conditions can make it difficult for people with care obligations and individuals with disabilities to participate in the labour force. Part-time work is

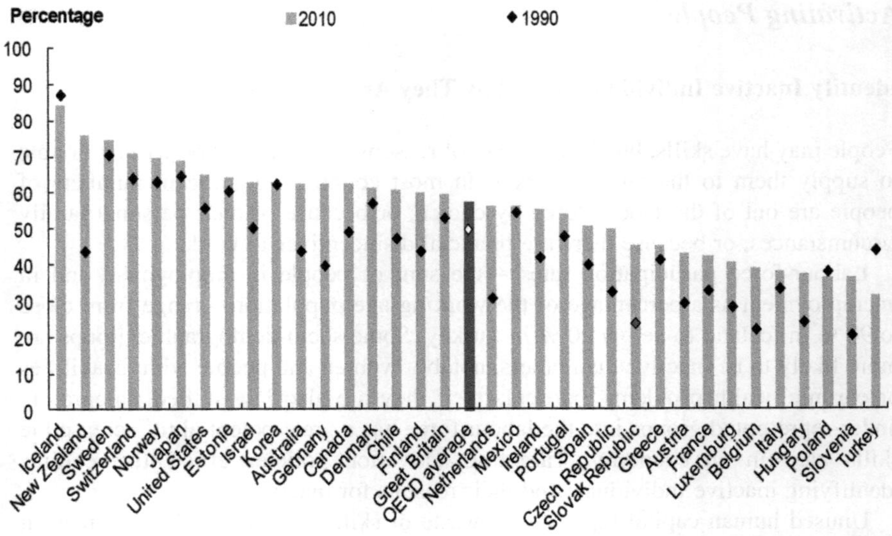

Fig. 3.6 Labour-force participation among older workers (OECD Statistics, n.d.. Notes: Percentage of the population aged 55–64, 1990 and 2010. The percentages were taken from 1991 for Iceland, Mexico and Switzerland; 1992 for Hungary and Poland; 1993 for Czech Republic; 1994 for Austria and Slovak Republic; 1996 for Chile and Slovenia)

increasingly seen as a way to activate these groups. Less rigid working-time arrangements and improved working conditions, particularly for workers with health problems, can also make employment more attractive to these traditionally inactive groups. Employers, trade unions and government can work in concert to design these policies. To be effective, however, these programmes have to be combined with efforts to reduce employers' reluctance to hire inactive individuals. In addition, since skills can atrophy or become obsolete during long periods of inactivity, these individuals may need re-training or up-skilling to improve their employability.

Retaining Skilled People

Contain Early Retirement

Some skilled workers might leave the labour market prematurely for various personal and work-related reasons. This is particularly a problem in countries with ageing populations (see Fig. 3.6). To keep older workers in the labour market, many countries have eliminated early-retirement schemes, increased the official pensionable age and corrected distorted financial incentives to retire early. To tackle demand-side barriers to employing older workers, some countries have tried to balance labour costs with productivity by reducing employers' social security contributions or providing wage subsidies for older workers. Lifelong learning and targeted training, especially in mid-career, can improve employability in later life and discourage early withdrawal from the labour market. A rise in the pensionable age lengthens the period of time over which employers could recover training costs; hence, it is likely to motivate more employers and older employees to invest in training.

Staunch Brain Drain

In certain countries, losing highly skilled individuals through migration to other countries, also known as brain drain, can create shortages of skills and result in a loss of the investment made in these skills. To reap the full benefits of initial investments in skills, countries where brain drain is a major concern should focus on retaining their skilled workers. But experience has shown that the best way to prevent brain drain is to provide incentives to stay, including by improving labour-market conditions locally, rather than by imposing coercive measures to prevent emigration. Brain drain also happens within countries, particularly between rural areas and urban centres. Local career-advice services can help to ensure that skilled people are fully aware and take advantage of the opportunities available within their nearby labour market.

How Can a Country Make the Best Use of Its Talent Pool?

Ensuring that People Use Their Skills Effectively

Developing skills and making them available to the labour market will not have the desired impact on the economy and society if those skills are not used effectively. The fact that skills shortages can co-exist with high unemployment, and that there is persistent evidence of mismatch between employees' skills and job requirements indicates that a population's stock of skills – and the investment made to develop those skills – may be partly going to waste. Skills mismatch on the job (see Fig. 3.7) can be a temporary phenomenon: sometimes, for example, the demand for skills takes time to adjust to the fact that there is a larger pool of highly skilled workers available. Thus, not all types of skills mismatch are bad for the economy. Skills surpluses, which can result from an under-use of skills in specific occupations, can serve as a skills reserve that may be used in other more advanced jobs and for building knowledge economies over the long term. However, the mismatch between workers' skills and their tasks at work can adversely affect economic and social outcomes (see Fig. 3.8). Over-skilling, or the under-use of skills, in specific jobs in the short to medium term can be a problem because it may lead to skills loss. Workers whose

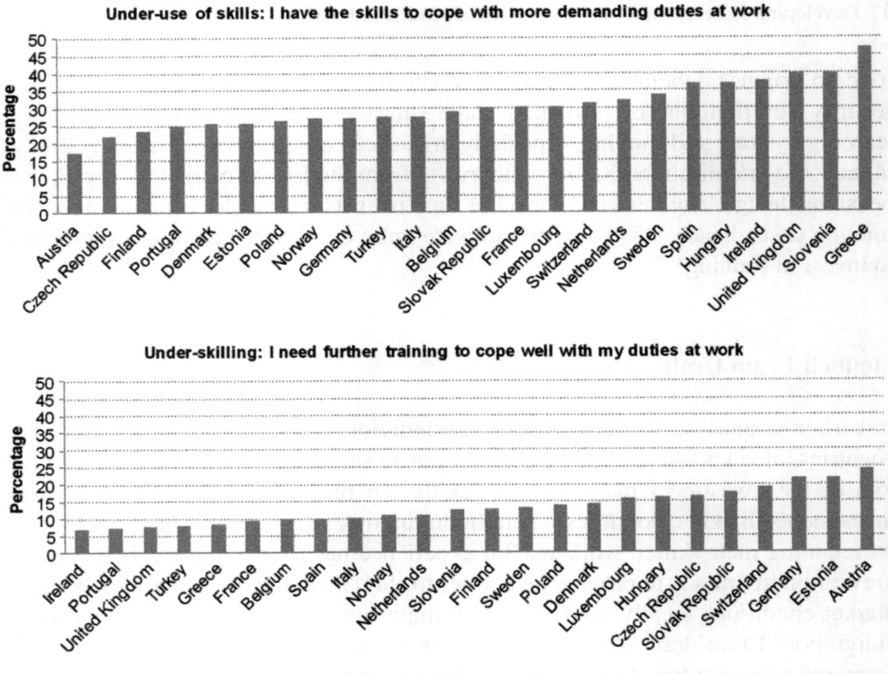

Fig. 3.7 The incidence of skills mismatch (Parent-Thirion, Fernández Macías, Hurley, & Vermeylen 2007. Notes: Incidence of self-reported over- and under-skilling in selected OECD countries, 2010. Data from Switzerland refer to 2005)

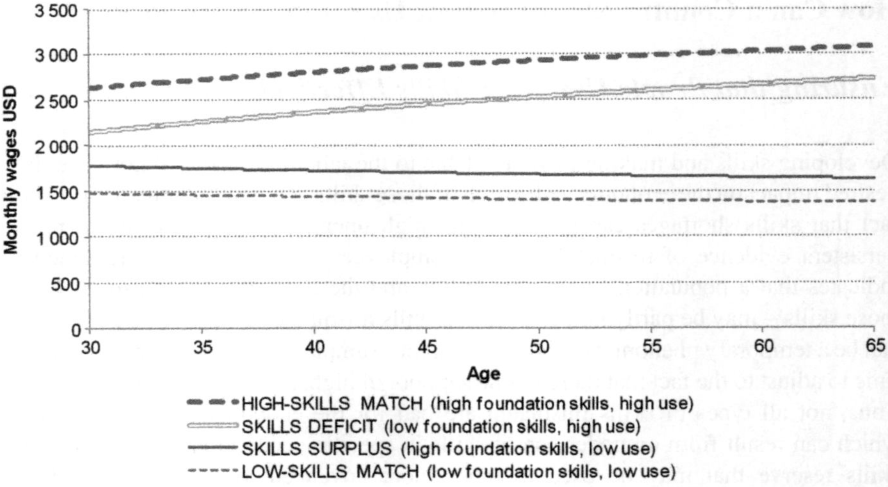

Fig. 3.8 The link between skills mismatch and earnings (PIAAC, 2010. Note: The figure uses preliminary data from the OECD Survey of Adult Skills, a product of the OECD's Programme for the International Assessment of Adult Competencies (PIAAC). Although these data are not based on representative samples, they illustrate trends)

skills are under-used in their current jobs earn less than workers who are well-matched to their jobs and tend to be less satisfied at work. This situation tends to generate more employee turnover, which is likely to affect a firm's productivity. Under-skilling is also likely to affect productivity and, as with skills shortages, slow the rate at which more efficient technologies and approaches to work are adopted.

Help Young People to Gain a Foothold in the Labour Market

Successful entry into the labour market at the beginning of a professional career has a profound influence on later working life. The 'scarring effects' of a poor start can make it difficult to catch up later. In 2011, the average youth unemployment rate among OECD countries was close to 17 % – 2.3 times higher than that of prime-age adults. While that figure reflects the impact of the global economic recession, high rates of youth unemployment were common even before the crisis. In addition, in Europe in 2005 close to one in five 15–29-year-olds were either trapped in unstable jobs or were neither in employment nor in education and training. Strong basic education, in conjunction with vocational education and training programmes that are relevant to the needs of the labour market, tend to smoothen the transition from school to work; so do hiring and firing rules that do not penalise young people compared with other groups, and financial incentives that make it viable for employers to hire young people who require on-the-job training. Such policies can help to prevent skills mismatch and unemployment later on.

Help Employers to Make Better Use of Their employees' Skills

Mismatch on the job, where it affects economic and social outcomes negatively, can be tackled in various ways. In the case of under-skilling, public policies can help to identify workers with low levels of foundation skills and offer an incentive to both employees and employers to invest in skills development to meet the requirements of the job. When the skills available are not adequately used, better management practices are needed. For example, employers can grant workers some autonomy to develop their own working methods so that they use their skills effectively. As workers assume more responsibility for identifying and tackling problems, they are also more likely to 'learn by doing', which, in turn, can spark innovation. Trade unions have an important role to play in improving the match between skills demand and supply.

Provide Better Information About the Skills Needed and Available

Under-skilling, under-use of skills, and unemployment can arise because of a lack of information and transparency in skills systems. The under-use of skills is often related to field-of-study mismatch, whereby individuals work in an area that is unrelated to their field of study and in which their qualifications are not fully valued. Under-skilling could be the result of skills shortages that force employers to hire workers who are not the best fit for the jobs on offer. Quality career guidance, thus, becomes a critical part of any skills strategy. Competent personnel who have the latest labour-market information at their fingertips can steer individuals to the learning programmes that would be best for their prospective careers. Coherent and easy-to-interpret qualifications can help employers to understand which skills are held by potential employees, making it easier to match a prospective employee to a job. Continuous certification that incorporates non-formal and informal learning over the working life is also essential, as is recognition of foreign diplomas. One of the biggest obstacles immigrants face when looking for work is that their qualifications and foreign work experience may not be fully recognised in the host country. As a result, many immigrant workers hold jobs for which they are over-qualified.

Facilitate Internal Mobility

One reason why skills shortages can co-exist with high unemployment is that people with the relevant skills are not in same geographical location as the jobs that require those skills. Reducing costs and other barriers associated with internal mobility helps employees to find suitable jobs and helps employers to find suitable workers. Importing skills from outside a country without first considering the potential for skills supply through internal mobility can have adverse consequences for overall employment and skills use in the country.

Increasing the Demand for High-Level Skills

Help Local Economies Move up the Value-Added Chain

In recent years there has been a growing trend, particularly in emerging economies, in mass-producing simple and effective products and services aimed at customers who do not have great purchasing power. When companies deliver standardised products to markets and attract customers mainly on the basis of costs, they tend to use technical means of production that are task- and routine-based. Thus, they have little incentive to attract skilled staff or to train new staff. Government programmes can influence both employer competitiveness strategies (how a company organises its work to gain competitive advantage in the markets in which it is operating) and product-market strategies, which determine in what markets the company competes. As companies move into higher value-added product and service markets, the levels of skills that they require, and the extent to which they use these skills, tend to increase.

Stimulate the Creation of More High-Skilled and High Value-Added Jobs

A good match between available skills and job tasks is not always a positive situation: people can be matched with their jobs, but at a very low level. Such low-skills equilibria can adversely affect the economic development of a local economy or region, or indeed an entire country. To tackle such a situation, policies can also 'shape' demand, rather than merely respond to it. By fostering competition in the market for goods and services, policymakers can promote productive economic activities that contribute to stronger economic growth and the creation of more productive and rewarding jobs. While such policies primarily fall into the realm of economic-development actors, education institutions focusing on new technologies and innovation can also be involved in developing the skills that will shape the economies of the future.

Foster Entrepreneurship

Entrepreneurs are made, not born. To be successful they need to know how to identify opportunities, turn them into successful ventures, and recognise and respond to difficulties and obstacles that may emerge. Teaching entrepreneurship in schools, universities and vocational training institutions can help instil these skills and competences in students. In promoting entrepreneurship, universities themselves need to be entrepreneurial and innovative. In some countries, for example, recruitment and career-development programmes for academic staff in many private and public universities now take into account entrepreneurial attitudes and prior experience, as well as work in mentoring entrepreneurs. Since migrants too can be entrepreneurs, policies can support recent immigrants in establishing their businesses by offering seminars and briefings on local labour law, and income and corporate tax and social-security legislation in addition to more traditional courses in financing, production and marketing.

Conclusion

Universally, skills transform lives and drive economies; and without the right skills, people are kept on the margins of society, technological progress does not translate into economic growth, and countries cannot compete in today's economies. But the toxic co-existence of unemployed graduates on the street and employers saying they cannot find the people with the skills they need shows that skills do not automatically translate into better economic and social outcomes.

Sound education policies are central to addressing the challenges and to ensure the economic and social well-being of individuals and nations. However, if skills are to be developed effectively with a lifetime perspective, then a broad range of policy fields are implicated.

Anticipating the evolution of the demand for skills is an essential antecedent. But education policy needs to respond by improving the quality of learning outcomes, putting the premium on skills-oriented learning throughout life instead of qualifications-focused education upfront. This is about fostering demand-sensitive and relevant learning. Schools and formal education institutions are the foundation for this. However, skills development will be far more effective if the world of learning and the world of work are linked. Compared to purely government-designed curricula taught exclusively in schools, learning in the workplace allows young people to develop 'hard' skills from modern equipment, and 'soft' skills, such as teamwork, communication and negotiation, through real-world experience. Hands-on workplace training can also help to motivate disengaged youth to stay in or re-engage with education and smoothen the transition to work. The social partners can make an important contribution to developing curricula that include broader, transferable skills and to ensure that good-quality training is available to all.

Education policy, in this broader sense, is everybody's business and countries need to deal with the tough question of who should pay for what, when and how, particularly for learning beyond school. Employers can do a lot more to create a climate that supports learning, and invest in learning. Some individuals can shoulder more of the financial burden. Governments can do much to design rigorous standards, provide financial incentives and create a safety net so that all people have access to high quality learning.

But even the best skills simply evaporate if they are not maintained and upgraded to meet the changing needs of societies. There are people who are highly skilled who have decided not to work. Why? They may be too busy caring for children or elderly parents, they may have health problems, or they may have calculated that it just does not pay to work. The answer is that countries need to make better use of their talent pool. Equally important, countries need to ensure that skills are used at work effectively. OECD data show that this is a genuine issue that is mirrored in the earnings prospects of people and therefore productivity.

What can education policy do about these issues that go beyond the immediate realm of educational institutions? Quality career guidance is essential: people who have the latest labour-market information can help steer individuals to the education or training that would best prepare them for their prospective careers. Helping young people to can gain a foothold in the labour market is fundamental too. Coherent and easy-to-understand qualifications are important to help employers identify potential employees who are suitable for the jobs they offer. And reducing the costs of moving within a country can help employees to find the jobs that match their skills and help employers to find the skills that match their jobs. There may be young people just starting out, who are well educated but have trouble finding jobs that put their education and training to good use. Here, public policy can help shape the demand for skills. There is much that governments and employers can to do promote knowledge-intensive industries and jobs that require high-skilled workers. Adding these kinds of high value-added jobs to a labour market helps to get more people working – and for better pay and to set the right signals for the initial education of future generations.

Last but not least, education that fosters entrepreneurships can help create jobs. Indeed, education is where entrepreneurship is often born. For that, education and educational policy need to become more entrepreneurial too.

Appendix 1 The Analytical Potential of the OECD Survey of Adult Skills

The OECD Survey of Adult Skills, a product of the Programme for the International Assessment of Adult Competencies (PIAAC), is the most comprehensive international survey of adult skills ever conducted. It gathers information from some 5,000 people aged 16–65 in each participating country.

Directly assessing adult skills has significant advantages over previous measures of human capital, such as those based on educational qualifications. A diploma does not certify a precise skill, even on the day it is awarded; one that was awarded many years prior to an assessment says even less about a person's current skills. The Survey of Adult Skills not only measures the level of skills, it also tries to assess how skills are associated with the success of individuals and countries. In addition, it examines how well education and training systems succeed in instilling these competencies, and how public policy might improve their effectiveness. The data gathered through the Survey of Adult Skills, which also includes information on participants' demographic characteristics (age, gender, immigrant status, etc.), education and training, job history, and the social aspects of their lives are broad and deep enough to offer insights into many different aspects of skills, including:

- The influence of skills on social and economic outcomes: The survey allows for in-depth analysis of the relationship between skills and labour-market outcomes as well as between skills, trust, political engagement, volunteering, and health. Information from the survey, combined with advanced econometric modelling, can provide insights into how the supply of skills and the quality of those skills affect economic growth.
- The use of skills in the workplace: Data from the survey can be compared against other measures of skills, such as occupations and qualifications or diplomas, while differences and similarities in how skills are used in the workplace can be examined and compared among countries, industries and enterprises. The data also offer a unique opportunity to develop a direct measure of mismatch by comparing observed individual skills levels to skills requirements at work. In addition to shedding light on the under-use of skills, its causes and consequences, the data will also allow for an examination of the reasons behind skills deficits.

(continued)

(continued)

- Developing skills over a lifetime: The survey allows for a study of some of the factors that are important for acquiring and maintaining skills, and how the acquisition of skills changes over time. These aspects of skills development can be studied at both the cohort and country levels. The comparative data on adult learning can also be used to identify international patterns of who is and who is not participating in adult learning, whether and where the opportunity to participate is not available to all, and the factors that motivate people to participate. The data can also help identify adults with poor skills and can also be used to develop strategies to improve their literacy.
- Immigrant skills and qualifications: The data from the survey can also be used to examine differences in skills levels between immigrants who acquired their skills in the host country and those who acquired their skills elsewhere, and between first- and second-generation immigrants. This information sheds light on such issues as whether returns to skills depend on where the qualifications, diplomas and work experience were acquired; the relationship between outcomes and measured skills, as opposed to formal qualifications; and the role of language proficiency in immigrants' labour-market outcomes and occupational choices.
- Digital literacy, problem solving in technology-rich environments, and using information and communication technologies: The survey will help build a better understanding of how well adults cope with an increasingly high-tech environment, both in and outside the workplace. They can be used to examine inequalities in cognitive foundation skills, particularly among young people, and the factors that drive those differences, including parental background, educational attainment, tracking, the quality of education and ICT-related practices.

References

Eurostat. (2005–2008). *EU adult education survey*. Retrieved from http://epp.eurostat.ec.europa.eu/portal/page/portal/education/data/database

ManpowerGroup. (2011). *2011 talent shortage survey*. Retrieved from http://www.experis.us/Client-File-Pile/Site-Documents/2011-Talent-Shortage-Survey.pdf

OECD. (2011a). *Education at a glance 2011: OECD indicators*. Paris: Author.

OECD. (2011b). *OECD employment outlook 2011*. Paris: Author.

OECD Statistics. (n.d.). *OECD labour market statistics*. Retrieved from http://stats.oecd.org

Parent-Thirion, A., Fernández Macías, E., Hurley, J., & Vermeylen, G. (2007). *Fourth European working conditions survey*. Retrieved from http://www.eurofound.europa.eu/pubdocs/2006/98/en/2/ef0698en.pdf

Programme for the International Assessment of Adult Competencies (PIAAC). (2010). *PIAAC field trial data*. Retrieved from http://nces.ed.gov/surveys/piaac

Chapter 4
Conceptualising Teacher Preparation for Educational Innovation: Singapore's Approach

Sing Kong Lee and Ee Ling Low

Setting the Context – How the 21st Century Competencies Framework Was Developed

The driving forces that have been identified to shape the twenty-first century include globalisation, rapid technological advancements, changing demographics (e.g., ageing populations), shifting economic weights (particularly with emerging markets in Asia), and major trends and issues such as climate change and pressure on resources. As the global landscape evolves, it is pertinent that countries and governments consider how to prepare their citizens for the future through the mapping of educational outcomes to fundamental workforce skills and competencies in order to remain competitive and relevant in the future. While academic qualifications remain an important entry requirement to the knowledge economy, it does not guarantee that qualified workers have the necessary competencies to thrive in the new economy, especially if they do not adapt to the rapidly changing demands in the global society and marketplace. Therefore, there is a strong push for educators to examine and incorporate within the education system the competencies paramount for survival in the twenty-first century.

An in-depth review of 21st century competencies (21CC) became topical when governments began to map education outcomes to workforce skills and competencies. Many councils and associations have been set up internationally and within government bodies to catalogue the essential competencies imperative in the twenty-first century, including the National Research Council (NRC), the

S.K. Lee (✉)
Director's Office, National Institute of Education, 1 Nanyang Walk,
Singapore 637616, Singapore
e-mail: singkong.lee@nie.edu.sg

E.L. Low
Office of Teacher Education, National Institute of Education, 1 Nanyang Walk,
Singapore 637616, Singapore
e-mail: eeling.low@nie.edu.sg

S.K. Lee et al. (eds.), *Educational Policy Innovations: Levelling Up and Sustaining Educational Achievement*, Springer Education Innovation Book Series 1,
DOI 10.1007/978-981-4560-08-5_4, © Springer Science+Business Media Singapore 2014

Table 4.1 Assessment and teaching of 21st century skills project: 21st century skills rates (Binkley et al., 2012)

Ways of thinking	1	Creativity and innovation
	2	Critical thinking, problem solving, decision-making
	3	Learning to learn, metacognition
Ways of working	4	Communication
	5	Collaboration (teamwork)
Tools for working	6	Information literacy
	7	ICT literacy
Living in the World	8	Citizenship – local and global
	9	Life and career
	10	Personal & social responsibility – including cultural awareness and competence

Assessment and Teaching of 21st Century Skills Project (ATC21S; see Table 4.1), to list a few.

ATCS21 developed a framework with descriptions that are able to quantify each of the 10 important skills, analysing them through the paradigm of Knowledge, Skills, and Attitudes, Values and Ethics, coined as the KSAVE framework. An example of the 'ways of thinking – critical thinking, problem solving, and decision making' is presented in Table 4.2.

The framework was formulated after collating the studies from various organisations and countries, which have attempted to map out the 21CC, which is listed in Table 4.3 (Binkley et al., 2012).

The NRC categorised the three domains of competencies as cognitive, intrapersonal and interpersonal. While the first two competencies have always been important, there is emerging attention on the importance of interpersonal skills in the twenty-first century, where the ability to collaborate and communicate ideas verbally and visually have become valuable skill-sets required to succeed. The NRC reported similar findings to those suggested by Binkley et al. (2012), albeit the NRC's reference was to the American market, with a greater focus on preparation for adulthood, career-readiness beyond mere academic performance. For some countries, it is not a matter of preference; instead, this framework provides an essential benchmark, a vision to work towards, without which, a country will fail to progress at a pace rapid enough to allow its citizens to be equipped with the skills essential for survival in the twenty-first century global workplace and society. Societies and individuals should resist the temptation to use the framework as a de-contextualised tool to measure performance but as a tool to guide progress instead.

In Singapore, as well documented by Goh and Gopinathan (2008), we have essentially entered an age which Reich (2001) calls the "age of terrific deal" (p. 13), where choices appear to be unlimited and it is not difficult for individuals to switch to the proverbial greener pastures as it were. As already alluded to earlier, social and economic forces are placing a strong pressure on educational change and the outcomes are likely to affect all sectors of society in Singapore. As Singaporeans are moving up the educational ladder, they are also increasingly well-travelled but the income gap is widening between the 'haves' and the 'have-nots'. The 'haves' will position their children for the best possible education they can afford, including

Table 4.2 KSAVE framework: ways of thinking – critical thinking, problem solving, and decision-making rates (Binkley et al., 2012)

Ways of thinking – critical thinking, problem solving, and decision-making		
Knowledge	Skills	Attitudes/ethics/values
Reason effectively, use systematic thinking and evaluate evidence	Reason effectively	Make reasoned judgments and decisions
Understand systems and strategies for tackling unfamiliar problems Understand the importance of evidence in belief formation Re-evaluate beliefs when presented with conflicting evidence	Use various types of reasoning (inductive, deductive, etc.) as appropriate to the situation	Consider and evaluate major alternative points of view Reflect critically on learning experiences and processes Incorporate these reflections into the decision-making
Solve problems Identify gaps in knowledge Ask significant questions that clarify various points of view and lead to better solutions	Use systems thinking Analyse how parts of a whole interact with each other to produce overall outcomes in complex systems. Examine ideas, identify, and analyse arguments Synthesise and make connections between information and arguments Interpret information and draw conclusions based on the best analysis. Categorise, decode, and clarify information Identify gaps in knowledge Ask significant questions that clarify various points of view and lead to better solutions Effectively analyse and evaluate evidence, arguments, claims, and beliefs Analyse and evaluate major alternative points of view Evaluate. Assess claims and arguments Infer. Query evidence, conjecture alternatives of view and draw conclusions Explain. State results, justify procedures, and present arguments Self-regulate, self-examine, and self-correct	Solve problems Be open to non-familiar, unconventional, and innovative solutions to problems and to ways to solve problems Ask meaningful questions that clarify various points of view and lead to better solutions

Table 4.3 Source documents on twenty-first century skills rates (Binkley et al., 2012)

Country/region	Document(s)
European Union	*Key Competencies for Lifelong Learning – A European Reference Framework*, November 2004 Recommendation of the European Parliament and of the Council of 18 December 2006 on key competences for lifelong learning Implementation of 'Education and Training 2010' work programme http://eur-lex.europa.eu/LexUriServ/LexUriServ.do?uri=OJ:L:2006:394:0010:0018:en:PDF
OECD	*New Millennium Learners Project: Challenging Our Views on ICT and Learning* http://www.oecd.org/document/10/0,3343,en_2649_35845581_38358154_1_1_1_1,00.html
USA (partnership for twenty-first century skills)	P21 Framework definitions P21 Framework flyer http://www.p21.org/documents/P21_Framework_Definitions.pdf
Japan	Center for Research on Educational Testing (CRET) http://www.cret.or.jp/e
Australia	Melbourne declaration on educational goals for young Australians http://www.mceecdya.edu.au/verve/_resources/National_Declaration_on_the_Educational_Goals_for_Young_Australians.pdf
Scotland	*A curriculum for excellence – the four capabilities* www.ltscotland.org.uk/curriculumforexcellence/index.asp
England	*The learning journey* *Personal learning & thinking skills – the national curriculum for England* http://curriculum.qcda.gov.uk/uploads/PLTS_framework_tcm8-1811.pdf
Northern Ireland	*Assessing the cross curricular skills* http://www.nicurriculum.org.uk/key_stages_1_and_2/assessment/assessing_crosscurricular_skills/index.asp
ISTE	*National educational technology standards for students, second edition, global learning in the digital age* http://www.iste.org/standards.aspx
USA. National Academies, science for the twenty-first century	*Exploring the intersection of science education and the development of twenty-first century skills* http://www7.nationalacademies.org/bota/Assessment_of_21st_Century_Skills_Homepage.html
USA, Department of Labor	Competency models A review of the literature The role of the Employment and Training Administration (ETA), Michelle R. Ennis

paying for many hours of after-school private tuition to help their children achieve better grades, whether their children academically require it or not. The so-called 'have-nots' do not have the financial means to provide their children who may be struggling to secure a pass at the end of each academic year's examinations with the extra private tuition support after school hours. The contribution of private tuition towards inflating the student achievement scores in internationally benchmarked tests has been observed by scholars and termed as the *shadow education industry*. Singapore needs to level out such achievement gaps, if any, caused by disparities in the ability to afford tuition for their children. In fact, studies ought to be done on whether there are indeed tangible benefits for students taking tuition lessons. Moving ahead, Singapore as a whole needs to prepare our young for the knowledge-based economy, as Goh and Gopinathan assert, in order to "sustain Singapore's competitiveness, strengthen their national identity, values, and social cohesion and, in the process, sustain Singapore's society regardless of race, language or religion" (p. 34).

Singapore is a small country with limited resources. Our people are our most important resource, and we invest heavily in building up our human capital in order to secure Singapore's future. Education is therefore a very important key enabler to equip our people with 21CC to thrive in a changing landscape. There is an urgent need for our education system to evolve and to be ready to meet this challenge. A holistic systemic response is required to produce learning outcomes of students to meet the demands of twenty-first century education. Responding to the demands and concerns of the ever-changing local and global educational landscape in the twenty-first century is not just the responsibility of teacher education institutes, but that of many stakeholders across the educational sector including the government agencies, schools, universities, parents, communities and unions.

The educational eco-system as a whole needs to respond in a coherent manner so that the reforms undertaken can truly help our students acquire the values, skills and knowledge critical for functioning effectively in the twenty-first century global workplace and society. Our small size makes it easy for the Ministry of Education (MOE) to directly support all our 365 public schools through their clusters and to directly support and develop our education service of more than 33,000 teachers, 2,200 allied administrators and 5,700 administrative staff.

MOE led a comprehensive review of the changes and demand of a twenty-first century landscape, by conducting an environmental scan of future trends and extensive research from both local and international sources (including focus-group discussions with employers, educators, etc.).

The 21CC framework in Singapore articulates a set of desired student outcomes we think the twenty-first century learner should possess (refer to Fig. 4.1). These are: a Confident Person, a Self-directed Learner, an Active Contributor, and a Concerned Citizen. These key competencies are underpinned by Core Values: Resilience, Responsibility, Respect, Integrity, Care and Harmony. These are supported by Social and Emotional Learning (SEL) skills: Self-Awareness, Self-management, Social Awareness, Relationship management and Responsible Decision-making.

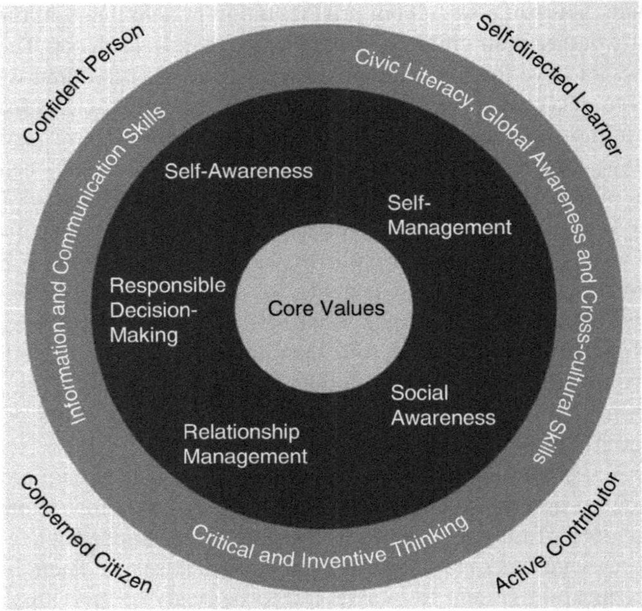

Fig. 4.1 Twenty-first century competencies and desired student outcomes rates (MOE, 2010)

How Do We Teach 21CC?

Understanding that Singapore's future is in the balance, we approached 21CC through changes to the national curriculum, pedagogy and assessment. MOE takes a total curriculum approach towards the teaching of 21CC, that is, all the different learning areas in the academic and non-academic curriculum (such as co-curricular activities) present opportunities for the development of 21CC. In the unique tripartite partnership between MOE, the National Institute of Education (NIE), NTU and schools, Singapore took up the challenge of creating a twenty-first century education system. This tight and strong partnership allows research to inform policy, and policy, in turn, to be translated seamlessly into schools.

Schools are given the autonomy to implement 21CC, with support from MOE in terms of provision of pedagogical exemplars, teacher training and professional sharing. MOE is also looking into developing standards and benchmarks for 21CC to establish a common point of reference for alignment among the different academic and non-academic programmes, teaching and learning and assessment in schools, working with like-minded countries in ATC21S and other forums. Subsequently, this led to the development of evaluation framework for 21CC (Chong-Mok, 2010) at both the systemic and school level.

Research has surfaced that outstanding teacher education programmes boast of at least the following attributes: seamless integration of courses that constructs a consistent learning environment throughout the programme; comprehensible standards of practices and performance; a core curriculum with emphasis on student learning, assessment and content pedagogy; use of problem-based teaching methods; active assessment using case studies and portfolios, drawing on the best practices of skilled veteran teachers in clinical experiences; and extending the amount of clinical exposure in the programme (Darling-Hammond, as cited in NIE, 2009). NIE took on board these research findings to enhance our teacher education model in order to prepare teachers who are able to meet the challenges of preparing their students for the realities of the twenty-first century global workplace and society.

Singapore's Response: Competencies Needed to Teach Twenty-First Century Skills

In 2009, NIE undertook a systematic review of our teacher education programmes in partnership with the MOE and the schools, using the revised National Curriculum and 21CC as a key guide. This collective and systemic effort led to the articulation of a set of Graduand Teacher Competencies (GTCs) outlining the professional standards, benchmarks and goals for graduands of our initial teacher preparation programmes (see Table 4.4).

Table 4.4 Graduand teacher competencies framework rates

Performance Dimensions	Core Competencies
Professional Practice	Nurturing the child
	Providing quality learning of child
	Providing quality learning of child in Co-Curricular Activities
	Cultivating knowledge:
	With subject mastery
	With reflective thinking
	With analytic thinking
	With initiative
	With creative teaching
	With a future focus
Leadership and Management	Winning hearts & minds
	Understanding the environment
	Developing others
	Working with others
	Partnering parents
	Working in teams
Personal Effectiveness	Knowing self and others
	Tuning into self
	Exercising personal integrity
	Understanding and respecting others
	Resilience and adaptability

Source: *TE21 Report*, NIE (2009, pp. 56–59)

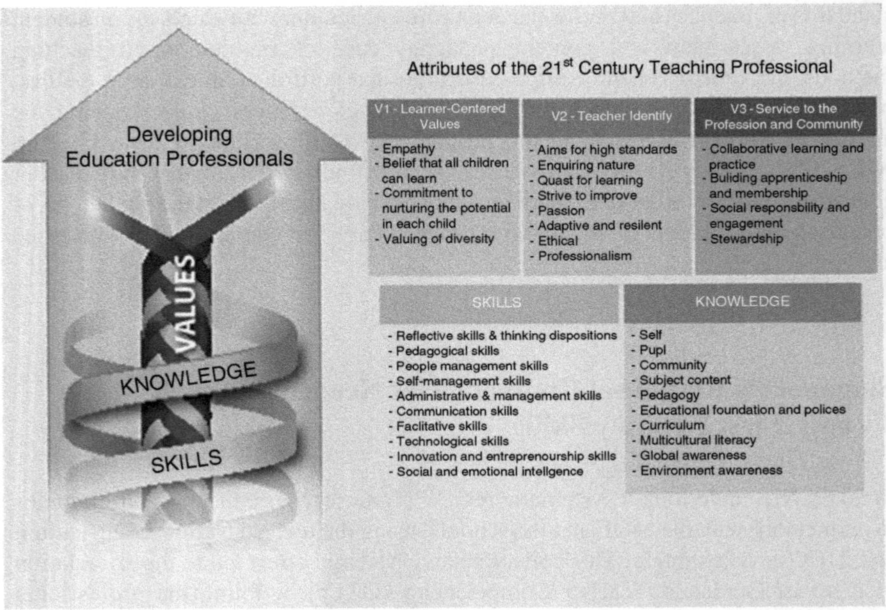

Fig. 4.2 V3SK rates (*TE21 Report*, NIE, 2009, p. 45)

GTCs is modelled after the Ministry's teacher appraisal system, Enhanced Performance Management System (EPMS), that spelled out three performance dimensions: professional practice, leadership and management, and personal effectiveness. GTCs indicate that beginning teachers emerging from our teacher preparation programmes will have been adequately prepared to deal with the core roles of nurturing the child and the quality of learning of the child, strong subject mastery and competencies related to the teaching and learning of the subject, working with and respecting others, and values pertaining to self.

We acknowledge that within a finite period, no pre-service teacher preparation programme can fully prepare teachers with all the competencies of a professional teacher. The teacher's professional development journey must be seen as a continuum. Hence, additional competencies can be acquired through continual professional development programmes during the span of a teacher's career. This is something that MOE is concurrently working on to ensure that in-service courses will build upon the foundation laid by pre-service teacher training.

The outcome of our review is the Teacher Education Model for the 21st Century (TE21; NIE, n.d. b), focusing on three key attributes of the twenty-first century teaching professional: Values, Skills and Knowledge, conceptualised as the V3SK framework shown in Fig. 4.2.

TE21: A Values-Driven Underpinning Philosophy

Our TE21 model is firmly anchored in values. As shown in Fig. 4.2, a three-pronged set of values forms the central pillar around which skills and knowledge deemed essential for the twenty-first century teacher are wrapped. The first value paradigm is learner-centredness, where the learner is placed at the centre of all our educational endeavours. The second value paradigm is developing a strong sense of teacher identity because research has established a clear linkage between teachers who develop a strong sense of identity and their eventual retention and contribution to the profession. Finally, our third value paradigm concerns service to the profession and the community. Our model strongly advocates that the professional teacher must contribute back to the community of teachers through developing an ability to mentor novice teachers and to build professional learning communities in order to collaborate with and learn from each other within the fraternity. The next section will explicate how each of these values has been translated into our teacher education curriculum.

Learner-Centredness: Belief that All Students Can Learn

The first set of values puts the learner at the core of the teachers' work. In our educational psychology core courses, our student teachers are introduced to key theoretical concepts about learners and learning, and then asked to reflect on how these concepts can help teachers to facilitate and maximise learning at optimal levels for all the students in their diverse classrooms. Such reflections help our student teachers to strengthen their beliefs that, indeed, every child can learn despite their diverse profiles.

Developing a Strong Sense of Teacher Identity

The second set of values is to enable teachers to develop a strong sense of professional teacher identity since research evidence shows that those with a strong identity will stay long and be able to contribute to the profession. This identity must manifest itself in terms of upholding the professionalism, integrity and values of the teaching fraternity. A constant emphasis and reminder of the Teachers' Pledge and the creed which further articulates each line of the Teachers' Pledge will strengthen their identity as to who teachers are and what they represent. The Teachers' Pledge is first recited during the Teachers' Compass Ceremony (TCC) organised by the Academy of Singapore Teachers (AST) at the start of the student teachers' teacher education programmes often held during the orientation week. During the TCC, each student teacher is welcomed by the Director-General

Teachers' Pledge
We, the teachers of Singapore, pledge that:
We will be true to our mission to bring out the best in our students.
We will be exemplary in the discharge of our duties and responsibilities.
We will guide our students to be good and useful citizens of Singapore.
We will continue to learn and pass on the love of learning to our students.
We will win the trust, support and co-operation of parents and the community so as to enable us to achieve our mission.

Fig. 4.3 Singapore's teachers' pledge rates (MOE, n.d.)

of Education (DGE) or her deputies, and the Director of NIE or NIE's Dean of the Teacher Education pre-service programmes. They also listen to an inspiring speech made by an award-winning educator, normally one of the Outstanding Youth in Education Award (OYEA) winners for educators who have contributed above and beyond their call of duty to the betterment of their students' learning and development, and who are aged 30 years or below. At the end of the ceremony, they are each presented with a compass, meant to symbolise a moral compass to guide them throughout their career from the pre-service to the professional teaching phases. The text of the Teachers' Pledge is shown in Fig. 4.3.

The next time that student teachers take the pledge led by DGE is at the exit point of their teacher education programmes, during their graduation ceremony known as the Teachers' Investiture Ceremony (TIC) where they are formally welcomed into the fraternity by MOE. It is hoped that the recitation of the teachers' pledge at the entry and exit points of their teacher preparation journey helps them to be aware of the ethos of the teaching profession and the onerous sense of duty and responsibility that they have undertaken.

Contribution to the Profession and the Community

The third set of values focuses on the professionalism of teachers in contributing back to the fraternity and the community at large. This is encouraged through the emphasis of group projects and collaborative learning whilst at NIE so that the seeds of professional learning and sharing communities can be sown at pre-service and be brought into the schools as they enter as beginning teachers (BT). More importantly, during the practicum postings (typically taking up 40 % of the 1-year postgraduate diploma in education and 22 weeks of the 4-year Bachelor of Arts and Science [Education] programmes), student teachers are mentored by experienced teachers who serve mainly as their cooperating teachers (CTs) in schools and who also chair the focused conversations where they are expected to share their learning from their pre-service programmes and also at the end of their practicum postings in schools.

Key changes in our Curriculum, Pedagogies, Assessment, Theory–Practice Linkages and Physical Infrastructure which have helped us to translate the theoretical recommendations of our TE21 model into actual implementation will be focused upon next.

Curricula Changes

Coherent Mapping of Courses across the Pre-service Programmes

It is well acknowledged from research literature that while the essential components necessary for preparing an excellent teacher may be present in a programme, it is the coherence and the clear linkages built between the components that contribute to the success or failure of pre-service teacher preparation. For this reason, the first thing we did was to establish a student teacher learning journey and concept mindmap detailing exactly which component of our programmes deliver which specific GTC, and which specific value, skill or knowledge dimension outlined in our TE21 model. This was done mainly through lecturer's self-reporting by filling up a form which indicated what their individual courses delivered in terms of either the GTC or the V3SK frameworks for each of more than 300 courses run by the institute. Thereafter, the coordinators help to consolidate the information into whether the attributes or competencies cover more or less than 50 % of the course. To achieve the overall programme mindmap for student teachers, only those attributes or competencies that cover more than 50 % of the course are reflected. The programme mindmap for the Postgraduate Diploma in Education programme is reflected in Fig. 4.4.

The original mindmap had an empty page for student teachers to map their own personal learning journeys but this is now being developed into an online electronic platform with the eventual aim of allowing student teachers to map their learning journeys automatically once they have tagged their entries via the e-Portfolio which will be described in further detail later in this chapter.

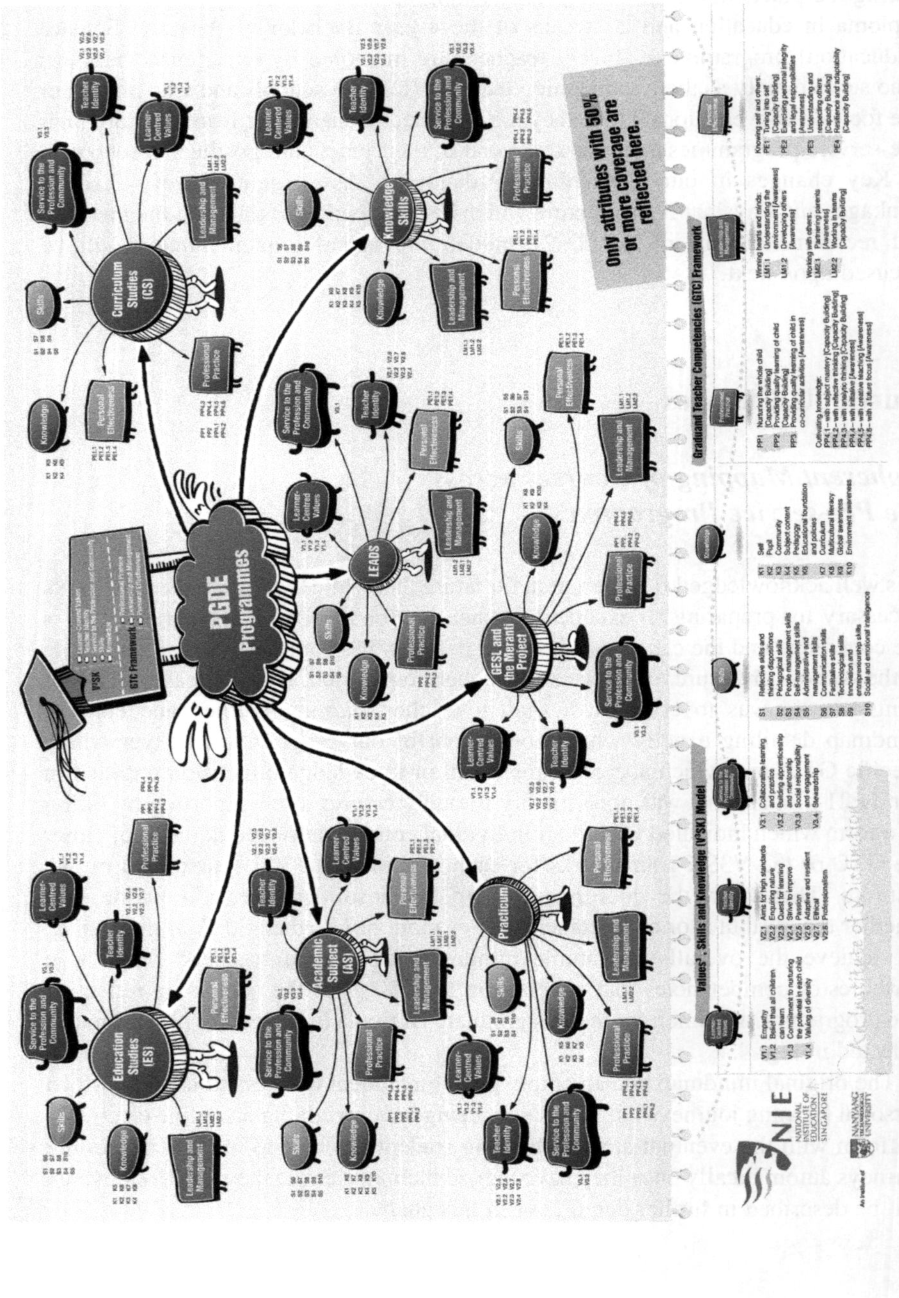

Fig. 4.4 TE21 Student teachers' learning journey and mindmap rates (NIE, n.d. c)

Core Mandatory Programmes Focusing on Values Development

Our teacher education programmes hold the philosophy that values can be both caught and taught. Values can be taught through the formal curriculum as well as caught through experiential learning platforms such as through service learning. For example, to ensure that values have a central focus in the teacher preparation programmes, all student teachers participate in two core mandatory programmes: the Group Endeavours in Service Learning (GESL), a community-involvement experiential learning project; and the Meranti Project (a personal and professional development 2-day non-residential workshop).

All student teachers participate in community projects of their choice in groups of 20. They plan and implement the project with the help of a staff facilitator. In the process, they are sensitised to issues confronting our community and they emerge confident of being able to facilitate community involvement projects in the future. At the end of the project, there is a celebratory programme known as Service Learning Day, where all groups get to exhibit their project in the form of a poster exhibition while selected groups present their projects and main learning points from the community to fellow student teachers, faculty members and representatives from MOE.

The Meranti Project (named after a tropical tree with extremely hard wood symbolising resilience) is a personal and professional development programme specially tailored for student teachers. The programme is experiential in nature where student teachers experience the core competencies of social emotional learning, share their personal aspirations with their peers and express their opinions about their chosen career in an open and supportive environment. Through informal dialogue with veteran teachers and school students, the Meranti Project gives student teachers the opportunity of learning first hand from teachers' experiences and student learners' perspectives.

At the end of the programme, student teachers have a better grasp of innovative approaches to National Education (NE), Character and Citizenship Education (CCE) and working in a multicultural classroom. The overall objectives of the Project include: helping student teachers to develop better self-awareness (better tuning into self); providing a clearer idea of what NE and CCE is all about and one's role in nurturing NE and CCE in innovative ways in the classroom; better ideas of working with diversity in the classroom; strategies for coping with being a teacher; and an affirmation of choosing teaching as a career.

Changes in Pedagogies and Assessment

Our teacher education programmes aim to produce thinking teachers who are effective instructors and facilitators of learning and good mediators and designers of learning environments. A few major pedagogical changes are highlighted below.

Self-directed and Real-world Learning

The major pedagogical change is that the ownership of learning is being transferred from the teacher (i.e., teacher educators) to the learner (i.e., student teachers). Two examples towards building self-directed, lifelong learners are:

1. **Problem-based learning**: In our Educational Psychology courses, real-life school-based scenarios are used as discussion focal points. Learners are presented with difficult classroom situations simulated using video-reenactments and are asked to consider what solutions they can propose to solve such different scenarios when presented with them. Learners act as active problem solvers while teachers act as mediating coaches.
2. **Social context of education**: A core Education Studies course provides student teachers the platform to organise student-led lessons where educational policies are discussed and reflected upon. Some critical questions that are being posed to students could be, for example, "What are my roles in upholding these policies as a teacher even if I personally don't agree with them?" Such questions then form the basis of seminar discussions, which are often student-led and lecturer-facilitated.

Modelling the Enabling Power of Technology

Twenty-first century teachers require new paradigms and competencies to prepare them to be mediators and designers of learning environments to engage their digitally native students. We have recently developed our own Apple apps to enhance independent learning on the go, anytime and anywhere. One example is NIE's *mVideo* app that allows students to watch the videos at their own pace, test their understanding on key concepts, and participate in online discussions. This app is designed with the flipped classroom in mind: content delivery is done outside the classroom while homework is done in the classroom.

In addition to the development of innovative software for enhancing pedagogical development, the sharing of good pedagogical practices across the different academic groups within the institute is also made possible through platforms such as an institute-wide 1-day professional sharing session known as The TE21 Summit in November 2010 which comprised workshops and sharing sessions sharing about effective pedagogical approaches informed by research and the latest development of technological tools that can enrich teaching and learning in the classrooms. To sustain the impact that such a powerful professional sharing day has created, there is a need to keep up the conversations started on an annual basis. To do this, we have the annual e-fiesta with the same intentions and goals to advance pedagogical development institute-wide.

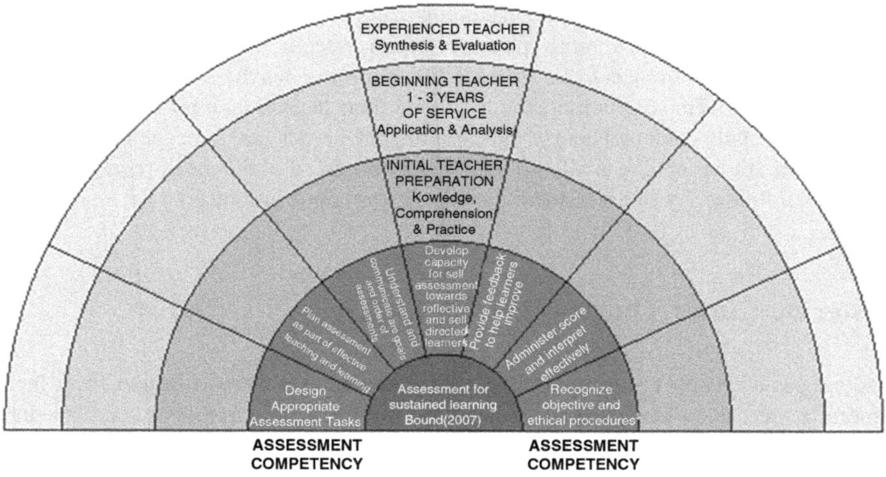

Fig. 4.5 Assessment Competency Framework rates (NIE, 2007)

Assessment for and as Learning

The Assessment Competency Framework for twenty-first century teaching and learning spells out a set of assessment literacy outcomes to be acquired and developed by teachers from the pre-service through to the professional teaching stage (see Fig. 4.5).

Faculty were first asked to map out the current assessment literacies covered in all the pre-service courses that are outlined in the assessment competency framework as adapted from Boud and Falchikov (2007), namely,

- Designing appropriate assessment tasks
- Planning assessment as part of effective teaching and learning
- Understanding and communicating goals
- Developing the capacity for self-assessment in order to build reflective and self-directed learners
- Providing feedback to help learners improve
- Administering, scoring and interpreting effectively
- Recognising objective and ethical procedures (as cited in NIE, 2009, p. 96)

In order to ensure that there is continuity in the assessment competency coverage from different areas of study, key assessment literacies introduced and covered in the Education Studies core courses are provided to the subject-specific Curriculum Studies coordinators to ensure alignment. An online site accessible to all student teachers covers the information on key assessment terminologies and hosts key readings on assessment of and for learning. Additionally, there is also a plan to mount a stand-alone basic assessment literacy course under the Education Studies area of study to ensure that by the time the Curriculum Studies courses begin, all student teachers have a baseline understanding of core assessment literacies at a broad level, and they go on to have more subject/discipline-specific focus in their respective Curriculum Studies subjects. To ensure that returning teachers and Diploma in Education crossovers who come back to pursue their degrees are not left out of the picture, a specially designed course on Assessment Literacy that is pegged at a Level 2 Education Studies course is offered to them as well. In all of our assessment literacy efforts, the philosophy of assessment for and of learning is embraced.

Fostering Closer Theory–Practice Linkages

Teaching is a complex activity and what teachers need is often different from the general expert-knowledge teacher educators often present to student teachers. In NIE, the link between the two is strengthened when student teachers are taught to reflect on their own action and experiences, and asked to document and articulate their own learning and growth in the teacher education programmes. There is strong emphasis on inquiry-based and experiential learning, and close partnerships with schools are forged in an attempt to harness the theory–practice nexus.

Purposeful Reflection

The focus in TE21 is to develop reflective practitioners and develop the kind of reflection that is planned and structured as part of teacher inquiry, collaborative learning and purposeful conversation. Reflection takes place through the Teaching and Learning e-Portfolio, sharing with peers, or discussions with university professors, mentors and practitioners.

Teaching and Learning e-Portfolio

NIE's teacher education programmes have strong inter-linking components but student teachers need to have the 'metacognition' to put the pieces together While the student teachers' mindmaps help to map a 'model answer' to piece together the different areas of study in the student teachers' learning journeys in the pre-service programmes, student teachers have to maintain a Teaching and Learning e-Portfolio, which is intended to help them form conceptual connections between their pedagogical method courses, content knowledge and practical experiences.

The e-Portfolio is an electronic collection of authentic and diverse evidence of a student teacher's learning and achievement over time, on which he/she has reflected and designed for personal development. It serves as a platform to promote learning and development, encourage self-assessment and reflection, provide evidence for assessment and accountability, support conversations about student teachers' growing understandings of what constitutes good teaching in relation to GTC, and to document student teachers' growth and development of personal teaching philosophy over time.

It is conceptualised as a Teaching and Learning e-Portfolio as it is meant to integrate and aggregate a student teacher's learning journey and the development of their personal teaching philosophies over time and to emphasise its role in charting the development of a student teacher from pre-service to his/her eventual development from a beginning teacher to eventually, that of a professional teacher. There is also a close linkage between the Teaching and Learning e-Portfolio and the enhanced practicum model because student teachers are expected to present artefacts from their e-Portfolios during the first and fourth session of the Focused Conversation sessions that take place during their practicum. The first session focuses on learning that has taken place at NIE up to the practicum posting, and the last session focuses on learning that has taken place on-site in schools in terms of how their teaching competencies have been developed during the practicum postings.

The actual implementation process of the e-Portfolio required both faculty members and student teachers to be familiar with the process, implementation, key practices and deliverables of the e-Portfolio (NIE, 2012). Dedicated 1 h per week time-tabled slots for a course entitled, "Using e-Portfolio for Learning and Teaching", were used to cover topics like the what and the why of a Teaching and Learning e-Portfolio, the crafting of one's personal teaching philosophy, the importance of reflective practice and the model for reflective teaching, and the sharing of artefacts during the practicum posting, to name a few. Technical implementation details are that the Google Sites platform was eventually selected as the electronic platform for use and that additional technical support was given by the Centre for e-Learning (CeL) who conducted training for new faculty members coming on board and served as a helpdesk for student teachers who had technical questions/issues to resolve. The main implementation challenge involved getting faculty to buy in to the concept of a Teaching and Learning e-Portfolio rather than portfolio as an assessment tool and to embrace the need for such a portfolio above and beyond 'business as usual' activities in the pre-service teacher education programmes.

Enhanced Practicum Model and Strengthening of Mentorship

NIE also made changes to our practicum model to strengthen theory–practice links through stronger mentoring and closer partnership with schools. For instance, as mentioned in the section above, Focused Conversations (FC) were introduced to provide an avenue for student teachers to have purposeful conversations with their School Coordinating Mentors (SCMs) and supervisors about their learning in NIE and in schools, and to articulate their learning in terms of developing their teaching competencies. Pre- and post-practicum conferences with supervisors were also introduced.

FCs are to take place four times over the span of a 10-week posting in schools. The enhanced practicum model also spells out the rough timing of the sessions, for example, the first should take place during Week 1, the second during Weeks 3 and 4, the third during Weeks 5 and 6, and the fourth during Weeks 9 and 10. As mentioned in the section detailing the Teaching and Learning e-Portfolio, the first and fourth sessions are dedicated to portfolio sharing but the second and third sessions are meant for student teachers to talk about managing teaching and learning in schools, specifically with regard to issues encountered during their lessons or with their pupils. SCMs (i.e., those who coordinate the practicum experience for the student teachers posted to their schools) had to be prepared for a mindset change as they were taking on roles as developmental mentors rather than as evaluators of the student teachers out on practicum postings in their schools (NIE, 2012). This required the practicum team conducting frequent dialogues that focused on competency and capacity building for SCMs and are available via e-mail throughout the 10-week practicum postings.

Transformation of Physical Infrastructure

In tandem with the pedagogical innovations, the physical infrastructure for teaching and learning must be transformed to support such innovations and skill acquisitions. If we want to transfer the learning back to the students, the classrooms must be reconfigured. Accordingly, NIE has reconfigured our 72 tutorial classrooms to be 'collaborative classrooms', empowered by technology, to facilitate collaborative and interactive learning by students in groups. This effort was undertaken with the 'teacher-as-facilitator' philosophy in mind and the reconfiguration was done in close consultation with faculty members who could voice their say in terms of the design of the classrooms that could bring about maximal interaction and collaborations between the student teachers (see Fig. 4.6 for a pictorial representation of the classroom).

The typical layout of the newly reconfigured classrooms involves six to eight hexagonally shaped tables that can seat five to six student teachers, and power plugs are located in concealed panels at the centre of each of these tables to enable each student to plug in their personal computer/handheld device. Surrounding the room is a panel of Liquid Crystal Display (LCD) screens which are designed to capture the notes from small-group discussions and flash them visibly in a common screen close to the group seating. Alternatively, the staff facilitator can also choose to flash on the LCD screens what he/she needs to show from the main facilitator's computer screen so that this is easily visible to all. The physical infrastructure of the collaborative classroom supports a technology-enabled and collaborative learning environment.

Fig. 4.6 Collaborative classrooms at NIE rates (NIE, 2009)

How Success Is Measured and Assured

It is important to ascertain the success or failure of any educational reform and Singapore is cognisant of the importance of conducting programme evaluations and research to inform the policy and practice of our teacher education programmes. A systematic research programme in the area of teacher learning spanning from the initial teacher preparation through to the formative years as the beginning teacher develops to become a professional teacher is critical to any teacher education institute. To this end, a number of competitively funded research projects on evidence-based Initial Teacher Education and evaluation of the impact of key TE21 initiatives provide NIE the basis for future directions. One such on-going funded study entitled, "To Build an Evidence-base for Teacher Education: A Longitudinal Study", aims to track the development of teacher competencies and identities of student teachers at various points in their pre-service career from the point of entry, to the point of exit via online quantitative and qualitative (open-ended questions) surveys. To triangulate the data found in the surveys, one-to-one interviews are also held with a percentage of the participants to find out more about their experiences in our pre-service programmes. Additionally, a component of the project which is unique is the video recording and coding of selected pre-service classrooms with willing award-wining faculty members known for their constant nomination and winning of teaching awards university-wide. The recordings are then followed by an in-depth interview of the faculty involved and their student teachers in order to ensure triangulation between the pedagogical coding results and the learning experiences of the student teachers.

Apart from these studies, the Office of Academic Quality Management (OAQM; NIE, n.d. a) also administers various surveys, for example, the Stakeholder Survey, the Programme Evaluation Survey, and the Graduate Preparedness Survey (GPS), to assess the quality of teaching and learning at strategic points of the teacher development process, and to track the impact of our TE21 implementation and reform efforts.

The stakeholders' survey asks schools leaders to rate beginning teachers' competencies. The raters are school management and supervising teachers and they rate beginning teachers who have been teaching for 1–3 years. The Programme Evaluation Survey is administered to graduating student teachers from NIE's Initial Teacher Preparation (ITP). The objective of this survey is to seek our graduating student teachers on their views on issues relating to programme content, programme implementation and delivery, and beliefs as well as their perceived readiness for their teaching role. GPS aims to obtain baseline evidence on the beginning teachers' level of preparedness for their role as a teacher in schools as well as the level of school support they received to help them settle into their new role. The target respondents for GPS are BTs who have taught for less than 3 years.

Learning from the High Performing Education Systems

Moving ahead, we acknowledge that no one educational model can be perfect or ideal for implementation in one's system. For this reason, it is important for us to continue to research on and learn from other high performing systems. To document current and exemplary practices in quality teacher preparation in secondary math and science, Singapore and the US are co-leading an Asia-Pacific Education Cooperation (APEC) Project on the Quality of Teacher Preparation with leading universities in eight countries, namely, Monash University, East China Normal University, University of Waikato, Moscow Institute of Open Education, NIE, Khon Kaen University, Harvard University, Columbia University, and University of Pennsylvania. More recently, Singapore and NIE became a member of the Global Cities in Education Network (GCEN) organised by the Asia Society (in the US). This network is a mechanism for educators and decision-makers in Asia and North America to collaboratively dream, design, and deliver internationally informed solutions to common challenges with which education systems are currently grappling. The GCEN Symposium is an important platform for participating countries to foster in-depth inquiry, planning and action to address specific topics related to the themes of transforming learning and achieving equity. So far, two symposia have been organised in Hong Kong and Singapore respectively, and the third will be held in Singapore in October 2013 with house delegates from Chicago, Denver, Hong Kong, Melbourne, Seattle, Seoul, Shanghai, Singapore and Toronto. At the Seattle Meeting in January 2013, Singapore was showcased as a successful case study in preparing and sustaining high quality teachers.

When S.K. Lee took over the helm of teacher education at the institute in 2007, he led in the conceptualisation of the institute's *3:3:3 Strategic Roadmap from 2007 to 2012* (NIE, 2007) and emphasised on the three success factors of relevance, responsiveness and rigor, which are required to help us realise three strategic directions of meeting the needs of our stakeholders, achieving international recognition through educational research and impacting the educational fraternity internationally. Ultimately, high quality teacher education programmes must be able to prepare teachers with the relevant attributes (values, skills and knowledge) to not just keep abreast with the times but also to be ahead of their time. We would like to re-emphasise that educating teachers for the twenty-first century cannot occur in a vacuum. Instead, it requires a holistic, systemic effort of all stakeholders within the educational community, including professional associations and teachers' unions, to come together to ensure that there is goal congruence and alignment in helping us to prepare our students to face the ever-changing demands and challenges of the twenty-first century global workplace and society. The secret of our educational success in Singapore therefore lies in the close tripartite relationship between NIE, MOE and the 365 schools in Singapore. Such a tight and close partnership ensures that policy formulation is research-informed and that any policy initiative can be implemented with fidelity across the system seamlessly and coherently.

Acknowledgments The authors would like to acknowledge the contributions of A/P Woon Chia Liu and A/P Kam Ming Lim when parts of these contents were written up as a speech for presentation at the International Summit of the Teaching Profession 2012. We would also like to acknowledge MOE for the use of Figs. 4.1 and 4.3; NIE's Strategic Planning & Corporate Services for the use of Figs. 4.2, 4.4 and 4.5 in this chapter; and Mr Jarrod Tam Chun Peng for the photography of the Collaborative Classroom in Fig. 4.6.

References

Binkley, M., Erstad, O., Herman, J., Raizen, S., Ripley, M., Miller-Ricci, M., et al. (2012). Defining twenty-first century skills. In P. Griffin, B. McGaw, & E. Care (Eds.), *Assessment and teaching of 21st century skills* (pp. 17–66). New York: Springer.

Boud, D., & Falchikov, N. (2007). Rethinking assessment in higher education: Learning for longer term. New York: Routledge.

Chong-Mok, W. Y. (2010). *Teaching and learning of 21st century competencies in schools.* Singapore: National Institute of Education, NTU. Retrieved from http://www.nie.edu.sg/files/EPD%20Presentation%20@%20TE21%20Summit_(final).pdf

Goh, C. B., & Gopinathan, S. (2008). The development of education in Singapore since 1965. In S. K. Lee, C. B. Goh, B. Fredriksen, & J. P. Tan (Eds.), *Towards a better future: Education and training for economic development in Singapore since 1965* (pp. 12–38). Washington, DC/Singapore: The World Bank/National Institute of Education, NTU.

Ministry of Education, Singapore (MOE). (2010). *MOE to enhance learning of 21st century competencies and strengthen art, music and physical education.* Retrieved from http://www.moe.gov.sg/media/press/2010/03/moe-to-enhance-learning-of-21s.php

Ministry of Education, Singapore (MOE). (n.d). *Singapore's teachers' pledge.* Retrieved from http://www.moe.gov.sg/about

National Institute of Education (NIE). (2007). *3:3:3 roadmap 2007–2012*. Retrieved from www.nie.edu.sg/files/333%20Roadmap%202007%20-%202012.pdf
National Institute of Education (NIE). (2009). *TE21: A teacher education model for the 21st century*. Retrieved from http://www.nie.edu.sg/files/spcs/Te21_online_ver.pdf
National Institute of Education (NIE). (2012). *TE21: An implementation report – NIE's journey from concept to realisation – A teacher education model for the 21st century* (TE21). Retrieved from http://www.nie.edu.sg/files/booklet_web.pdf
National Institute of Education (NIE). (n.d. a). *Framework for OAQM processes: Office of Academic Quality Management*. Retrieved from http://www.nie.edu.sg/office-academic-quality-management/framework-processes/framework-oaqm-processes
National Institute of Education (NIE). (n.d. b). *Teacher education 21*. Retrieved from http://www.nie.edu.sg/about-nie/teacher-education-21
National Institute of Education (NIE). (n.d. c). *TE21 student teachers' learning journey and mindmap*. Retrieved from http://www.nie.edu.sg/about-nie/teacher-education-21
Reich, R. (2001). *The future of success*. New York: Alfred A. Knopf.

Chapter 5
Singapore's Performance in PISA: Levelling Up the Long Tail

Laik Woon Teh

Introduction

Singaporean students' high mathematics, science and literacy performance at international studies has attracted significant world-wide attention. Starting from TIMSS 1995, Singapore has reported high average performance and also high proportion of students obtaining top scores. In the latest PISA 2009, Singaporean students have again performed well in terms of average performance in literacy, mathematics and science. However, in terms of other measures, for example, 5th percentile scores and the difference between mean and 5th percentile scores, Singapore does not perform as well as the other top-performing countries such as Hong Kong, SAR, South Korea and Finland. This may be one of the reasons that sparks discussions about the Singaporean's 'long-tail' in performance distributions.

The focus of this paper will not be on Singapore's PISA 2009 results as there are many reports from OECD and other sources that cover this topic. Instead, this paper will situate Singapore's PISA performance in its context, both social and historical. It will also highlight some observations about Singapore's efforts in 'levelling up' its lower achieving students and will end with a short discussion.

A Recap of Singapore's Performance in PISA 2009

I refer the 'long-tail' in terms of 5th percentile scores and the difference between mean and 5th percentile scores. As mentioned above, Singaporean students are ranked 5th, 2nd and 4th in terms of absolute mean scores in literacy, maths and science in PISA 2009, respectively. However, in terms of absolute 5th percentile

L.W. Teh (✉)
Office of Education Research, National Institute of Education, Nanyang Technological University, 1 Nanyang Walk, Singapore 637616, Singapore
e-mail: laikwoon.teh@nie.edu.sg

S.K. Lee et al. (eds.), *Educational Policy Innovations: Levelling Up and Sustaining Educational Achievement*, Springer Education Innovation Book Series 1,
DOI 10.1007/978-981-4560-08-5_5, © Springer Science+Business Media Singapore 2014

scores, Singaporean students ranked lower, namely 9th, 6th and 13th. And because of Singaporean students' relatively lower 5th percentile scores than their higher absolute mean scores, Singaporean students ranked high in terms of the differences between mean and 5th percentile PISA scores – 16th in reading, 2nd in math and 6th in science. While there are other top-ranking countries which also have similar rankings as Singapore in terms of both 5th percentile ranking and mean-5th percentile ranking (e.g., New Zealand which ranked 15th and 10th in terms of 5th percentile and mean-5th percentile in literacy; Chinese Taipei which ranked 12th and 4th in maths; and Japan which ranked 14th and 7th in science), the observation that Singapore ranked relatively lower in 5th percentile scores and higher in mean-5th percentile scores consistently in the three domains is of interest to many both in and outside Singapore. (For details please refer to Table 5.1.)

Proportion of Students Not Speaking Language of Assessment at Home and Their Performance Relative to Those Who Speak the Language of Assessment

Another interesting observation from PISA 2009 is the variation in the proportion of students who did not speak the language of assessment at home across the participating countries and economies, and their respective PISA scores. Referring to Table 5.2, PISA 2009 data shows about 59 % of Singaporean students do not speak the language of assessment at home. This percentage is the highest among the top 20 education systems with the highest mean PISA 2009 reading scores.

The unique language pattern of Singaporean students (coupled with other observations, e.g., Singapore's socioeconomic gradient is significantly higher than OECD mean but not the percentage of variance explained by PISA ESCSI index, see OECD, 2010a, Table II.4.4), may have contributed to Singapore's lower 5th percentile scores and higher difference between the mean and 5th percentile scores. However, a discussion of the distribution of Singaporean students' academic performance will not be complete without an understanding of Singapore's social-political context seen from a historical perspective.

Social-Political Context of Singapore Education System and Singaporean Students' Academic Achievement Over Last Decades

Students' academic achievement is influenced by its broader social context. This section provides a brief description of Singapore's social context which may play a role in influencing the overall status and the spread of the academic distribution of Singaporean students. It also highlights progress made by Singaporean students

Table 5.1 Mean score, variation and rank of 5th percentile in student performance on the reading scale (OECD, 2010a, Table I.2.3)

					All students					
					Mean score		Standard deviation		5th percentile	
Country	Rank of mean	Rank of 5th percentile	Rank of mean-5th percentile	Mean-5th percentiles	Mean	S.E.	S.D.	S.E.	Score	S.E.
Shanghai, China	1	1	59	139	556	−2.4	80	−1.7	417	−5.2
Korea	2	2	61	139	539	−3.5	79	−2.1	400	−7.6
Finland	3	3	39	154	536	−2.3	86	−1.0	382	−3.4
Hong Kong, SAR	4	4	42	153	533	−2.1	84	−1.7	380	−5.5
Singapore	5	9	16	169	526	−1.1	97	−1.0	357	−3.4
Canada	6	5	35	156	524	−1.5	90	−0.9	368	−2.9
New Zealand	7	15	10	177	521	−2.4	103	−1.7	344	−5.8
Japan	8	19	8	181	520	−3.5	100	−2.9	339	−9.8
Australia	9	17	12	172	515	−2.3	99	−1.4	343	−3.8
Netherlands	10	6	56	144	508	−5.1	89	−1.6	365	−4.7
Belgium	11	31	9	180	506	−2.3	102	−1.7	326	−6.1
Norway	12	14	34	157	503	−2.6	91	−1.2	346	−4.5
Estonia	13	7	58	142	501	−2.6	83	−1.7	359	−5.3
Switzerland	14	21	24	164	501	−2.4	93	−1.4	337	−4.1
Poland	15	13	37	154	500	−2.6	89	−1.3	346	−5.6
Iceland	16	26	17	169	500	−1.4	96	−1.2	331	−4.9
United States	17	18	30	161	500	−3.7	97	−1.6	339	−4.2
Liechtenstein	18	10	55	144	499	−2.8	83	−3.5	355	−12.1
Sweden	19	30	15	171	497	−2.9	99	−1.5	326	−5.3
Germany	20	23	22	165	497	−2.7	95	−1.8	333	−4.8

Table 5.2 Proportion of students speaking the language of assessment at home and mean Reading score by country (OECD, 2010a, Table II.4.4)

	Students speaking the language of assessment at home		Students speaking another language at home		All students	
Country	% of students	Mean reading score	% of students	Mean reading score	Mean reading score	5th percentile reading score
Shanghai, China	98.7	558	1.3	493	556	417
South Korea	99.9	541	0.1	—	539	400
Finland	96.3	539	3.7	477	536	382
Hong Kong, SAR	92.8	539	7.2	480	533	380
Singapore	40.8	562	59.2	506	526	357
Canada	85.8	530	14.2	513	524	368
New Zealand	85.5	531	14.5	475	521	344
Japan	99.9	522	0.1	—	520	339
Australia	90.9	519	9.1	510	515	343
Netherlands	93.8	514	6.2	477	508	365
Belgium	78.6	520	21.4	483	506	326
Norway	92.8	509	7.2	451	503	346
Estonia	97.3	504	2.7	464	501	359
Switzerland	84.8	515	15.2	461	501	337
Poland	99.4	503	0.6	—	500	346
Iceland	96.9	502	3.1	436	500	331
United States	87.1	507	12.9	472	500	339
Liechtenstein	85.2	512	14.8	435	499	355
Sweden	92	507	8	436	497	326
Germany	89.8	511	10.2	455	497	333

over the last few decades. Further details can be found in other sources (see Gopinathan, 1985; Lee, Goh, Fredriksen, & Tan, 2008; Yip & Sim, 1990).

Today, Singapore is a small and highly urbanised city state. It has a total population of 4.987 million with a population density of 7,022 per sq km in 2009 (Department of Statistics, Singapore [DOS], 2010). Its per capita GDP of S$53,143 (or US$36,537) is one of the highest in Asia. Based on the latest official estimates, Chinese, Malays and Indians make up 74 %, 13 % and 9 % respectively of the Singapore resident population today. The remainders are classified as 'Eurasians' (i.e., from European and Asian descent) or 'Others' (Immigration and Checkpoints Authority Singapore, 2010). In 2009, the non-resident population of Singapore was estimated to be about 25 % of the total population.

The diversity and size of the Singapore population are mirrored in its education system. Singapore has a small education system with a relatively short history. Its school population is ethnically diverse. There are about 180 primary schools (Grades 1–6), 170 secondary schools (Grades 7–10), and about 20 junior colleges, centralised institute and specialised schools that offer academic pre-university curriculum (Grades 11–12). All publicly funded schools employ English language as the medium of instruction and cater to almost all Singaporean students of school-going age. The proportion of Singaporean children attending privately funded schools is very small. Currently, principals have substantial autonomy in managing the learning programme of the schools within Ministry of Education, Singapore (MOE) guidelines. The typical size of each Primary 1 cohort is about 40,000 and the enrolment of a typical Singapore school is approximately 1,300. Schools are relatively well resourced. The pupil to teacher ratio is 19.6 in primary schools and 16.4 in secondary schools (Ministry of Education, Singapore [MOE], 2010). The Singapore government's total expenditure (both recurrent and development) on primary, secondary and pre-university education in FY2009/2010 was S$4,924 million or about 2 % of Singapore's annual Gross Domestic Product (GDP). This is relatively lower than the typical OECD figures of 5.5 % of GDP in Nordic countries and approximately 3 % in Japan, Luxembourg and the Slovak Republic (OECD, 2010b).

The Singaporean educational system today is highly centralised and regulated following three decades of reorganisation, rationalisation, consolidation and reformation. Over the last 4 or 5 years, there has been a significant decentralisation of pedagogical authority to individual schools. Virtually all Singaporean students study in one of the publicly funded schools, and virtually all the school leaders and teachers in these schools (except a small number of independent schools and specialised schools) are recruited, paid and managed (in terms of appointment and promotion) by the MOE. The highly centralised school system allows it to leverage substantial economies of scale which may partly explain the lower education expenditure as a percentage of GDP relative to other OECD countries.

Nevertheless, this highly centralised and highly efficient education system is a relatively recent development. The transformation that Singapore education system has undergone since late 1950s, when Singapore achieved self-governing status from the United Kingdom, is significant. Until the early 1980s, the Singapore education system was a system with four different languages of instruction (i.e., English, Chinese, Malay and Tamil) in essentially one single academic stream. In 1959, less than half or 47.4 % of all Singaporean students were in English stream (with English as medium of instruction). Although this percentage grew to 88.9 % by 1979, (Goh, 1979), even until the end of the 1980s, there were still Singaporean students whose medium of instruction was not English.

As recent as in 1979, about 90 % of Singaporean secondary school students studied a common syllabus. Streaming of students into different academic tracks with different curricula and syllabi only started after 1979. In 2010, about 62 % of the Secondary 4 students were in the 4-year Express stream leading to General Certificate of Education (GCE) Ordinary level ('O'-level) examinations, another 25 % were in the 4-year Normal Academic (NA) stream leading to GCE Normal level ('N'-level) examinations (about 70 % of these will sit for the GCE 'O'-level examinations in a 5th year) and the remaining 13 % were in the 4-year Normal Technical (NT) stream. The NT curriculum is designed to prepare the students for vocational and technical training in the Institute of Technical Education (ITE), where most of the NT students would progress to.

Academic achievement of Singaporean students in the end of the 1970s was low. In 1978, it was reported that fewer than 40 % of each primary 1 cohort managed to obtain three or more GCE ‘O’-level passes, which is generally viewed as a threshold qualifications for lifelong learning. By 1993, this percentage has risen above 90 % (MOE, 2000). The percentage of Primary 1 cohort with more than five GCE ‘O’-level passes, which is a more stringent benchmark, also rose from 65 % in 1987 to 82.1 % in 2010.

The other key education and social statistics of Singapore from 1980s also show remarkable development. The GDP per capita in 1980, 1990, 2000 and 2010 were respectively S$10,685, S$23,101, S$40,364 and S$61,071 at current market prices. The rise in public expenditure on education during the same time periods was equally steep. The total public expenditure on education in the respective years was S$686 million, S$2,056 million, S$5,868 million and S$9,910 million (DOS, 1983, 2010; MOE, 2003).

The rapid changes in the education structure, public expenditure on education and GDP were mirrored in standard indicators of education outcomes. For example, based on the data released by MOE, 93.2 % of students progressed to post-secondary institutions (i.e., pre-university courses, polytechnics and ITE) in 2010. While official data from 1980s was not available, the figure was likely to be close to 60 % (see Table 5.3 for more information).

Based on anecdotal evidence as well as the steepness in the trajectory of the social, economic and education indicators presented earlier, it was perhaps between the mid-1980s and the mid-1990s that the academic achievement of Singaporean students saw a steep improvement. The only available data that allows the academic achievement of Singaporean students to be compared with those from the other countries in the 1980s was from the Second Science Study conducted by IEA in 1986 (Keeves, 1992; see Table 5.4). Singaporean students’ performance in this study was at best mediocre. Singaporean 10-year-old students ranked 15th out of the 18 participating countries and the 14-year-old students ranked 16th out of the 24 participating countries.

Given that Singaporean students performed extremely well in TIMSS 1995, it is therefore likely that the academic performance of Singaporean students saw rapid improvement between 1986 and 1995.

Singapore’s Efforts in Levelling Up Academically Low-Achieving Students

After Singapore had achieved universal participation in primary and secondary education in 1970s, the Singapore education system focused its efforts on improving the efficiency of the system to up-lift the overall quality of its students. The following levelling up initiatives have been adopted by MOE. They reflect the background and needs of Singaporean students.

Table 5.3 Percentage of the respective primary 1 cohort with 5 'O'-level passes, GCE 'O' mathematics passes, and progressed to post-secondary education institutions (i.e., Pre-University, Polytechnics, ITE; MOE, 1997, 2000, 2005, 2011)

	Percentage of the respective primary 1 cohort with 5 'O'-level passes				Percentage of the respective primary 1 cohort with GCE 'O' maths pass				Percentage of the respective primary 1 cohort that progressed to post-secondary education institutions (i.e. pre-university, polytechnics, ITE)		
Ethnicity	1987	1990	2000	2010	1987	1990	2000	2010	1990	2000	2010
Chinese	69.5	72.6	82.6	86.5	86.9	88.6	91.8	93.2	64.7	83.8	95.5
Malay	39.1	43.1	52.8	62.1	44.1	53.3	64.2	70.1	35.9	68.3	86.2
Indian	53.3	58.2	66.2	72.3	55.5	65.8	73.3	78.2	39.2	66.6	89.8
Others	57.4	57.4	75.8	81.2	66.5	70.0	84.5	90.2	88.2	79.4	93.2
All	65.2	68.9	77.8	82.1	80.5	83.9	87.1	89.0	83.9	87.1	89.0

Table 5.4 Performance of participating countries in Second IEA Science Study (Keeves, 1992)

Science 10-year-olds	Mean percent correct	Science 14-years-olds	Mean percent correct
Japan	66.4	Hungary	70.7
Korea	66.0	Japan	66.8
Finland	65.7	Netherlands	63.7
Sweden (Gr 4)	62.8	Canada (Eng)	61.6
Canada (Eng)	61.7	Korea	61.0
Hungary	61.7	Sweden (Gr 8)	60.3
Canada (Fr)	61.4	Finland	60.3
Italy	59.2	China	60.0
U.S.	57.6	Italy (Gr 9)	59.8
Australia	56.9	Poland	59.5
Norway	55.5	Norway	59.3
England	53.8	Australia	58.5
Poland	52.5	Canada (Fr)	61.4
Israel	52.2	Israel	58.5
Singapore	51.8	Thailand	56.7
Hong Kong	50.9	Singapore	56.4
Philippines	42.3	England	55.9
Nigeria	35.1	Papua New Guinea	55.3
		Hong Kong	55.0
		U.S.	54.6
		Ghana	46.7
		Zimbabwe	42.8
		Nigeria	42.2
		Philippines	39.7

Lower Primary Curriculum That Focuses on Literacy

Because of Singapore's unique linguistic pattern, the lower primary curriculum (the foundation stage of Primary 1–4 or P1–4) has a heavy focus on literacy in English language (EL) and in Mother Tongue languages. More than 1/3 of the curriculum time for P1 and P2 is allocated to EL. This provides pupils who are weak in EL sufficient exposure time to the language early, to level them up so that they can possess a threshold level of English language competency to be ready for upper primary and secondary education.

Streams and Courses That Provide Differentiated Curriculum for Low Academically Achieving Students

In the 1980s and 1990s, the levelling up strategy MOE focused on was the systematic channelling of academically low-achieving students into courses/streams that provided them with a differentiated curriculum designed by MOE to meet the needs of these students, including a longer time to cover curriculum materials. It is important to note that the system also provided 'ladders and bridges'. Hence, students in these lower streams but have subsequently performed well and can catch up can be transferred to the more academically demanding course/stream. Students assigned to the lowest stream/course (i.e., EM3 course[1] or NT stream) were also allocated more resources than students in the average stream/course. For example, NT students are in smaller classes and have access to newer equipment (e.g., computer). In terms of academic progression and career preparation, NT curriculum prepares students for vocational and technical training, and most NT students articulate to Singapore's ITEs. Students in ITE receive per capita funding which is at least on par as that received by students in the polytechnics and the junior colleges/centralised institutes pursuing the pre-university course (MOE, 2011).

Early Intervention for Lower Achieving Students

Since 1998, MOE has implemented early intervention programmes in the lower primary levels (P1 and P2) of all schools, that is, the Learning Support Programme (LSP) to help pupils who are weak in English language level up. LSP includes daily

[1] Pupils were streamed at Primary 5 to the EM1, EM2 and EM3 (English and Mother Tongue at 1st, 2nd and 3rd language levels respectively) streams. Since 2008, the MOE has altered this streaming system, catering to pupils who are academically weaker to undertake only subjects that they are weak in at 'Foundation' level.

lessons with smaller groups of pupils taught by specially trained teachers. The programme uses structured teaching approaches that meet the learning needs of these pupils. It was reported to be successful in reducing the number of pupils who are not 'school-ready' due to low English proficiently. In 2007, LSP was extended to provide early intervention for P1 and P2 pupils who are weak in mathematics (MOE, 2008a).

Specialised Schools for Academically Weak Students

In 2007, a specialised school was piloted to provide a different education programme customised to meet the needs of students who failed Primary School Leaving Examinations (PSLE) once or more times (MOE, 2006). The NorthLight School (NLS) was given additional resources and flexibility to provide education experience that better suit these students but was difficult to implement in the mainstream secondary schools which admit students from all the three academic streams. Based on the successful experience of NLS, a second specialised school, the Assumption Pathway School (APS) was set up in 2009 (MOE, 2008b). In 2013 and 2014, another two specialised schools for the NT stream will be set up to cater to students who are among the bottom 10 % of those who pass PSLE and are assigned to the NT stream. Leveraging on the experience from NLS and APS, these new specialised NT schools will also be provided additional and different resources, and the flexibility to design curriculum/programmes to suit the needs of the students. While NLS and APS have received much accolade from the wider society for transforming their students, a few more years may be needed before a sustained and systemic impact can be observed.

Discussion

The underlying cause of the longer 'tail' (as defined by mean-5th percentile score) in Singapore PISA 2009 score distribution is likely to be complex. One of the contributing factors could be the diverse home language pattern among Singaporean students. As mentioned in the earlier section, PISA 2009 data shows that 59 % of Singaporean students did not speak the language of assessment at home. Even though these students performed very well compared to students from the other countries who did not speak the language of assessment, their average score was 56 points lower than that of Singaporean students who spoke English at home. Given the rapid change in language pattern in Singapore homes, as more and more Singaporean students speak English more frequently at home (DOS, 2006), the spread in English language achievement among Singaporean students (and the long-tail) is likely to narrow over time.

Notwithstanding Singapore's larger mean-5th percentile score in PISA 2009, students in Singapore have made significant progress in their academic achievement over last three decades as observed from student performance in Singapore national examinations and in international studies. The main contributing factors to this improvement are, however, not conclusive. Even though streaming or differentiated curriculum, is the key feature of the Singapore education system throughout these three decades, there has been insufficient evidence available to infer the causal impact of streaming on Singaporean student achievement. There are many other possible factors which could lead to this improvement. They include the rapid economic expansion Singapore experienced during the same period, and the quantitative and qualitative changes in Singapore's teaching force during these three decades (Lee et al., 2008). However, the more recent levelling up initiatives, such as LSP and specialised schools, are not likely to have contributed much to this improvement as it takes time to see their effects.

While there is insufficient evidence to conclude what the underlying factors behind the observed improvement in Singapore education system over the last three decades are, the underlying philosophy behind Singapore's levelling up initiatives is clear and obvious. Since the introduction of streaming policy in late 1970s, MOE has repeatedly affirmed its abhorrence of a one-size-fit-all curriculum. Instead, students with different academic achievement, and different learning needs and dispositions (whether real or perceived) are thought to be best served with differentiated curriculum. The provision of a small number of fixed curriculum offerings to students grouped according to their examination results was MOE's chosen way of delivering differentiated curriculum. This is probably to maximise efficiency and economies of scale. This approach is particularly relevant in the early 1980s when resources were limited and policies that could achieve rapid overall improvement in the education system within the constraints were chosen, even when there might be individual losses. This pragmatic and hard-headed manner of addressing problems is typical of the survival and efficiency driven phases of the development of the Singapore education system (Mourshed, Chijioke, & Barber, 2010).

Another philosophy which has influenced the conceptualisation and implementation of Singapore's levelling up efforts is its perspective of viewing equity as equalising opportunities instead of equalising outcomes, especially narrowly defined academic outcomes. It is again possible that Singapore embraces this perspective partly because of practical limitations. As mentioned, Singaporean society is highly diverse and this is reflected in its student population. Especially in the 1970s, it would be impossible to conceptualise, let alone implement, an education system that could equalise the education outcomes of all Singaporean students. A system that aims to provide the education opportunities that are most suitable to the characteristics and needs of the students would be more pragmatic. This focus on providing equalising education opportunities is in a way analogous to experience in public health care where focus is given to providing a sufficiently high standard of care for all citizens, regardless of an individual ability to pay, and not on the provision of identical care or on equalising of health outcomes to all

(Jordan, 2010). Nevertheless, what constitutes 'sufficiently high standard of education' for students with diverse characteristics is a highly controversial question.

Questions for Deliberation

This commentary will end with three questions that Singapore education system may need to contend with in the future.

First, Singapore today no longer faces the same resource constraints which limit its education policy options in the 1970s and 1980s. MOE has also announced that it is no longer in an efficiency-driven phase of education development, and has moved into the ability-driven and values-driven phases (Heng, 2011). However, in practice during the formulation of policies and programmes, it is not as clear how trade-off in programme efficiency and cost-effectiveness (often based on quantifiable indicators) would be made. Should policy decisions be balanced with more attention given to qualitative measures of programme quality and learning experience? Or should policy formulation and programme design be more motivated by values, principles or even ideology? Particularly, how can the education system balance trade-off between monetary cost and less quantifiable public goods such as inclusivity, well-being and passion of students? Furthermore, many studies have demonstrated that there is positive link between academic achievement and emotion well-being and socio-acceptance (Nisbett, 2011).

Second, despite high GDP and living standards, many of Singapore's fundamental challenges still persist. It remains a highly diverse multi-ethnic and multilingual society despite three decades of concerted effort to adopt English as the medium of instruction for all students in schools, to engender a common school experience for young Singaporeans and to uplift economic opportunities for all Singaporeans. In fact, as Singapore participates actively in globalised trade, there has been a rising income inequality and the accompanying social challenges can be substantial (Bhaskaran et al., 2012). Singapore may therefore wish to consider if the long-standing focus on equalising opportunities can be augmented by also acknowledging that a system would need to at least make genuine efforts to equalise outcomes. This is relevant because a system that conceived equity as equal opportunities (or equal treatment) may be desensitised to persistent gaps in the learning outcomes among students, to the extent that the society may not critically reflect about the education policies and pedagogical practices and identify specific elements that may contribute to these gaps. This omission could be simply because of its premise which is that students are treated fairly and given equal opportunities (Rousseau & Tate, 2003). However, it is important to note that uniformity in overt education structure at the system and school levels alone, that is, equal access and equal provisions, may not lead to equalised education outcomes or processes. According to the PISA2009 results, countries with low horizontal differentiation in selecting and grouping students at the system and school levels (e.g., Australia, Finland, New Zealand, Sweden; see OECD, 2010c) can have very different mean-5th percentile scores according to Table 5.2. Also, after formal tracking was dismantled in American high schools, in-school inequality in terms of learning experience and learning outcomes continue to persist (see Lucas, 1999).

Third, if Singapore decides to balance its perspective of equalising opportunities with equalising outcomes, then the choice of education outcomes to equalise becomes crucial. There are many major international education reforms which narrowly defined education outcomes as academic achievement measured with a single yardstick (e.g., *No Child Left Behind*). In a diverse society and rapidly changing world, making sure that disadvantaged students meet centrally and narrowly defined benchmarks alone, without an appreciation of what these students need is not likely to provide them with a life transforming learning experience to open more doors and to do what they want in life. There is a case for education outcomes to be also seen from the fundamental perspective of the care that our students need and deserve, regardless of their background and characteristics. Instead of sole reliance on scientific and formulaic education, Singapore may wish to also draw motivation from an alternative more holistic curriculum, one that is not divided according to the traditional disciplines but focusing on care for one's self, for others, for our environment, human elements and ideals (Noddings, 1992). Perhaps, Singapore MOE's recent mention about student-centric, values-driven education (Heng, 2011) could be an indication that it is thinking in this direction.

References

Bhaskaran, M., Ho, S. C., Low, D., Tan, K. S., Vadaketh, S., & Yeoh, L. K. (2012). *Background paper: Inequality and the need for a new social compact. Singapore perspectives 2012 – Singapore inclusive: Bridging divides*. Singapore: Institute of Policy Studies, Lee Kuan Yew School of Public Policy. Retrieved from http://www.spp.nus.edu.sg/ips/docs/events/p2012/SP2012_Bkgd%20Pa.pdf

Department of Statistics, Singapore (DOS). (1983). *Economics and social statistics Singapore, 1960–1982*. Singapore: Author.

Department of Statistics, Singapore (DOS). (2006). *General household survey 2005 – Statistical release 1: Socio-demographic and economic characteristics*. Retrieved from http://www.singstat.gov.sg/pubn/popn/ghsr1.html

Department of Statistics, Singapore (DOS). (2010). *Yearbook of statistics Singapore, 2011*. Retrieved from http://www.singstat.gov.sg/pubn/reference/yos11/statsT-education.pdf

Goh, K. S. (1979). *Report on the Ministry of Education 1978*. Singapore: Singapore National Printers.

Gopinathan, S. (1985). Education in Singapore: Progress and prospect. In J. S. T. Quah, H. C. Chan, & C. M. Seah (Eds.), *Government and politics of Singapore* (pp. 197–232). Singapore: Oxford University Press.

Heng, S. K. (2011, September 22). Opening Address by Mr Heng Swee Keat, Minister for Education, at the Ministry of Education (MOE) Work plan seminar at Ngee Ann Polytechnic Convention Centre. Retrieved from http://www.moe.gov.sg/media/speeches/2011/09/22/work-plan-seminar-2011.php

Immigration and Checkpoints Authority. (2010). *Singapore demographic bulletin October 2010*. Retrieved from http://www.ica.gov.sg/data/resources/docs/Media%20Releases/SDB/SDB_October2010.pdf

Jordan, W. J. (2010). Defining equity: Multiple perspectives to analyzing the performance of diverse learners. *Review of Research in Education, 34*, 142–178.
Keeves, J. P. (1992). *Learning sciences in a changing world, cross-national studies of science achievement: 1970 to 1984*. Amsterdam: IEA.
Lee, S. K., Goh, C. B., Fredriksen, B., & Tan, J. P. (Eds.). (2008). *Toward a better future: Education and training for economic development in Singapore since 1965*. Washington, DC: The World Bank.
Lucas, S. R. (1999). *Track inequality: Stratification and mobility in American high school*. New York: Teachers College Press.
Ministry of Education, Singapore (MOE). (1997). *Performance by ethnic group*. Retrieved from http://www.moe.gov.sg/media/press/1997/pr02397.htm
Ministry of Education, Singapore (MOE). (2000). *Performance by ethnic group*. Retrieved from http://www.moe.gov.sg/media/press/2000/pr30082000.htm
Ministry of Education, Singapore (MOE). (2003). *Essential statistics digest, 2004*. Retrieved from http://www.moe.gov.tt/media_pdfs/publications/Statistical%20Digest.pdf
Ministry of Education, Singapore (MOE). (2005). *Performance by ethnic group 1995–2004: Improvement in overall performance for PSLE, 'O' & 'A' levels* [Press release]. Retrieved from http://www.moe.gov.sg/media/press/2005/pr20050910.htm
Ministry of Education, Singapore (MOE). (2006). *New school to offer enhanced vocational programme in 2007*. Retrieved from http://www.moe.gov.sg/media/press/2006/pr20060308.htm
Ministry of Education, Singapore (MOE). (2008a). *Enhanced learning support programme has benefited pupils*. Retrieved from http://www.moe.gov.sg/media/press/2008/01/enhanced-learning-support-prog.php
Ministry of Education, Singapore (MOE). (2008b). *In assumption pathway school to start in 2009*. Retrieved from http://www.moe.gov.sg/media/press/2008/03/assumption-pathway-school-to-s.php
Ministry of Education, Singapore (MOE). (2010). *Essential statistics digest, 2010*. Retrieved from http://www.moe.gov.sg/education/education-statistics-digest/files/esd-2010.pdf
Ministry of Education, Singapore (MOE). (2011). *Essential statistics digest, 2011*. Retrieved from http://www.moe.gov.sg/education/education-statistics-digest/files/esd-2011.pdf
Mourshed, M., Chijioke, C., & Barber, M. (2010). *How the world's most improved school systems keep getting better*. London: McKinsey & Company.
Nisbett, R. E. (2011). The achievement gap: Past, present & future. *Daedalus, the Journal of the American Academy of Arts & Sciences, 140*(2), 90–100.
Noddings, N. (1992). *The challenge to care in schools – An alternative approach to education*. New York: Teachers College Press.
OECD. (2010a). *PISA 2009 results: Overcoming social background – Equity in learning opportunities and outcomes* (Vol. 2). Paris: Author. doi:10.1787/9789264091504-en.
OECD. (2010b). *Education at a glance 2010*. Paris: Author.
OECD. (2010c). *PISA 2009 results: What makes a school successful? – Resources, policies and practices* (Vol. 4). Paris: Author. doi:10.1787/9789264091559-en.
Rousseau, C., & Tate, W. F. (2003). No time like the present: Reflecting on equity in school mathematics. *Theory into Practice, 42*, 210–216.
Yip, J. S. K., & Sim, W. K. (Eds.). (1990). *Evolution of educational excellence: 2 years of education in the Republic of Singapore*. Singapore: Longman.

Chapter 6
Singapore's English Language Policy and Language Teacher Education: A Foundation for Its Educational Success

Ee Ling Low

Introduction

At the heart of Singapore's educational success, cautious language planning and policy implementation, coupled with a rigorous language teacher education programme, have contributed significantly towards Singapore's sustained performance in internationally benchmarked tests of student achievement. As a point of reference, Singapore emerged top of the league tables in the recently released results of the Trends in International Mathematics and Science Study (TIMSS) and Progress in International Reading and Literacy Study (PIRLS) held in 2011, emerging top in mathematics at the fourth grade and second at the eighth grade, and top in science achievement at both the fourth and eighth grades. Singapore's performance in the PIRLS was also amongst the top five performers at the fourth grade level. Although a myriad of factors have to be realistically considered in order to gain a holistic picture of Singapore's educational success, this chapter will focus the contribution of Singapore's English language policy and language teacher education as a foundation for its educational success.

The home language patterns among our students are diverse (see Chap. 5 in this volume). It is reported that 59 % of Singaporean students did not speak English at home (the language used for assessment of the Progress in International Student Achievement [PISA] by test-takers in Singapore) and yet, they out-performed their counterparts in other countries. However, a careful look at the data shows that if one compares the achievement scores between Singaporean students who spoke English and did not speak English at home, students who did not speak English at home performed on average 56 points lower than those who do (see Fig. 5.2 in this volume). Thus, undeniably, language competency has been established as one of the most significant factors that impact academic achievement. In this chapter, we

E.L. Low (✉)
Office of Teacher Education, National Institute of Education, 1 Nanyang Walk, Singapore 637616, Singapore
e-mail: eeling.low@nie.edu.sg

S.K. Lee et al. (eds.), *Educational Policy Innovations: Levelling Up and Sustaining Educational Achievement*, Springer Education Innovation Book Series 1,
DOI 10.1007/978-981-4560-08-5_6, © Springer Science+Business Media Singapore 2014

shall approach Singapore's educational success through the lens of how prudent language policy and planning, coupled with a carefully thought through and judiciously implemented pre-service programme for English language teaching, has set Singapore firmly on achieving and possibly being able to sustain its educational success.

Historical and Cultural Background of Singapore's Language Planning Policies

The previous chapter has devoted a section on the sociopolitical context of the Singapore education system. Kuo and Jernudd (1994) have asserted that in the case of Singapore, government involvement in the education system is especially evident in the language planning policies. Hence, this section will focus specifically on Singapore's language planning policies, and the education policies that have a language focus will also be mentioned. Low and Brown (2005, Chapter 3) have provided a broad overview of Singapore's main language planning policies post-independence, and Alsagoff (2012) has given a thorough and comprehensive coverage of Singapore's language policies from pre-independence to the present delving mainly into primary sources of reference for her chapter. The main milestones will be presented in this chapter.

The language policies just pre-independence to the late 1970s arose out of the 1956 All-Party Committee Report (All-Party Committee on Chinese Education, 1956) established specifically to address the problem of the linguistic diversity that existed in a newly independent Malaya at that time. Several main policies were introduced as a result of this report (Bokhorst-Heng, 1998), namely, the declaration of English, Mandarin, Malay and Tamil as the four co-official languages of Singapore in order to ensure that no ethnic group was favourably biased over the other; Malay was also declared as the national language in full cognisance of the predominantly Malay neighbours in the region; and the seeds of the bilingual education policy were sown as from the 1960s the learning of a second language became compulsory at the primary level.

Following the All-Party Report, several language policies came into effect from 1979 to 1990 as documented in Pakir (1991) and Gopinathan (1994), and cited in Low and Brown (2005). Firstly, the Speak Mandarin Campaign was introduced in 1979 in order to simplify the linguistic diversity caused by the different dialect groups of the Chinese population in Singapore, to provide a lingua franca for communication amongst the Chinese Singaporeans and to create a Mandarin-speaking environment that can help Chinese Singaporeans to successfully attain bilingualism. Subsequent to the introduction of the Speak Mandarin Campaign, in 1981, the Romanisation of the names of Chinese pupils using *Hanyu Pinyin* ensured that the dialect grouping of pupils was not immediately recognisable from the spelling of their names. Secondly, streaming was introduced as part of the recommendations made by the Goh Report chaired by the then Defence Minister Goh Keng Swee, where at Primary 3, all students undergo a streaming examination to ascertain whether they continue to take English and a second language up to Primary 6 (normal or bilingual stream) or whether they can concentrate on only reading English as a first language in school, also known as 'the monolingual stream'. From 1985 onwards, all students seeking entry into the National University of Singapore are required to have a pass in both English as a first language and a second language. This was to ensure that bilingual attainment was a prerequisite for entry into higher education locally.

Pakir (1991) was the first to apply the term 'English-knowing bilingualism' to refer to the concept of bilingualism in the Singapore educational context. She defines this as

> the linguistic ability in the first language (English) and in a second school language – one of the following ethnically defined mother tongues (viz. Mandarin for the Chinese community, Malay for the Malay community, and Tamil for the Indian community). In other words, education is conducted mainly in English with class periods set aside for second language learning in Mandarin, Malay or Tamil. (p. 167)

Since the implementation of the bilingual education policy back in the 1960s, the population of English-knowing bilingual speakers has been steadily increasing. According to the Singapore Census of Population 2010 (Department of Statistics Singapore, 2011), since the last census data release in 2000, the percentage of bilingual speakers among residents has increased by 13.5 % (see Table 6.1). What is also important to note is the increase in the percentage of the population literate in English language of close to 10 %.

Bilingual Education Policy and Its Advantages

In an *Education Week* blog article commissioned by the Asia Society based in New York, Low (2013) spoke about Singapore's bilingual language policy and its educational success. In that article, she expounds the many advantages that the policy gave to Singapore. For a start, bilingualism provides key stakeholders in the educational domain such as policymakers, educational leaders, and teachers the ability to linguistically access and therefore the opportunity to learn from other English-speaking education systems. Singapore began its important task of nation building through its education system via accessing important knowledge gleaned through teaching resources, curricular development, teacher education, school administration and leadership development. Through the different critical phases of educational development in Singapore from the survival-driven (1960s and 1970s) to the efficiency-driven (late 1970s–1980s) to the ability-driven phase (late 1990s to the present), educators have had international access to the wealth of resources written in English worldwide in order to learn from best practices around the world.

Table 6.1 Literacy among resident population aged 15 years and over (Department of Statistics Singapore, 2011)

Indicators	2000 (%)	2010 (%)
General literacy rate	92.5	95.9
Literate in English language among literate resident population	70.9	79.9
Literate in two or more languages among literate resident population	56.0	70.5

Beyond the educational arena, competency in the English language remains the most important asset for international trade. The world economic powers seem to be moving towards Asia with the rise of the economies of China and India, and bilingual ability can only grow in importance for the purpose of engaging in international business and trade. English-knowing Malay bilingualism is also an important quality for those wishing to engage in partnership possibilities with our Malay-speaking neighbours and to forge closer diplomatic relations and cultural understandings.

The declaration and subsequent adoption of four co-official languages in Singapore signals the celebration of not just bilingualism but multilingualism in Singapore. It also ensures that competence in the use of English as an international language does not compromise on our cultural ties and heritage since mastering a second language linked to one's ethnic mother tongue is upheld as an educational policy, as Low (2013) expressed,

> This policy therefore has the ingenuity of uniting us in a language that none of the racial groups can claim to be ethnically biased while allowing us to celebrate the diversity of the tongues that come along with our multi-ethnic, multi-cultural make-up.

Language Competency and Academic Achievement

Looking beyond the local arena, the link between language competency and one's academic achievement has also been established in previous research. Language competency has long been established as a strong determiner for academic success. Internationally benchmarked tests of English language proficiency such as the Test of English as a Foreign Language (TOEFL) and the International English Language Testing System (IELTS) have been used as basic admission requirements for higher education in many English-speaking countries including Singapore, the United States, United Kingdom and Australia. Establishing the importance of language competency in English is one of the most fundamental reasons why Singapore has achieved and sustained educational achievement over the years.

Bernstein (1970) argues that the acquisition of an elaborated linguistic code is necessary for one to succeed in schooling, and as a child advances into higher levels of schooling, higher levels of abstract and analytical thinking are required.

Consequently, children whose family environment limits their access to codes (rich language) will find it increasingly difficult to achieve in schools (Lee, 1997). Bilton (1977) points out the four main advantages that children who possess elaborated language codes have in schools. First, these children are accustomed to expressing themselves and, therefore, are easily understood by their teachers and peers in relation to their written work and oral communication. Second, they are less likely to be misunderstood by their teachers compared to children who have restricted codes. Unlike children who possess the appropriate tone, register and vocabulary, children with restricted codes may appear to be rude, and are more likely to perceive their teachers as cold. Third, school is an extension of a child's family environment where he or she is used to the elaborated code, but children with restricted code embedded in their family environment may face discontinuity in their language development and might develop negative feelings towards language and schools.

The perspective that language competency had an impact on educational achievement was very strong in the 1960s to 1970s. The Newsom Report in 1963 reported:

> The evidence of research increasingly suggests that linguistic inadequacy, disadvantages in social and physical background and poor attainment in school, are closely associated. (Newsom Report, 1963, p. 15)

The importance of language competency and its impact on educational achievement has always been grounded on certain sociocultural frameworks. However, Halliday (1973) cautions that educational failure could not be restricted solely to the lack of language proficiency. Language competency is one of the variables that can help to explain educational achievement, but one must also explore other contributing factors as well.

Are Singaporeans Native or Non-native Speakers of English?

The previous section has established the strong link between language competence and academic achievement. Singaporeans' exposure and subsequent mastery of two languages from primary school onwards ensures that they have a firm foundation in building strong language competency from a young age and this can be seen as a precursor to ensuring academic success in the future. From Table 6.1, it is clear that 79.9 % of the population is literate in English, and there is a need to question whether Singaporeans are native or non-native speakers of the language. This question is important if we wish to consider the impact of native/non-native status of English teachers in Singapore and its impact on the quality of language teaching in Singapore.

To answer this question, we need to scour the literature on what or who qualifies to be a native speaker. Bloomfield (1927) describes native speakers as those who speak the language as a first language from a very young age or who learnt how to speak it whilst at "one's mother's knee" (p. 151). Paikeday (1985) takes a step further to define the native speaker as one who "has a mother tongue or first language" (p. 15) and provides a second definition based on competence where one is both competent and able to use the language to conform to "the syntactical, grammatical, or structural form peculiar to a language" (p. 24).

Kachru's (1992) seminal concentric circles of World Englishes uses the concept of native, first and second language to divide up the spread of Englishes around the world according to how English is acquired and its functions in the different parts of the world. According to Kachru, the Inner Circle comprises countries such as the United Kingdom, United States, Australia, New Zealand and Canada where speakers use English as a first language while the Outer Circle comprises countries where English was spread through early phases of British or American colonisation, where English has become institutionalised and where speakers generally use it as a second language. Within this circle, Kachru lists Singapore along with Malaysia, Hong Kong, the Philippines, India and some 50 other countries. Therein lies the inherent paradox because while English has been the medium of instruction since 1987 and where in present-day Singapore, according to the 2010 population census data, 79.9 % are literate in English, but according to the seminal Kachruvian circle, Singapore is still listed as using English as a second language.

Our answer may be sought by referring to Davies' (2003) definition of a native speaker, which is based on three criteria: birthright, competence and exposure. A basic definition of a native speaker is one who is born in one of the five Inner Circle English-speaking countries mentioned earlier. A second perspective is via exposure where the speaker has been exposed to the English language from a very young age or who immigrated in their early childhood years to the Inner Circle countries. It is the third perspective which is relevant to the Singapore context where a native speaker is defined as someone who has psycholinguistic, linguistic, sociolinguistic and communicative competency in the language. If we accept Davies' third perspective of a native speaker, then most Singaporeans can technically be considered native speakers of the English language as long as they have acquired a level of competency in the language that is at least equivalent or that may even surpass that of a native speaker. Since English has been adopted as the medium of instruction in schools since 1987, it is not surprising that there could well be many speakers of English in Singapore whose proficiency levels are comparable to or who may even surpass the levels of speakers in native English-speaking countries.

Given the close relationship between language competence and academic achievement, to ensure that proficiency in English is not left to chance, policies ensuring stringent teacher selection and quality language teacher education are essential. The next few sections will be devoted to talking about how teachers are selected based on their proficiency in the English language and the type of teacher preparation programme they are required to undergo.

Teacher Selection

English language proficiency is a key requirement in order to enter into Singapore's pre-service initial teacher education programmes. Even without going into the exact grading criteria for entering any of the pre-service programmes, whether it be the 2-year non-graduate Diploma in Education programme, the 4-year Bachelor of Arts/ Science (Education) programme or the 1-year (or 2 years if one specialises in Physical Education and Sports Science) Postgraduate Diploma in Education programme, candidates are required to have at least a General Certificate of Education 'Ordinary' (GCE 'O'-level) pass in English language and/or a pass in the General Paper at H1 level in order to be considered. Additionally, all candidates must take and pass the English medium of instruction unless they have performed well enough in previous milestone examinations to warrant an exemption. Candidates who are going to teach the Mother Tongue languages (Chinese, Malay and Tamil) have their own Mother Tongue language requirements to meet but are not subject to the same English language proficiency requirements although they might be encouraged to pass the English Language Entrance Proficiency Test (EL EPT) if they wish to be considered for teaching another subject in the English medium in the future. Should candidates fail the EL EPT, they can retake it until such a time when they pass it.

From 2013 onwards, the Ministry of Education (MOE), Singapore has commissioned the Singapore Examinations and Assessment Board (SEAB) to administer the test, which comprises a speaking component and writing component. Candidates will be required to introduce themselves, read a passage aloud and deliver a monologue followed by a few minutes of dialogue with the examiner for the speaking component and to complete a piece of situational writing followed by a short expository essay for the writing component. Exemption from the EL EPT is possible if the candidate fulfils the requirements listed in Table 6.2.

English Language Teacher Preparation

This section will cover the theoretical underpinnings in the design of our English language teacher education programmes, a full description of the coverage of the courses falls outside the scope of this section but examples of course coverage that fit into the underlying framework will be provided. The theoretical underpinning of our programme is guided by Shulman's (1986, 1987) and Shulman and Grossman's (1988) proposal about the knowledge base that is required in teacher education which he derived from observing how knowledge of pedagogy and content knowledge evolve from the perspective of novice teachers. Banegas (2009) provides a comprehensive review of this concept. Shulman (1986, 1987) proposes three main categories of knowledge required by teachers: subject matter knowledge, pedagogical knowledge and knowledge of context. Accordingly, our teacher education

Table 6.2 Exemption from English language entrance proficiency test (EL EPT; Ministry of Education, Singapore [MOE], n.d. a)

Candidates who fulfil any of the criteria below are exempted from the EL EPT
Honours degree/Pass with merit/Pass degree graduates/Final year undergraduates with English Language or English Literature as the major Subject OR
Applicants who scored at least a Grade B3 in General Paper (English)/Grade B in H1 General Paper/Grade B in H2 Knowledge and Inquiry at the GCE 'A'-level Examination OR
Applicants who scored at least a Grade B3 in English Language (EL1) at the GCE 'O'-level Examination OR
Applicants who scored at least a Grade B3 in English Paper 121, 1120 or 1119 at SPM OR
Applicants who scored at least a Grade 5 in English at the International Baccalaureate Examination OR
Applicants who scored at least an overall cap of 3.5 in English Language in the NUS High School Diploma

programme is guided by the need to cover subject matter knowledge, pedagogical knowledge and knowledge of context (professional preparation) and each of these will be further explained in the sections that follow.

Subject Matter Knowledge

Subject matter knowledge helps student teachers to acquire content mastery of the subject that they are required to teach, in this case, the English language. In the review of the literature on the type of content knowledge required for teacher education (see Banegas, 2009), the type of content knowledge required by English language teachers in particular comprises not just mastery of the knowledge about language but also about the different contributing factors to achieving the mastery of communicative competence. According to Hymes (1972) and Canale and Swain (1980), communicative competence involves the ability to use language both grammatically and appropriately. There are four aspects of communicative competence, namely, grammatical, sociolinguistic, discoursal and strategic. Grammatical competence refers to knowledge about the linguistic rules of a language (phonetics, phonology, syntax, lexicon and semantics). Sociolinguistic competence refers to the ability to use the language appropriately according to audience (who), domain (the setting in which the conversation is taking place), timing (when the conversation is taking place) and the topic (what one is talking about) and to help understand language as used in its context. Next, discoursal competence refers to aspects of cohesion (how a text is linked) and coherence (knowledge of how to logically connect ideas in a text). Finally, strategic competence is the ability to repair breakdowns in communication in order to achieve the goals of communication. Apart from helping student teachers to achieve communicative competence, subject matter knowledge also covers courses that help students to build awareness of aspects of linguistics that are directly relevant to the contexts of language

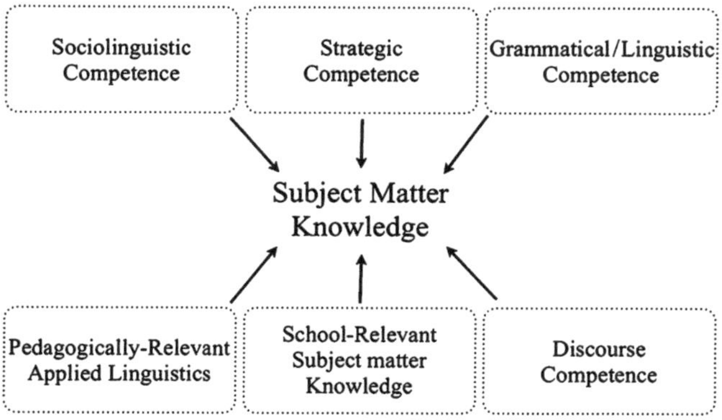

Fig. 6.1 Goals of subject matter knowledge instruction

classrooms that they will be facing in their future roles as classroom teachers of the English language. I will term this group of subjects as pedagogically relevant applied linguistics. This is in tandem with Bartels' (1999) suggestion where he advocates that linguistic knowledge for teachers can only be useful when relevance is drawn to application in the language teaching classroom. Finally, we also consider school-relevant subject matter knowledge in the conceptualisation of our programme.

The goals of our subject matter knowledge instruction may be summarised in Fig. 6.1 which details how, within our English language teacher education programme, we aim to help student teachers achieve communicative competence via the mastery of linguistic, sociolinguistic, discoursal and strategic competence and how we also aim to cover pedagogically relevant applied linguistics and school-relevant subject matter knowledge.

In terms of programme delivery, two main types of courses help us to realise the goals of our subject matter knowledge instruction: academic subjects and subject knowledge. English Language as an academic subject is only offered within the 4-year Bachelor's programme as it covers the disciplinary breadth and depth that is required of any student majoring in the English language as a discipline in their undergraduate studies. The key difference within our programme is that our courses within the academic subjects help to develop all aspects of competence listed in Fig. 6.1. A brief explanation will be provided in the sections that follow.

Developing Grammatical/Linguistic Competence

Within the study of English language as an academic subject, we have specific courses aiming to help student teachers to develop grammatical/linguistic competence. The courses begin with an introduction to the major branches of language study, investigating the nature, history and structure of the English language and it then moves on to introduce basic phonetics and grammar to student teachers and different approaches surrounding their study. At the higher levels of study, student teachers can opt as electives to be introduced to Halliday's (1973) systemic functional grammar and the interpersonal, textual and experiential nature of texts. They are also introduced to the history, compilation and innovations in the design of lexical resources for language learners. They can also opt to delve deeper in the topics in phonetics and phonology where they are also introduced to the main research methods in conducting acoustic phonetic research that can inform phonological theory. Other elective topics include going into a study of the history of linguistics, translation theory and comparative linguistics. The higher level courses build on the strong foundation of the introductory courses with the view of preparing student teachers to undertake research in these areas if they choose to pursue their higher degrees in linguistics in the future as can be seen in the electives on research methods and undertaking independent reading and research.

Developing Sociolinguistic Competence

Another group of courses are designed in order to help student teachers master sociolinguistic competence within the study of the English language as an academic subject. These courses start at an introductory level where student teachers are developed to become critical observers of how language is used both in written and spoken forms to achieve purposeful communication. They are also given a thorough introduction to basic concepts of sociolinguistics and language in relation to society and how language varies according to purpose, topic, audience and domain. As an elective, student teachers can opt to study the linguistic features of Singapore English, understand deeper the history, development and variation existing in Singapore English and consider the implications of such varietal variation when using English as the medium of instruction for teaching. An advanced level elective focuses on both the development of English in new cultural contexts and considers the roles and functions of the development of new varieties of English around the world again with an eye to discuss the implications for teaching English as an international language. Another elective looks at bilingual education from the perspective of language policy and planning and the effects of societal bilingualism on language, culture and identity. These electives are purposefully designed with the sociolinguistic situation of Singapore in mind and with the ultimate goal of allowing our student teachers to master sociolinguistic competence of the English language and the other languages that they speak in their repertoire.

Developing Discoursal Competence

The courses aim to help student teachers to acquire the concept of semiosis or meaning-making and explore the relationship between texts, people and contexts in order to understand the roles that written, spoken and visual discourse plays in our everyday lives and in the context of education. The more advanced level course on

Critical Discourse Analysis (CDA) looks at how power and ideology are realised through language and relies mainly, though not exclusively, on the Hallidayan framework for analysing texts and a wide variety of discourses are looked at from various perspectives such as the media, gender and politics.

Developing Strategic Competence

The courses are designed to show how we use meaning in English in the contexts of real interaction and language use; and how meanings in language start off conventionally, the relation between forms and meaning, different meaning relationships; and how meanings can change as a result of the creative use of language and over time. It then proceeds to a more advanced level showing how meanings are generated in real-life contexts and conversations and the different theoretical aspects of pragmatics help student teachers to make sense of how to develop pragmatic competence which is essential for the avoidance of miscommunication and to help them to achieve their communicative goals.

Developing Pedagogically Relevant Applied Linguistics Knowledge

These groups of courses are mainly offered as electives and they add a special dimension as they introduce aspects of applied linguistics that are pedagogically relevant, that is, necessary for helping our student teachers to fulfil their future roles as teachers of the English language. Student teachers are exposed to the centrality of the English language and its role in the Singapore education system as it is both used as a medium of instruction and as the means to convey the message, that is, the English language is both the medium and the message, and the issue of how language can be used to improve the quality of student learning outcomes is critically explored. Aspects of becoming literate from the social, cognitive and linguistic dimensions are also covered in another elective and in an elective for third and fourth year undergraduates, the issue of multiliteracies available in the language classroom is explored from the perspective of how best to engage the learners to become effective users of the language. Reading and writing are looked at from theoretical perspectives and how latest research has informed earlier theoretical understandings. The roles that reading and writing play in language learning process are also explored. In the age of interactive digital media, the role of information technology as an enabling tool in the language classroom is elucidated and explored. Student teachers are also taught basic assessment literacy skills in order to use language assessment of learning, for and as part of the language learning process. Language across the curriculum, also known as Disciplinary Literacy, looks at how language is used in various disciplines in order to enable more effective student learning outcomes. Finally, the elective on special topics allows student teachers to work one-on-one in an educationally related linguistic topic of their choice and to explore this topic or work of an educational linguist in greater depth. The ultimate goal of this group of courses is to ensure that the linguistics in our teacher education programmes have future relevance and application to student teachers' roles as language teachers.

Developing School-Relevant Subject Matter Knowledge

These courses have been conceptualised in order to help reinforce mastery of subject content relevant to teaching in primary schools. In this regard, close coverage of the latest primary school English language syllabus is a key feature of the courses. Student teachers explore grammatical structures in selected English text types, analyse different types of fiction and non-fiction text types written for children and move on to cover how the latest English language syllabus and latest policy initiatives on language teaching and learning by the MOE is being implemented in the primary schools.

Pedagogical Knowledge

This group of courses helps to impart pedagogical knowledge and I define this concept in two ways. Firstly, it is imparting knowledge about how to teach a particular subject, including introducing the latest theories and research-based practices about the latest pedagogical methodologies/strategies for teaching a particular subject area. Secondly, it is also about imparting knowledge of the latest curriculum/syllabi goals for the subject. In our teacher preparation programmes, this group of courses is known as Curriculum Studies (CS).

The CS courses are designed to help student teachers to develop the competencies and knowledge, strategies and approaches for the teaching of the main language skills such as reading, writing and oral communication (both speaking and listening) and are differentiated according to the primary and secondary levels. Special attention is placed on the intended curriculum goals of the English language syllabus at the primary and secondary levels.

Knowledge of Context (Professional Preparation)

The third and final knowledge base that our teacher education programmes is to allow student teachers to have a grasp of the knowledge of the professional contexts for which they will be using the English language. In this group of courses, student teachers are given exposure to the specific contexts for language use that is relevant to their future roles as teachers. Of course, the clinical field experience or the teaching practicum postings form an essential part of our teacher education programmes in terms of exposing our student teachers to the actual context of the language classrooms in developmental phases throughout their teacher education programmes which I will elaborate upon after I have described the professional preparation courses.

The Communication Skills for Teachers (CST) course is designed to provide all pre-service student teachers with the necessary oral and written skills to function effectively as communicators in the professional communicative contexts they will encounter in their future roles as teachers, such as in interacting with their peers and senior colleagues, with parents and other community partners. Voice care tips are given as is a thorough introduction to phonetic transcription with a view to helping them check out pronunciations of words in dictionaries.

Hands-on opportunities are provided for giving oral and written presentations. Academic Discourse Skills is offered to undergraduate students only with a view to helping them to acquire the necessary conventions of academic discourse for writing their coursework assignments and for future research purposes such as writing research reports and later on, writing theses and dissertations.

Another group of courses for undergraduate students not reading the English language as an academic subject discipline but who will still be expected to teach English language courses is known as Certificate in English Language Studies (CELS; National Institute of Education [NIE], n.d.). These student teachers are mandated by MOE to complete English language content and proficiency enhancement courses leading to the award of the CELS. Spread over the first, second and third years of the degree programme, CELS courses are designed to benefit student teachers in two ways: to equip them with the content knowledge for teaching English confidently, that is, content enhancement and to enhance their language and communication skills so that they can serve as good models of spoken and written English (language skills enhancement).

The final aspect of professional preparation is to expose student teachers to the real context of practice teaching through four school postings that take place over the course of the 4 years of undergraduate study totalling 22 weeks of exposure in schools. The first posting is known as School Experience and takes place over 2 weeks at the end of the first year of study. The first week is spent at a primary school and the second in a secondary school. No independent teaching is expected at this posting but mentoring and observing a senior colleague is the main focus. The second posting is known as Teaching Assistantship and takes place over 5 weeks at the end of the second year of study. Here, student teachers are expected to write weekly reflections and to be given the opportunities not just to observe but to start teaching classes on their own. Teaching Practice I takes place at the end of the third year of study where student teachers are expected to be observed teaching classes on their own. The final practicum posting is known as Teaching Practice II and takes place for 10 weeks during the second term of the student teachers' fourth year of study. Here, student teachers are expected to present their teaching and learning portfolios described earlier in Chap. 3 during the first week and the final weeks of their teaching practicum posting, first to showcase their learning during the coursework component done at the National Institute of Education (NIE) and then to showcase what they have learnt during their Teaching Practice II posting.

This section has given detailed coverage of how our English language teacher education programmes within the pre-service programme are organised around the principles of helping our student teachers to acquire crucial knowledge bases deemed essential for preparing an English language teacher for our Singapore classrooms through helping them attain mastery of subject matter and pedagogical knowledge and most importantly, equipping them with knowledge of the contexts in which they will function as English language teachers.

English Language Teacher Professional Development

Coverage of the professional development opportunities for our English language teachers is beyond the scope of this chapter. However, suffice to say that like all other teachers in Singapore, English language teachers can be developed along three career pathways specially customised and developed by MOE. English language teachers can select to be on the teaching, specialisation or leadership tracks depending on their strengths and preferences and their career pathways can be developed in discussion with their reporting officers. In terms of professional development opportunities, a slew of courses are offered by a host of service providers such as NIE and the English Language Institute of Singapore (ELIS), to name a few. Higher degree opportunities tenable at NIE and funded by MOE's Professional Development Continuum model are also possible. ELIS was officially launched by Mr Lee Kuan Yew in September 2011 and the mission of ELIS as reflected on their website is as follows:

> to drive excellence in the teaching and learning of English language in Singapore schools, in order to support the wider strategic objectives of raising the general command of both spoken and written English language among all our students, while achieving the best international standards among our most able. (English Language Institute of Singapore [ELIS], n.d.)

To constantly encourage excellence in English language teaching in Singapore, since 2010, 27 teachers have been awarded the Inspiring Teacher of English Award by *The Straits Times* (Singapore's local newspaper) and the Speak Good English Movement (SGEM) with the support of MOE. The award is meant for English language teachers in Singapore schools who have ignited a love for the English language in their students, use innovative methods to engage students and help them speak and write better, and are passionate about making English interesting and relevant to students. Another award, the prestigious MOE Overseas English Language Teachers Study Award presents outstanding English language teachers with a scholarship overseas to conduct research, participate in university courses, teach and observe English language classes, and helps develop these teachers as international teachers of English. When these teachers return to Singapore, they conduct sharing and participate in workshops for educators and school leaders at national level to promote innovative ideas for language teaching that have sparked off from their overseas stint and among interaction from other schools.

Future Challenges and Concluding Remarks

While it does seem that Singapore's language planning policies vis-a-vis the role of English in relation to the other languages spoken in Singapore and the careful thought given to the selection, preparation and development of English teachers appears to put Singapore firmly in the global league of English-speaking nations, it is undeniable that further challenges do lie ahead in our quest for excellence. The first has to do with uneven levels of proficiency mastered by the community of English language speakers in Singapore mainly caused by differences in home language backgrounds of our students. Having established the strong correlation between language competence and academic achievement and bearing in mind the data cited by Teh (see Chap. 5 in this volume) mentioned earlier in this chapter where students from non-English speaking homes performed 56 points lower than their counterparts from English-speaking homes, it is important to level out the performance both in terms of language and academic competence of the students who come from non-English speaking homes. Such is indeed the aspiration of the English Language syllabus released in 2010, where it is envisaged that

> All should attain foundational skills, particularly in grammar, spelling and basic pronunciation. They should be able to use English in everyday situations and for functional purposes, such as giving directions, information or instructions and making requests. The majority of our pupils will attain a good level of competence in English, in both speech and writing. Some in this group who have a flair for the language will find this an advantage in frontline positions and various service industries. At least 20 % will attain a high degree of proficiency in English. They will help Singapore keep its edge in a range of professions, and play an important role in teaching and the media. Further, within this group, we can expect a smaller group of Singaporeans to achieve mastery in their command of the language that is no different from the best in English-speaking countries. (MOE, n.d. b)

A concern over falling standards of English spoken in Singapore led the government to set up the Speak Good English Movement (SGEM) in 2000. The movement is a nation-wide effort to promote the use of good English in Singapore and whose main mandate is "to encourage Singaporeans to speak grammatically correct English that is universally understood" (Speak Good English Movement [SGEM], n.d.).

While English-knowing bilingualism has been a policy upheld since the 1960s and while English has been used as a medium of instruction in all schools since 1987, the real challenge is whether the standard of English proficiency is equivalent to those of English-speaking countries so that our current leading performance in internationally benchmarked tests of student achievement can be sustained over the years and that we can level up the tail-end performers, especially those from

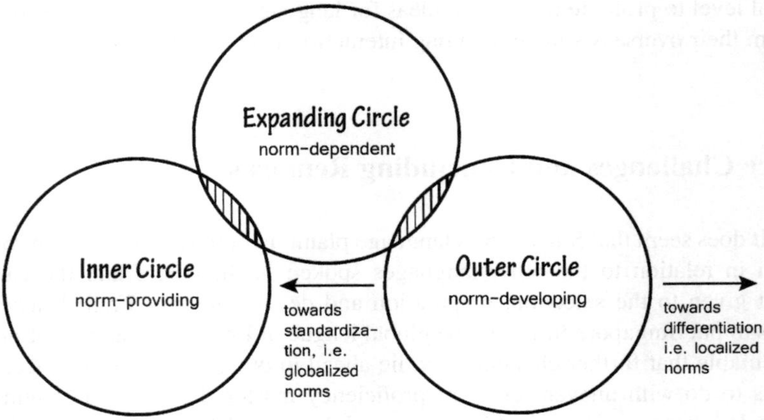

Fig. 6.2 Low's Venn diagram representing the rhythmic patterning of the *three circles* of English (Adapted from Low, 2010)

non-English speaking homes and to eventually equalise the achievement levels throughout the nation.

Two remaining but inter-related challenges confront the future of English language in Singapore. The first has to do with competing global and local norms in relation to the model of English to aspire towards. Alsagoff (2007) came up with the 'cultural orientation model' where she describes

> two opposing macro-cultural orientations – at one end are practices and orientations representing a globalist perspective, and at the other those associated with the local(ist) perspective. Each of these perspectives is associated with a cluster of referential ideologies relating to culture, capital and identity. (p. 38)

Put simply, Singaporeans are torn between aspiring towards a more globalised norm in the use of English which symbolises economic and social attainment and a localised norm which is closely linked with the expression of their culture and identity as Singaporeans using English. Which norm should be encouraged system-wide and what ramifications might this have on the system is a question that remains to be answered.

Low (2010) presents a realistic picture of the type of norm that is developing in the use of English in Singapore by providing empirical evidence from examining the pronunciation features used by educated Singaporeans in formal speech. She found evidence at least by looking at the rhythmic patterning of the English spoken in Singapore that Singaporeans had significantly different linguistic patterns (at least in the rhythmic domain) compared to a native English-speaking country such as Britain. Based on that finding and the similarities she found with the rhythmic patterning of Chinese English, she came up with her Venn diagram for explaining the development of norms within the Kachruvian circles (Kachru, 1982). She argued that Kachru's three concentric circles for the spread of World Englishes should instead be conceptualised as a Venn diagram instead (see Fig. 6.2).

Low's findings provides concrete evidence that the English spoken in Singapore is moving away from Inner Circle native English-speaking norms and shows evidence of developing our own norms. The challenge presented here is that while it is good that Singapore English is ready to evolve our own norms, the challenge of remaining internationally intelligible arises. For a nation that relies heavily on international trade for economic success, this can potentially be a serious issue.

Ultimately, while Singapore's prudent language planning policies and fidelity in the implementation of these policies system-wide with great coherence has been a foundational cornerstone explaining Singapore's high performing education system thus far, it is important to cast our eye on potential challenges that lie ahead so that we can not only sustain but continue to scale new peaks of success in our educational achievement that has so far been lauded by other systems around the world.

References

All-Party Committee on Chinese Education. (1956). *Report of the all-party committee of the Singapore legislative assembly on Chinese education*. Singapore: Government Printing Office.

Alsagoff, L. (2007). Singlish: Negotiating capital, culture and identity. In V. Vaish, S. Gopinathan, & Y. B. Liu (Eds.), *Language, capital, culture: Critical studies of language and education in Singapore* (pp. 25–46). Rotterdam: Sense Publishers.

Alsagoff, L. (2012). The development of English in Singapore: Language policy and planning in nation building. In E. L. Low, & A. Hashim (Eds.), *English in Southeast Asia: Features, policy and language in use* (pp. 137–154). Amsterdam: John Benjamins Publishing.

Banegas, D. L. (2009). Content knowledge in teacher education: Where professionalisation lies. *English Language Teacher Education and Development, 12*, 44–51.

Bartels, N. (1999). How teachers use their knowledge of English. In H. Trappes-Lomax, & I. McGrath (Eds.), *Theory in language teacher education* (pp. 46–56). Harlow, UK: Longman.

Bernstein, B. (1970). Elaborated and restricted codes: Their social origins and some consequences. In K. Danziger (Ed.), *Readings in children socialization*. Oxford, UK: Pergamon.

Bilton, T. (1977). *Introductory sociology*. London: Macmillan.

Bloomfield, L. (1927). Literate and illiterate speech. *American Speech, 2*, 432–439.

Bokhorst-Heng, W. (1998). Language planning and management in Singapore. In J. A. Foley, T. Kandiah, Z. Bao, A. E. Gupta, L. Alsagoff, C. L. Ho, I. S. Talib, & W. Bokhorst-Heng (Eds.), *English in new cultural contexts: Reflections from Singapore* (pp. 287–319). Singapore: Oxford University Press.

Canale, M., & Swain, M. (1980). Theoretical bases of communicative approaches to second language teaching and testing. *Applied Linguistics, 1*, 1–47.

Davies, A. (2003). *The native speaker: Myth and reality*. Clevedon, UK: Multilingual Matters.

Department of Statistics Singapore. (2011). Singapore census of population 2010: Statistical release 1: Demographic characteristics, education, language and religion. Retrieved from http://www.singstat.gov.sg/Publications/population.html#census_of_population_2010

English Language Institute of Singapore (ELIS). (n.d.). *Vision and mission*. Retrieved from http://www.elis.moe.edu.sg

Gopinathan, S. (1994). Language policy changes, 1979–1992: Politics and pedagogy. In S. Gopinathan, A. Pakir, W. K. Ho, & V. Saravanan (Eds.), *Language, society and education in Singapore* (pp. 65–91). Singapore: Times Academic Press.

Halliday, M. A. K. (1973). *Explorations in the functions of language*. London: Edward Arnold.

Hymes, D. H. (1972). On communicative competence. In J. Pride, & J. Holmes (Eds.), *Sociolinguistics* (pp. 269–293). Harmondsworth, UK: Penguin.

Kachru, B. B. (1982). South Asian English. In R. W. Bailey, & G. Manfred (Eds.), *English as a world language* (pp. 353–383). Ann Arbor, MI: University of Michigan Press.

Kachru, B. B. (1992). Teaching world Englishes. In B. B. Kachru (Ed.), *The other tongue: English across cultures* (2nd ed., pp. 355–365). Urbana, IL: University of Illinois Press.

Kuo, E., & Jernudd, B. H. (1994). Balancing macro- and micro-sociolinguistics perspectives in language management: The case of Singapore. In S. Gopinathan, A. Pakir, W. K. Ho, & V. Saravanan (Eds.), *Language, society and education in Singapore* (pp. 26–46). Singapore: Times Academic Press.

Lee, W. O. (1997). Social class, language and achievement. In G. A. Postiglione, & W. O. Lee (Eds.), *Schooling in Hong Kong: Organisation, teaching and social context* (pp. 155–174). Hong Kong, SAR: Hong Kong University Press.

Low, E. L. (2010). The acoustic reality of the Kachruvian circles: A rhythmic perspective. *World Englishes, 29*(3), 394–405.

Low, E. L. (2013, February 25). Singapore: Bilingual language policy and its educational success [Web log post]. *Education Week*. Retrieved from http://blogs.edweek.org/edweek/global_learning/2013/02/singapore_bilingual_language_policy_and_its_educational_success.html

Low, E. L., & Brown, A. (2005). *English in Singapore: An introduction*. Singapore: McGraw-Hill (Education) Asia.

Ministry of Education (MOE), Singapore. (n.d. a). *English language entrance proficiency test* (*EL EPT*). Retrieved from http://www.moe.gov.sg/careers/teach/applying/entrance-proficiency-test/english

Ministry of Education (MOE), Singapore. (n.d. b). *English language syllabus 2010* (*EL Syllabus 2010*). Retrieved from http://www.moe.edu.sg/education/syllabuses/languages-and-literature/files/english-primary-secondary-express-normal-academic.pdf

National Institute of Education (NIE). (n.d.). *Certificate in English language studies* (*CELS*) *programme*. Retrieved from http://www.nie.edu.sg/files/ell/tldc/CELS/CELS%20Information%202013.pdf

Newsom Report. (1963). *Half our future: A report of the Central Advisory Council for Education*. London: HMSO.

Paikeday, T. M. (1985). *The native speaker is dead!* Toronto, Canada: Paikeday Publications.

Pakir, A. (1991). The range and depth of English-knowing bilinguals in Singapore. *World Englishes, 10*, 167–179.

Shulman, L. S. (1986). Those who understand: Knowledge growth in teaching. *Educational Researcher, 15*(2), 4–14.

Shulman, L. S. (1987). Knowledge and teaching: Foundations of the new reform. *Harvard Educational Review, 57*(1), 1–22.

Shulman, L., & Grossman, P. (1988). *The intern teacher casebook*. San Francisco: Far West Laboratory for Educational Research and Development.

Speak Good English Movement (SGEM). (n.d.). *What we do – Speak good English movement*. Retrieved from http://www.goodenglish.org.sg/category/movement/about-us

Chapter 7
Purposeful Policy and Practice for Equity and Quality – A Finnish Case

Hannele Niemi

The Purpose of the Chapter

Finnish students' outstanding success in PISA studies (OECD, 2003, 2006, 2010) during the last decade has been a great joy to educational practitioners and decision-makers in Finland. It has been amazing how the Finnish education system, with only average monetary investments, a very small amount of homework and lesson hours, and extremely light education evaluation (no inspection system) can reach such results in high quality and equality in international comparisons (Reinikainen, 2012).

The purpose of this chapter is to reflect on factors that are and have been the major reasons promoting high quality education in Finland. The article starts with a short historical and cultural description of contextual factors. Thereafter, policy level decisions and trends for the comprehensive school and teacher education are introduced. The chapter also summarises how equity and lifelong learning are connected together to provide equal opportunities to all learners. The chapter will focus on the factors that are important for keeping up the high quality in the Finnish system. Finally, the chapter will also bring some major challenges for the future.

This chapter is based on strategic national policy documents, especially governmental programmes and their action plans, decision documents of the Finnish National Board of Education and Ministry of Education and Culture, the University Act and Teacher Education Decrees. The analysis is based on the principles and contents in which students' learning is the focus. National evaluations and research projects on teaching, learning and teacher education have also provided important knowledge about the strengths and weaknesses of the Finnish educational system.

H. Niemi (✉)
Institute of Behavioral Sciences, University of Helsinki,
P.O. Box 9, Siltavuorenpenger 5 A, 00014 Helsinki, Finland
e-mail: hannele.niemi@helsinki.fi

S.K. Lee et al. (eds.), *Educational Policy Innovations: Levelling Up and Sustaining Educational Achievement*, Springer Education Innovation Book Series 1,
DOI 10.1007/978-981-4560-08-5_7,

National and Cultural Context – A Brief History

Roots of Educational Values in a National History

In the national history of Finland, learning and education have been central values for a long time. Thus, in Finland, we like to think that our success in the PISA surveys has been only a side product in the development of our educational system. A major cultural influential background factor is a strong sense of Finnish national identity. Having first been part of the Swedish realm from 1249 to 1809, then from 1809 to 1917 existing as a Grand Duchy of the Russian Empire, Finland finally became independent in 1917. From the late nineteenth century onwards, a strong Finnish nationalist movement, known as the Fennoman Movement, grew. The main message of the representatives of the Finnish national movement was the education of a nation. They advocated that the power of a nation depends especially on competent leaders and the quality of the civil servants and teachers. Teacher education was seen as a necessary means for national education. Teacher education has had a close relationship with universities since its beginnings in the nineteenth century. Respect for learning and teachers' work has had long historical roots in Finland and has been a deep cultural feature in Finnish society. Teachers were considered to be important actors in local communities. They were often responsible for cultural activities in villages when 6-year basic education became compulsory for all children in 1921. Teachers, nicknamed 'candles of the nation', very often educated the whole village and people in local regions by organising choirs, theatre performances and parental education in addition to their normal school work. This education process was strongly supported by the Finnish Lutheran Church that had demanded literacy as a requirement for obtaining permission to marry since the fifteenth century until the school system in society took responsibility for basic education and literacy (Niemi, 2012a).

Towards a Comprehensive School

The baby boom after the Second World War increased the number of pupils enrolled in Finnish schools in the 1950s. At the same time, the concept of a welfare society emerged. Education was seen as a crucial factor for upholding equity in society. An important part of this process was the idea that free education is a basic right for all citizens. After many contradictory and heated debates, wide consensus could finally be found among politicians that a small country has to promote equality in education by implementing a system that provides educational opportunities for as long as possible to all those who are motivated to learn, regardless of their socioeconomic status, gender or place of residence. At the time, Finland had a parallel system in education in place in which 10-year-old children had to decide on their future prospects and careers. One had either to pass entrance examinations into academically oriented schools or go on routes that led to vocational fields. If they selected the vocational route, they could not seek entrance to higher education. The educational system put individuals into one of two categories at a very early stage of their lives, thus creating a divided nation. The academic schools very often had tuition fees, which further strengthened the divide.

Moving to a new school system that would be the same for all children was not an easy process in spite of a common general vision of the importance of education. After a very tough political debate in the 1960s, it was decided in 1968 that the parallel school system should be replaced by a national 9-year basic education that would represent the ideology of comprehensive education (Jakku-Sihvonen & Niemi, 2007; Laukkanen, 2006, 2008; Sahlberg, 2011). When the government delivered its bill to parliament in 1967, one of the arguments for the common 9-year comprehensive education for all was that it was too early to judge individual capacities after only 4 years of basic education. In the beginning of the new system, streaming was allowed but it was abolished in the 1980s because of unwanted consequences. It did not increase learning outcomes but strengthened the divide between different learners. In the 1970s and 1980s, the comprehensive school was a very centralised system. It was a time when a new concept of pedagogy had to be developed and teacher education was reformed radically. In the 1980s, a general decentralisation in all administrations was implemented in Finland and also in educational policy. It gave more freedom as well as responsibility to local educational providers. The teacher education system was also developed to provide new teachers with better competences to meet the whole age cohorts and to take more responsibility for curriculum development. During the 1980s and 1990s, there were many political debates about the relevance of the common comprehensive school for all. Critical voices demanded more attention especially to gifted children. However, the comprehensive school model remained. The main policy was that the comprehensive school could have different profiles locally and support students' individual qualities without streaming or having separate schools, for example, gifted pupils.

Educational Policy for Equity Throughout the System

Equity has been a leading principle of Finnish education policy and it covers the whole educational system from early education to higher education as well as adult education (Kumpulainen & Lankinen, 2012; OECD, 2005). This objective can be seen in every governmental programme for the past 20 years even though there have been different political parties in the government. It is included also in the national curricula of all levels of the educational system (Finnish National Board of Education [FNBE], 2004a, 2004b). The principle entails that everyone needs sufficient learning skills and opportunities to educate and develop themselves in different learning environments throughout their lifespan (Ministry of Education and Culture, Finland [MEC], 2011). The Finnish official policy can be summarised in the following way:

> The main objective of the Finnish education policy is to offer all citizens equal opportunities to receive education, regardless of age, domicile, financial situation, sex or mother tongue. Education is considered to be one of the fundamental rights of all citizens. (FNBE, 2012a, 2012b)

Since the late 1960s, Finnish basic education has been logically developed towards the comprehensive model, which guarantees everybody equal opportunities in education irrespective of sex, social status, ethnic group, among others, as outlined in the constitution. According to education researchers (Jakku-Sihvonen & Niemi, 2007; Laukkanen, 2006; Schleicher, 2007; Simola, 2005; Välijärvi, 2004), the educational policy has purposefully aimed at equity in education, which is the main reason for its good learning outcomes. Finland has built an education system with the following uniformed characteristics: free education, free school meals and special needs education. The principle of inclusion has been an important guideline. In the 1980s, all Finnish students in basic education began to have the same goals in mathematics and foreign languages. In so doing, the Finnish Government was realistic. In reality, these goals are attained by individuals with different levels of success. However, with extra support for the weakest students, we can considerably raise the performance of the whole age group.

Laukkanen (2006) summarises the most important decisions as: (1) the discontinuation of streaming; (2) the strong allocation of affordable educational resources to lower secondary education; (3) the decentralisation of decision-making powers; (4) the qualification of primary school teacher education was also raised to the MA level; (5) support for weak students was taken care of, and (6) different stakeholders were invited to express their opinions on educational policy.

One of the aims of the Finnish education system is to have an educational infrastructure that is devoid of so-called ‘dead-ends’. Compulsory education is the 9 years of comprehensive school, but the national aim is to keep all children in connection with the educational system for at least 12 years and to provide several routes for lifelong learning after that. The aim of the system is to enable an individual’s education to continue. Nearly 100 % of each age cohort completes the 9 years of comprehensive schooling. Of those who finish the 9th grade of comprehensive school, 94 % continue their studies in the same year either in upper secondary general school or upper secondary level vocational education (Statistics Finland, 2009). The 6 % of the age cohort, who do not continue their studies, are in danger of exclusion. Municipalities have launched various programmes to keep them in touch with education and learning so that they will be able to find pathways to further education. Without additional education they are in danger of being excluded from the labour market. The aims related to equity and the enablement of all people’s development through learning and education set special requirements on teachers, the teaching profession and teacher studies at universities.

An inclusion policy and special needs education are extremely important in promoting all students’ rights to learn. The basic principle is that all students with learning difficulties must be given help and support to overcome these difficulties.

They can have extra tuition hours or/and special needs instruction integrated into their own class, and temporary or more permanent help in special classes or groups. In each school there is a multi-professional student care group which consists of a principal, teachers as well as special need teachers, social workers and a nurse. According to a new decree passed in 2011, every teacher is responsible for identifying students' learning difficulties at the earliest stage possible (FNBE, 2012a, 2012b). This widens teachers' and local level actors' responsibility to seek solutions for supporting these students. Inclusion has been the main principle in the last decade and the new law from 2011 strengthens this trend.

Equity and Lifelong Learning (LLL) Are Connected

Niemi and Isopahkala-Bouret's study (2012) has revealed that the curricula and strategic plans of all levels had as common objectives: a readiness to continue studying at the next level, learning to learn consisting of increasing responsibility for one's own learning, and learners' personal growth. These LLL objectives are important within formal education. The same qualities are also needed when new technologies change the internal and external processes of knowledge creation in informal learning contexts, such as work organisations. (See Fig 7.1 for a schematic representation of this lifelong learning framework.)

In Finnish LLL policy, the equity principle is related to societal and economic purposes. In the governmental programme of 2011, equity is not only set as the aim for individuals' learning paths for all ages but also for the nation's welfare and growth of productivity. The Council for Lifelong Learning (2010) also emphasised the value of LLL from the perspective of Finnish society as a whole:

> Skilled people are Finland's primary resource and the foundation for successful welfare and business...The joy of learning and the possibility to apply new skills in life are the best sources of motivation. Learning provides individuals and communities the skills to tackle changes in the environment. Lifelong learning also prevents social exclusion. (p. 2)

According to the core curriculum of pre-school education, the major task of LLL is to promote learning opportunities by supporting and following up children's physical, mental, social, cognitive and emotional development (FNBE, 2000). This happens by enhancing their well-being and perception of themselves and increasing their opportunities for participation. The important objectives are to provide positive learning experiences, which strengthen children's healthy self-esteem, prevent learning difficulties, and advance social skills by providing social interaction with other people (2000). In pre-school, while children learn basic skills and abilities, they also learn "learning to learn" skills (p. 7). According to the core curriculum, learning by playing is central to children at this age. The basic objective is also to guarantee equal opportunities for every child to start comprehensive school.

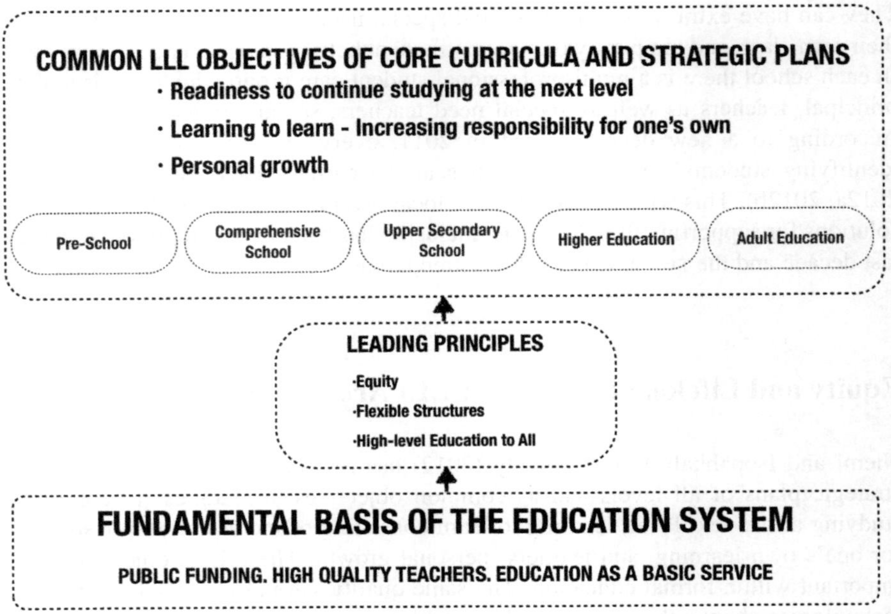

Fig 7.1 The leading principles and major LLL objectives in the Finnish lifelong learning policy (Niemi & Isopahkala-Bouret, 2012)

Comprehensive School

The national core curriculum for comprehensive schools provides the main objectives for the active learning of different subject matter and aims for the generic skills needed in LLL (FNBE, 2004a). The core curriculum emphasises that the main aim is to awaken a desire for lifelong learning. The objectives related to LLL are the following:

- To steer pupils to develop their abilities and to take responsibility for their learning, to assess it, and seek feedback to reflect on their own learning behaviour;
- To facilitate pupils to become aware of their own learning and to help them to find opportunities to affect it; and
- To provide opportunities for pupils to develop their own learning strategies and apply them in new situations. (p. 8)

Pupils must learn skills needed for their own learning at school and for their future learning outside the formal school system. LLL skills are generic, such as thinking and problem-solving skills, collaboration and interaction skills, self-knowledge and responsibility, and participatory and active citizenship skills. An important LLL objective in the core curriculum is to extend learning into different informal learning environments, including the new technology-based environments (2004a).

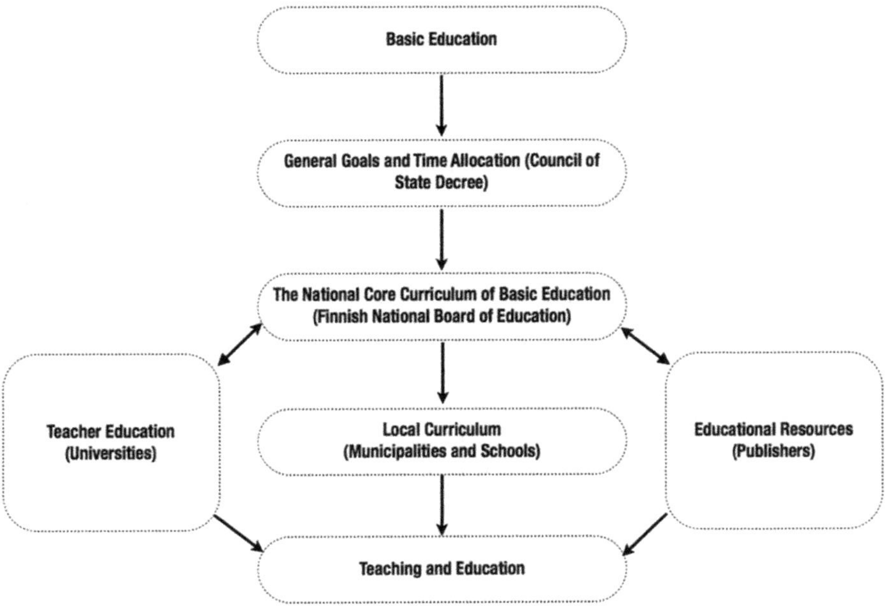

Fig. 7.2 The steering system of basic education (Vitikka, Krokfors & Hurmerinta (2012, p.86))

Responsibility for Quality at a Local Level

Finland has also balanced between a centralised and decentralised administration of education. At the beginning, comprehensive schools were very centralised, but in 1985 the municipalities' freedom and responsibility increased. The status of the then new national curricular guidelines was to create a framework for curriculum design in the municipalities (Laukkanen, 2006). Ten years later, in 1994, the National Board of Education only gave very broad aims and content guidelines for teaching different subjects. The municipalities and, ultimately, the schools set up their own curricula on the basis of the national core curriculum. Since 1999, new legislation has been provided to mainstream decentralisation. Providers of education – meaning municipalities, coalitions between municipalities and private foundations – have been given a lot of freedom when it comes to writing their local curricula. Still, the local curricula have to be drawn up in accordance with the National Core Curriculum for both comprehensive and upper secondary schools.

The local curricula have to determine the teaching and educational practices of the schools concerned. The curricula must be drawn up in such a way that they take into account the schools' operating environments, local value choices and special resources. The education provider may decide about the implementation of curriculum in cooperation with interest groups. The aim is to ensure a high standard of general education, with relevance to society and commitment from the community as a whole to the jointly determined objectives and procedures. As it concerns pupils' welfare and home–school cooperation, the curriculum must be drafted in collaboration with authorities charged with tasks that are part of the implementation of the local authority's social and health services (FNBE, 2004a, 2004b).

Halinen and Järvinen (2008) point out that municipalities and schools are granted great autonomy in organising education and implementing the core curriculum. This is to ensure freedom to make individual choices based on the local needs of different schools, with the core curriculum serving as a common national basis. Local decision-making is also seen as a means of increasing local officials' and teachers' commitment to the implementation of the curriculum. Their active involvement in the process and therefore their ownership of the curriculum is reinforced by the autonomy and freedom they enjoy. (See Fig. 7.2 for the overall steering system of basic education in Finland.)

Vitikka, Krokfors, and Hurmerinta (2012) argue that textbooks and other materials produced by private publishers have a strong effect on teaching and learning but in Finland, textbooks and other learning materials are not authorised by the government. Previously, the National Board of Education approved all textbooks, but now private publishers independently interpret curricula into educational resources. Teachers have the freedom to choose what teaching and learning materials they use and whether they use textbooks or not.

Enhancement-Led and Formative Evaluation Policy for Promoting Quality

The quest for good learning outcomes is on the educational agenda of many countries. Globally, much controversy exists over what is the best way to use assessment as a tool to achieve high learning outcomes. Some countries have chosen standardised testing, which stresses competition between schools and focuses on measurable performances. Other countries have applied more formative aspects of evaluation. The Finnish choice has been enhancement-led evaluation at all levels of education. The assessment of outcomes is regarded as an important tool to improve education.

There is no inspection system to control the educational arrangements at schools or institutions (Jakku-Sihvonen & Niemi, 2007; Sahlberg, 2011). Instead of inspection, there is an evaluation system in place. For basic education, following up on whether schools have reached the national goals for learning outcomes set in the national core curriculum for basic education is done by national sample based assessments. Upper secondary schools have their own statute-based final examination system.

Since the mid-1990s, the Finnish National Board of Education has conducted national assessments of learning outcomes, mostly in the 9th grade of basic education (FNBE, 2012a, 2012b). Regular assessments have been carried out in mathematics, the students' mother tongue (either Finnish or Swedish) and literature, and occasionally in other subjects as well. National assessments produce information about the quality and results of education and training in relation to objectives stated in the national core curricula. These assessments are sample based and thus do not cover the whole age group. This is because the results are used for the development of education. Recently, evaluations have also been started, for example, at the end of the second grade. The purpose of this is to enhance the use of evaluation for formative purposes. All schools who are being sampled in an assessment receive an individual feedback report. These reports are delivered to schools as soon as possible after the assessment data has been collected, as fresh results are more interesting for schools than results that were conducted months ago. Recently, feedback has been received as soon as 2 months after the data was collected (Laukkanen, 2006). At the local level, municipalities are encouraged to produce internal and external evaluations to develop education. Policymakers are informed about the status of education by assessments and special up-to-date reports organised by the Ministry of Education. Evaluations are implemented to find evidence to support the continuous development of education and learning (Kumpulainen & Lankinen, 2012).

The aim of the national evaluation system is to support the local/municipal education administration and the development of schools as goal-oriented and open units, and to produce and provide up-to-date and reliable information on the context, functioning, results and the effects of the education system (Niemi & Lavonen, 2012). The Ministry of Education is responsible for general education policy and financing educational evaluations. National evaluations are organised by the following special councils: The Finnish Educational Evaluation Council (2012) is responsible for evaluating general education, vocational education and adult education. Evaluation of school achievement/learning outcomes in basic education is carried out by the Finnish National Board of Education (2012a, 2012b). The Finnish Higher Education Evaluation Council (2012) is an independent expert body assisting universities, polytechnics and the Ministry of Education in matters relating to evaluation and quality assurance systems. Besides the national evaluations, international evaluations are important in developing Finnish education. Since 2000, PISA has provided important information for the development of Finnish basic education (Jakku-Sihvonen & Niemi, 2007; Reinikainen, 2012).

Enhancement-led evaluation concerns also higher education and teacher education at Universities (Niemi & Lavonen, 2012). Society's trust in universities' degrees as well as teachers' competences are mediated via trustworthiness of the universities and makes them accountable. Trust is not a stable and permanent status. Results and quality must be assessed and evaluated systematically. Therefore universities' own quality assurance methods are important. All Finnish universities were audited by 2011 (Niemi & Lavonen). Teacher education has also been evaluated several times nationally and internationally in the last two decades. Evaluations have been enhancement-led and their purpose has been to produce improvements in teacher education. There is a close cooperative relationship between universities and the Ministry of Education in teacher education issues.

Many teacher education research projects have also been carried out jointly. The recent recommendations from the Ministry of Education and Culture (MEC, 2007) stress the importance of strengthening research in and on teacher education. The Ministry of Education also requires universities to reorganise conditions for teacher education research.

Teacher Education as a Key Player

A Research-Based Approach as a Main Guideline

For decades, the Finnish orientation toward teacher education has committed itself to the development of a research-based professional culture (Jakku-Sihvonen & Niemi, 2007; Niemi, 2012b; Niemi & Jakku-Sihvonen, 2006). The critical scientific literacy of teachers and their ability to use research methods are considered to be crucial. Accordingly, many teacher education programmes in Finland require studies in both qualitative and quantitative research traditions. The aim of these studies is to train students to identify and analyse problems they may expect to face in their future work. Research studies provide students with an opportunity to complete an authentic project, in which they must formulate a research question in an educational field, be able to search independently for information and data, elaborate on their findings in the context of recent research in the area, and synthesise the results in the form of a written thesis. They learn to study actively and to internalise the attitude of researchers in the learning process (Niemi, 2011).

Professors have the responsibility to guide students in the research-oriented aspects of their education. The main objective of this guidance is not the completion of the Bachelor's or Master's thesis, but to actually engage students in becoming active participants of the education society. In this aspect of the degree programme, the processes of active working and thinking are integrated in various complex and sometimes unexpected ways. The aim of the guiding process is to help students to discover and tap his/her own intellectual resources and to enable him/her fully to utilise the resources of the study group in which he/she is working (Nummenmaa & Lautamatti, 2004).

The goal of Finnish teacher education is to equip teachers with research-based knowledge and with skills and methods for developing teaching, cooperating at school and communicating with parents and other stakeholders. The main guidelines are:

- **Teachers need a deep knowledge of the most recent advances of research in the subjects they teach**. In addition, they need to be familiar with the latest research concerning teaching and learning. Interdisciplinary research on subject content knowledge and pedagogical content knowledge provides the foundation for developing teaching methods that can be adapted to suit different learners.

Table 7.1 Inquiry-orientation in an individual Finnish teacher's work (Jyrhämä & Maaranen, 2012, p. 105)

Content class
Develop and educate (oneself)
Evaluate one's own action
Constructivist view of teaching
Using multiple methods in teaching
Cooperation with teachers or other people in the school
Active, societal and critical orientation in teaching
Inquiry as a method in teaching
Relationships with students and the class
Collects feedback
Evaluation
Subject (content) knowledge

- **Teacher education in itself should also be an object of study and research.** This research should provide knowledge about the effectiveness and quality of teacher education implemented by various means and in different cultural contexts.
- **The aim is that teachers internalise a research-oriented attitude towards their work.** This means that teachers learn to take an analytical and open-minded approach to their work, and to draw conclusions based on their observations, and experiences and that they develop their teaching and learning environments in a systematic way.
- **Teachers need independent thinking skills and reflection in their work.** Teachers' competence must include readiness to analyse a situation like a researcher, draw conclusions and take action. This means that teachers need a critical mind and the ability to reflect. Reflection can be in action or on action. Because many decisions have to be made rapidly – in action – teachers must have deeply internalised the knowledge and the moral code which will guide them as they adapt to changing situations.

Student teachers see research studies in their teacher education as very valuable for their professional development. They see that research studies have helped them particularly in the following competences: Critical thinking, independent thinking, inquiring, scientific literacy, and questioning phenomena and knowledge. Niemi (2011) also found that even if the general picture is very positive, student teachers gave also a lot of feedback on how to improve the quality of research studies e.g. connecting them better with practice and further developing also the cooperation between subject matter studies and educational research studies.

We have some studies (Jyrhämä & Maaranen, 2012) which show how teachers in schools see the value of research studies in their work. Teachers gave the following themes on the relevance and usefulness of research based orientation in their work (see Table 7.1).

Jyrhämä and Maaranen have (2012) summarised:

> As a whole, the relatively high means [of student performance] indicate that the students have, in principle, accepted the idea of a research-based approach in their studies. The students expected a more research-based approach in the courses actually contained.

> The students appreciated the high level of the master's degree studies. In other words, they thought it valuable that teachers have rather long academic studies instead of a more practical teacher training and they felt that it was important that methodological courses started sufficiently early in the studies. It seems that the students have comprehended the basic idea of the curriculum of teacher education and this is very encouraging. (p. 105)

Integration of Theory and Practice

Teachers' pedagogical studies include supervised teaching practice (approximately 200 contact hours). The aim of the guided practical studies is to support students in their efforts to acquire professional skills in researching, developing and evaluating teaching, and learning processes. In addition, student teachers should be able to reflect critically on their own practices and social skills in teaching and learning situations. During their supervised practice periods student teachers meet pupils and students from various social backgrounds and psychological orientations and have opportunities to teach them according to the curriculum.

Teaching practice is integrated with all levels of teacher education. The practice is supervised by university teachers, university training school teachers or local school teachers depending on the phase of the practice (Jyrhämä, 2006). The main principle is that practice should start as early as possible and support student teachers' growth towards expertise. At the beginning, student teachers observe school life and pupils from an educational perspective after which they focus on specific subject areas and pupils' learning processes. Finally, it supports student teachers as they take holistic responsibility for their teaching and their overall stay at the schools. This period can be tightly connected with their research studies and Master's dissertation.

University teacher training schools (so-called 'Normal' schools) play a crucial role in the Finnish teacher education. The Normal schools are state schools (as opposed to municipal schools) and their teachers have a different status than those in other schools. Normal school teachers have a dual role: on one hand, they teach pupils; and on the other, they supervise and mentor student teachers. Many of the Normal school teachers are active in research and development and are members of teams that produce learning materials for schools. There is frequent critique on carrying out practice only in the Normal schools and demands for having a substantial part of the teaching practice in more typical schools. Parallel to the Normal schools there is a network of so-called 'field schools' with an important contribution to the capacity and volume of teacher education in the times of high demand of qualified teachers (Meisalo, 2007). At the University of Helsinki, all student teachers have experiences in teacher training schools and local schools. Both practices are supervised.

When student teachers were asked to assess their teacher education in two big universities in Finland (Niemi, 2011, 2012b), they gave very good feedback.

According to the survey, the student teachers had achieved very good competences in teachers' basic skills, such as planning instruction, managing teaching content, and assessing students. They had a deep commitment to teaching profession and saw that teachers need to learn throughout their career. The student teachers thought they had good learning competence for their future work. However, they also saw they had not achieved enough competences to collaborate in the school community as well as outside it, for example, with parents. Student teachers also regarded they would need more competence to meet students' diversity and prepare them to the needs of the future.

Teachers as Professionals

Teachers in Finland are representatives of a high quality academic and ethical profession. Teachers have to take an active role in raising serious questions about what they teach, how they teach it, and the larger goals towards which they are striving. Teachers need to view themselves as public intellectuals who combine conception and implementation, thinking and practice in the struggle for a culture of democratic values and justice. Teachers have a right and an obligation to articulate educational needs and challenges in the society they serve. They also have to be active in public debates and decisions affecting the development of schools and education. As professionals, teachers cannot only be implementers of decisions, but are also partners in their nation's development. Teachers are expected to be able to take an active role in evaluating and improving schools and their learning environments. They are also expected to refresh their professional skills, to cooperate with parents and other stakeholders, and to be active citizens (Toom & Husu, 2012).

Finnish teachers are recognised as professionals, and the teachers' trade union considers this status to be very important. Almost all teachers belong to the same teachers' trade union Opetusalan Ammattijärjestö (OAJ), which is a very powerful agency. OAJ has been invited to play an active role as a partner in all major reforms of teacher education and school curriculum in the last decades. It has also promoted the policy of having a Master's degree as teachers' basic qualification (OAJ, 2013). Finland has no inspectorate, no probation time for newly graduated teachers' or national school achievement testing. Finnish society considers teachers to be professionals who are morally responsible for their work.

Teachers' work is contextually bound, depending on learners' age level, cultural conditions, available resources and the contents they are mediating to learners. Teachers and teacher education are clearly related to national goals and purposes. The welfare and economy of the society are related to the quality of educational outcomes, which are associated with teachers' competences. Besides being guided by national and local community-based goals, teachers' work also have more generic aims. Teachers open doors and windows to cultural enrichment and help people to understand other human beings and their cultural contexts. Teachers are key actors in promoting human rights, justice and democracy in a global world (e.g., Aloni, 2002; Biesta, 2009; Campbell, 2008; Carr & Hartnett, 1996; Darling-Hammond, 2010). In Finland, the school law contains values that promote these aims. Teachers are expected to implement them in their daily work. Since 2000, the Ethical Council for the Teaching Profession has worked to promote teachers' ethical awareness. Also, the teacher education programmes emphasise teachers' social and moral responsibility. A survey in 2010 showed that Finnish student teachers are committed to the teaching profession and are aware of the ethical bases of teaching (Niemi, 2011).

Teachers are working in conditions where they must identify, observe and understand complexity of educational processes and face the evidence that is coming from different sources. They also need to be open to acquire and assess local evidence. Scardamalia and Bereiter (2003) have examined the behaviour of experts. The feature that really distinguishes experts from others is their approach to new problems. The pattern recognition and learned procedures that lead to intuitive problem-solving are only the beginning. The expert invests in what Bereiter and Scardamalia call progressive problem-solving, that is, tackling problems. This increases expertise rather than reduces problems to previously learned routines.

According to Schön (1991), experts always face problems in situations that are unique and consist of uncertainties, value conflicts and other tensions because of their complexity. They work in complex situations and therefore need various kinds of evidence. This sets special requirements on their knowledge base. Experts' knowledge is rational knowledge, but this is not sufficient. They also need principles, rules and role models, and to know how to apply scientific theories and techniques to complex problems. Teachers' work comprises so many uncertainties and changing elements that they cannot be provided with directly applicable knowledge or practice for their work.

Future Challenges

The concepts of equality and equity are often used with the following meanings: equality refers to an ideal and aim that people should have the same rights with each other without considerations of their sex, status or race. Equity is a policymaking concept that embodies the quality of being fair and reasonable in a way that gives equal treatment to everyone. The Finnish educational policy has aimed to operate under an umbrella that encompasses both meanings. The educational policy has systematically reinforced practices that provide equal opportunities for different learners.

In future, Finnish society will face several challenges related to ensuring current high quality learning opportunities for all learners as Finland becomes a multicultural society. It is important to ensure that everyone will have equal opportunities for education and learning. The last PISA results (OECD, 2010) showed signs of slightly widening differences between schools. Aspects related to multicultural education, for example, Mother Tongue teaching, religious education and location of multicultural pupils in all the schools in a city, are continuously considered in Finnish educational decision-making. In the next PISA measurements, multicultural education and learning outcomes of different ethnic groups will be a special national focus area.

Another threat is the diversity in the provision of education, by the municipalities who are responsible for the quality of education at the local level. There are considerable differences in their financial bearing capacity, and this has clear consequences for educational services. In 2012 National Board of Education set a working group to find out what is the national situation and make recommendations how to prevent unequal development.

Diversity and different learners are taken into account by identifying and supporting them at the early stages of their difficulties, by organising special needs education at local schools and classrooms, and by offering multi-professional support through pupil welfare groups welfare groups in which a principal, special education teacher, school nurse and school social worker, and often also school psychologist work together. Finnish schools subscribe to an inclusive policy for organising special needs education. The aim is to organise support for all learners – not by making problem students repeat classes, but by keeping all the youngsters with their peers as they progress through the educational system. A new law for special needs support in 2011 requires every teacher to identify learning difficulties as early as possible. The purpose of this is that students will get support in time and are able progress in their development. This is a real challenge both for pre- and in-service teacher education.

Summary and Conclusion

Biesta (2009) has analysed what is good education. He criticises the thought that there can be good education based only on external and instrumental aims. A position in a rankings table or PISA achievement test cannot be the main purpose for education. The same message comes also from leadership studies (Day & Johansson, 2008). Biesta advocates values when seeking good education. He suggests that education serves (at least) three different functions:

- Qualification, consisting of the ways in which education contributes to the acquisition of knowledge, skills and dispositions that qualify us for doing something – a 'doing' which can range from the very specific (such as the training for a particular job) to the very general (such as in the case of liberal education).
- Socialisation, through education, individuals become part of existing socio-cultural, political and moral 'orders.' This is the socialisation function of education. Schools partly engage in socialisation deliberately, for example, in the form of values education, character education, religious education or citizenship education. According to Biesta, socialisation also happens in less visible ways, for example, through the hidden curriculum and we can also see that education may serve the reproduction of social inequality.

- Individuation, a third function of education is different from both qualification and socialisation. This function is related to the ways in which education contributes to the individuation – or, as Biesta prefers to call this subjectification – of children and young people. Individuation consists ways of being that hint at independence from such orders, ways of being individuals, not simply a 'specimen' of a more encompassing order. It is about the ways in which education makes a contribution to human freedom.

On reflection, we may see a clear connectedness with values in the Finnish educational system. Equity has been the main leading principle for the past 30 years. Proving good lifelong learning skills to all learners throughout their life spans is linked with equity. This requires a very flexible educational system and structures in which learners always have an opportunity to continue their schooling. The Finnish system does not have a national curriculum. There are only national core curricula for different levels of the educational structure and they consist of a set of values for teaching and learning and set as objectives much wider purposes than mere success in international tests. Values are related to both social and individual growth processes and promote students to become active citizens, responsible and cooperative contributors in society. These same values also guide students how to self-regulate one's own learning and have agency in one's life. Teacher education is also connected with major educational values and the educational system even though teacher education is provided in universities. Teachers are expected to work as high quality professionals and their ability to reflect on their profession is one of the most important aims in the Finnish teacher education.

Connecting equity and quality requires a purposeful and persistent work for these aims. Without a strong political will and continuity across governments these aims are very difficult to achieve. Society, business and industry, technology, people's life conditions are changing continuously. No educational system is ever fully perfect and it cannot develop without active and honest evaluations and feedback on its functionality and ability to achieve its aims. This is also a case in Finland. It has taken a long time to mature to this phase. The Finnish educational system wades between success and challenges. The future is developed by decisions today and visions for the long term. There are many challenges to keep equity and quality together. So far, there has been commitment at different levels of education to continue in the selected path. However, it requires and will require persistent work for education.

References

Aloni, N. (2002). *Enhancing humanity: The philosophical foundations of humanistic education*. Boston: Kluwer Academic Publishers.

Biesta, G. (2009). *Good education: What it is and why we need it*. Inaugural lecture at The Stirling Institute of Education, Stirling, Scotland, UK.

Campbell, E. (2008). Preparing ethical professionals as a challenge for teacher education. In K. Tirri (Ed.), *Educating moral sensibilities in urban schools* (pp. 3–8). Rotterdam, The Netherlands: Sense Publishers.

Carr, W., & Hartnett, A. (1996). *Education and the struggle for democracy: The politics of educational ideas*. Buckingham, UK: Open University Press.

Council for Lifelong Learning. (2010). *Lifelong learning – Opportunity for growth and employment*. Retrieved from http://www.minedu.fi/opencms/opencms/handle404?exporturi=/export/sites/default/OPM/Koulutus/aikuiskoulutus_ja_vapaa_sivistystyoe/elinikaisenoppimisenneuvosto/liitteet/eng_teesit.pdf

Darling-Hammond, L. (2010). Teaching and educational transformation. In M. Fullan, A. Hargreaves, A. Lieberman, & D. Hopkins (Eds.), *Second international handbook of educational change* (pp. 505–522). New York: Springer.

Day, C., & Johansson, O. (2008). Leadership with a difference in schools serving disadvantaged communities: Arenas for success. In K. Tirri (Ed.), *Educating moral sensibilities in urban schools* (pp. 19–34). Rotterdam, The Netherlands: Sense Publishers.

Finnish Educational Evaluation Council. (2012). *Introduction. Mission*. Retrieved from http://www.edev.fi/portal/english5/basis_for_operation

Finnish Higher Education Evaluation Council. (2012). *Duties*. Retrieved from http://www.finheec.fi/index.phtml?l=en&s=28

Finnish National Board of Education (FNBE). (2000). *National core curriculum for pre-school education in Finland*. Retrieved from http://www.oph.fi/download/123162_core_curriculum_for_pre_school_education_2000.pdf

Finnish National Board of Education (FNBE). (2004a). *National core curriculum for basic education*. Retrieved from http://www.oph.fi/english/sources_of_information/core_curricula_and_qualification_requirements/basic_education

Finnish National Board of Education (FNBE). (2004b). *National core curriculum for upper secondary schools*. Retrieved from http://www.oph.fi/english/sources_of_information/core_curricula_and_qualification_requirements/basic_education

Finnish National Board of Education (FNBE). (2012a). *Pupil assessment*. Retrieved from http://www.oph.fi/english/education/basic_education/pupil_assesment

Finnish National Board of Education. (2012b). Basic education. Retrieved from http://www.oph.fi/english/education/basic_education

Halinen, I., & Järvinen, R. (2008). Towards inclusive education: The case of Finland. *Prospects, 38*(1), 77–97.

Jakku-Sihvonen, R., & Niemi, H. (2007). Introduction. In R. Jakku-Sihvonen & H. Niemi (Eds.), *Education as societal contributor* (pp. 9–20). Frankfurt am Main, Germany: Peter Lang.

Jyrhämä, R. (2006). The function of practical studies in teacher education. In R. Jakku-Sihvonen & H. Niemi (Eds.), *Research-based teacher education in Finland: Reflections by Finnish teacher educators* (pp. 51–70). Turku, Finland: Finnish Educational Research Association.

Jyrhämä, R., & Maaranen, R. (2012). Research orientation in teachers' work. In H. Niemi, A. Toom, & A. Kallioniemi (Eds.), *Miracle of education: The principles and practices of teaching and learning in Finnish schools* (pp. 97–114). Rotterdam, The Netherlands: Sense Publishers.

Kumpulainen, K., & Lankinen, T. (2012). Striving for educational equity and excellence: Evaluation and assessment in Finnish basic education. In H. Niemi, A. Toom, & A. Kallioniemi (Eds.), *Miracle of education: The principles and practices of teaching and learning in Finnish schools* (pp. 82–96). Rotterdam, The Netherlands: Sense Publishers.

Laukkanen, R. (2006). *Finnish strategy for high-level education for all*. Paper presented at the educational systems and the challenge of improving results conference, University of Lausanne, Lausanne, Switzerland.

Laukkanen, R. (2008). Finnish strategy for high-level education for all. In N. C. Sognel & P. Jaccard (Eds.), *Governance and performance of education systems* (pp. 305–324). Dordrecht, The Netherlands: Springer.

Meisalo, V. (2007). Subject teacher education in Finland: A research-based approach – The role of subjects didactics and networking in teacher education. In R. Jakku-Sihvonen & H. Niemi (Eds.), *Education as societal contributor* (pp. 161–180). Frankfurt am Main, Germany: Peter Lang.

Ministry of Education and Culture, Finland (MEC). (2007). *Opettajankoulutus 2020* [Teacher Education 2020]. Helsinki, Finland: Author.

Ministry of Education and Culture, Finland (MEC). (2011). *Education*. Retrieved from http://www.minedu.fi/OPM/Koulutus/?lang=en

Niemi, H. (2011). Educating student teachers to become high quality professionals – A Finnish case. *Center for Educational Policy Studies Journal, 1*(1), 43–66.

Niemi, H. (2012a). The societal factors contributing to education and schooling in Finland. In H. Niemi, A. Toom, & A. Kallioniemi (Eds.), *Miracle of education: The principles and practices of teaching and learning in Finnish schools* (pp. 82–96). Rotterdam, The Netherlands: Sense Publishers.

Niemi, H. (2012b). Teacher education for high quality professionals. An analysis from the Finnish perspective. In O. S. Tan (Ed.), *Teacher education frontiers: International perspectives on policy and practice for building new teacher competences* (pp. 43–70). Singapore: CENSAGE Learning.

Niemi, H., & Isopahkala-Bouret, U. (2012). Lifelong learning in Finnish society – An analysis of national policy documents. *International Journal of Continuing Education and Lifelong Learning, 5*(1), 43–63.

Niemi, H., & Jakku-Sihvonen, R. (2006). Research-based teacher education. In R. Jakku-Sihvonen & H. Niemi (Eds.), *Research-based teacher education in Finland: Reflections by Finnish teacher educators* (pp. 31–50). Turku, Finland: Finnish Educational Research Association.

Niemi, H., & Lavonen, J. (2012). Evaluation for improvements in Finnish teacher education. In J. Harford, B. Hudson, & H. Niemi (Eds.), *Quality assurance and teacher education: International challenges and expectations*. Oxford, UK: Peter Lang.

Nummenmaa, A. R., & Lautamatti. L. (2004). *Ohjaajana opinnäytetöiden prosesseissa: Ryhmäohjauksen käytäntöä ja teoriaa* [As a supervisor in a thesis processes: Praxis and theory of group guidance]. Tampere, Finland: University Press.

OAJ. (2013). Qualifications (in Finnish Kelpoisuudet). Retrieved from http://www.oaj.fi/portal/page?_pageid=515,452376&_dad=portal&_schema=PORTAL

OECD. (2003). *First results from PISA 2003: Executive summary*. Retrieved from http://www.oecd.org/education/preschoolandschool/programmeforinternationalstudentassessmentpisa/34002454.pdf

OECD. (2005). *Equity in education thematic review*: *Finland country note*. Retrieved from www.oecd.org/document/3/0,2340,en_2649_34531_36296195_1_1_1_1,00.html

OECD. (2006). *PISA 2006 science competencies for tomorrow's world*. Retrieved from http://www.oecd.org/edu/preschoolandschool/programmeforinternationalstudentassessmentpisa/pisa2006results.htm

OECD. (2010). *PISA 2009 results: What students know and can do: Student performance in reading, mathematics and science* (Vol. I). Paris: Author.

Reinikainen, P. (2012). Amazing PISA results in Finnish comprehensive schools. In H. Niemi, A. Toom, & A. Kallioniemi (Eds.), *Miracle of education: The principles and practices of teaching and learning in Finnish schools* (pp. 3–18). Rotterdam, The Netherlands: Sense Publishers.

Sahlberg, P. (2011). *Finnish lessons: What can the world learn from educational change in Finland?* New York: Teacher College Press.

Scardamalia, M., & Bereiter, C. (2003). Knowledge building environments: Extending the limits of the possible in education and knowledge work. In A. DiStefano, K. E. Rudestam, & R. Silverman (Eds.), *Encyclopedia of distributed learning*. Thousand Oaks, CA: Sage Publications.

Schleicher, A. (2007). Can competences assessed by PISA be considered the fundamental school knowledge 15-years-olds should possess? *Journal of Educational Change, 8*(4), 349–357.

Schön, D. A. (1991). *The reflective turn: Case studies in and on educational practice*. New York: Teachers Press, Columbia University.

Simola, H. (2005). The Finnish miracle of PISA: Historical and sociological remarks on teaching and teacher education. *Comparative Education, 41*(4), 455–470.

Statistics Finland. (2009). *Statistics. Education.* Retrieved from http://tilastokeskus.fi/til/kou_en.html

Toom, A., & Husu, J. (2012). Finnish teachers as 'makers of the many': Balancing between broad pedagogical freedom and responsibility. In H. Niemi, A. Toom, & A. Kallioniemi (Eds.), *Miracle of education: The principles and practices of teaching and learning in Finnish schools* (pp. 39–54). Rotterdam, The Netherlands: Sense Publishers.

Välijärvi, J. (2004). The system and how does it work – Some curricular and pedagogical characteristics of the Finnish comprehensive schools. *Educational Journal, 31*(2), 2003 & *32* (1), 2004, 31–55.

Vitikka, E., Krokfors, L., & Hurmerinta, E. (2012). The Finnish national core curriculum: Structure and development. In H. Niemi, A. Toom, & A. Kallioniemi (Eds.), *Miracle of education: The principles and practices of teaching and learning in Finnish schools* (pp. 82–96). Rotterdam, The Netherlands: Sense Publishers.

Chapter 8
The Light and Shadow of Educational Achievement in South Korea with Suggestions for Levelling Up

Youngdal Cho

Introduction

South Korean education has become the centre of increasing interest in the world because of South Korean students' high performance in internationally benchmarked tests such as PISA and TIMSS. This might be the reason behind U.S. President Obama's comments about South Korea's education in his speech. Concurrently, many third world countries also look to South Korea's educational system as a successful model because of South Korea's high performance in international benchmarking tests.

However, in South Korea itself, there has been serious self-criticism about South Korean education; among others, the lack of higher cognitive skills – such as scientific problem awareness and situation explanation ability – this was evidenced by the 11th ranking for mean scores in the PISA results for 2006. The issue of educational inequality has also been a serious concern in South Korea.

This chapter will attempt to provide an answer to the question about 'how to make sense of educational achievements in South Korea' by identifying and analysing the factors and suggestions for policy implications for the improvement of education in South Korea not only in terms of attaining higher scores in PISA, TIMSS and other international tests of student achievement, but also about increasing the level of educational equality in the country. This is because both high achievement and equality are important in helping an individual to maximise their social and personal potential and to exercise their freedom as South Korean citizens. In section "The culture, context and tradition of education in South Korea", this chapter will analyse South Korea's cultural context and tradition of education. Section "Education reforms in South Korea" will discuss recent educational reforms and analyse the impact of such changes on South Korean education.

Y. Cho (✉)
Department of Social Education, College of Education, Seoul National University,
1 Gwanak-ro, Gwanak-gu, Seoul 151-742, South Korea
e-mail: ydcho@snu.ac.kr

S.K. Lee et al. (eds.), *Educational Policy Innovations: Levelling Up and Sustaining Educational Achievement*, Springer Education Innovation Book Series 1,
DOI 10.1007/978-981-4560-08-5_8, © Springer Science+Business Media Singapore 2014

This is because, I believe, today's educational attainment is grounded upon both the cultural context (section "The culture, context and tradition of education in South Korea") and the South Koreans' efforts to reform (section "Education reforms in South Korea") South Korean education. Based on the discussions in sections "The culture, context and tradition of education in South Korea" and "Education reforms in South Korea", this chapter will discuss the overall achievements of South Korean education. As mentioned above, South Korea's educational achievements have two sides – including both the light (or 功, its merits) and the shadow (or 缺, its demerits). The discussion provided in section "The South Korean education system under scrutiny" also closely scrutinises the educational system in South Korea. The final section "Conclusion: overcoming barriers and looking ahead in South Korean education", based on the preceding discussions, will include a conclusion and policy implications for enhancing South Korean education.

The Culture, Context and Tradition of Education in South Korea

Tradition and Influence of Confucianism

Confucianism, since the Chosun dynasty (from AD 1392 to 1907), has embedded a foundation of beliefs, values, and traditions within the South educational system. The Confucian ethic emphasises 'seeking truth with righteous mind by himself/herself' (格物致知 誠意正心), and serving others and society with those attitudes. It teaches that only persistence and hard work for the truth by self-cultivation. When the study yields results in school, one then will seek further contributions in life and for the society (修身 齊家 治國 平天下). In Confucianism, education is a starting point from which a man/woman can reach the truth of Heaven (天命: 'God') through their human nature (性). This kind of Confucian philosophy, starting from China, has been promulgated throughout East Asia. Especially in South Korea and in Japan, its influence is much stronger than in the other regions.

Confucianism is characterised by a strong emphasis on formal education which symbolises social mobility. Confucian philosophy stresses the importance of learning as a vehicle to self-betterment. Until recently, education had been regarded as the major means by which young people can raise their social stature, regardless of their family background.

In this context, South Korea and the South Koreans have invested heavily in the human capital, and have significantly increased their educational spending as a proportion of the central government's budget. As a consequence, there has been an expansion of secondary and higher education in South Korea.

Based on the great value that they South Koreans place on the family, they strongly desire to have children. Traditionally, South Korean families' priority has been to bear sons who are seen to be able to maintain the family's inheritance and who can contribute actively to society (立身揚名). To fulfil these goals, compliance of all family members to the head of a family (father, in general) was required, and education was considered as the key factor for the success story of the family. To obtain a level of educational achievement sufficient to pass the *Kwako* (科擧, the national civil service examination system for highest ranking officials) was a wish or a dream for all families. The designated head of the family had specific rights and duties.

Ogbu's (1987) 'cultural model of success' describes the impact of Asian Americans' culture in relation to their high academic performance. South Korean students have unique home environments, parental assistance, and much social pressure to deal with. Traditional culture, along with its beliefs and values, are passed on to the South Korean children (Ogbu, 1988) and it is thought that these values help them excel academically and become resilient.

'Education Fever' and Preparation for the College Entrance Exam

The 'education fever' (or 教育熱), high zeal and demand for education, is a major factor helping to explain the expansion and workings of South Korean education (Burt & Park, 2008). The education fever can be observed in the way the applicants prepare for the College Entrance Examinations and other high-stakes examinations.

Why does the education fever exist in South Korea? Park and Weidman (2000) identified six perspectives: the historical and cultural perspective, the social environment perspective, the human capital perspective, the radical perspective, the educational stratification perspective, and the education war perspective.

According to Burt and Park (2008), while the historical and cultural perspective explains the education fever with the factors associated with South Korea's history, Confucian culture, and past education systems, the social environment perspective views it in terms of increasing GDP per capita, demographic characteristics of the national population, and the changing school system. The human capital perspective regards the expansion of education to be resulting from governmental planning to develop human capital and technological advancement. However, the radical perspective, assuming that society is characterised by a high level of social class conflict, views individuals as being deprived of autonomy, and sees education expansion as means of the dominant social class to legitimate their use of political power to control student movements and as a result, education is a means of serving the interest of the elites (Burt & Park).

Contrary to all these views, the educational war perspective asserts that

> the South Korean context cannot be described adequately by the terms struggle or competition, rather to the South Korean people, it is actually a war for survival due to insufficient natural resources, high population density, inadequate job opportunities, and conflict over government policies which are interpreted by many people as aiming at various types of social and economic control. This war for survival has spilled over to the education sector,

> pushing people into increasingly intense battles over education (Park & Weidman, 2000, p. 194).

From the educational war perspective, therefore, the education fever is viewed in terms of extremely competitive social and economic conditions, processes of structuring social class, school choice based solely on students' academic ability, job distribution mainly based on academic achievement, and schooling as the best tool for social class change (Burt & Park, 2008).

Shadow Education (Private Tuition)

One problematic aspect of the 'education fever' is the inadvertent encouragement of private tutoring in addition to formal schooling. Private tutoring is referred as the 'shadow education industry' in South Korea. Some studies reported that South Korean students had four times more private tuition than their peers in the USA (Hwang, 2001).

Why is 'shadow education' prevalent in South Korea? Lee, Lee, and Jang (2010) explained it according to three levels. At the macro-level, the issue of 'credentialism', that is, a social value system where educational credentials, such as a high school diploma and college degree, play an important role. At the middle level, it is high-stakes examinations that determine access to the higher education. Finally, at the micro or individual levels, it is the South Koreans' conviction that shadow education will improve academic performance, which in turn will increase the possibility to be accepted in selective universities that will lead up to a pathway for prestigious jobs. From this perspective, Lee et al. (2010) concluded that South Koreans were pushed towards the desire for shadow education by their subjective expectation of its positive effects on educational outcomes. It also reflects their low level of satisfaction with the provision of public education.

Following a recent study about factors leading to private tuition, as education shares characteristics of 'positional goods', the investment in shadow education is not to support the public education but to uphold a dominant position in society in order to secure positional goods. In economic theory, it is believed that people, after being supplied with public goods, tend to desire the consumption of positional goods. According to Hirsch (1977), education has a characteristic of being considered as positional goods and the investment on education expands as household income increases.

Hirsch also believes that competitive investment in education for acquiring positions is exacerbated because of the specific political and economic environments in South Korean. For instance, the demand for competitive investment, that is, private tuition, will be acute because the ideal of 'education for general skills' is quite widespread in South Korea, but there is no secured social safety net for the general skills. Consequently, in order to minimise the risks of unemployment and low wages, people competed in their investment in education in order to secure a better position, as far as the reputation and rank of a university are considered to reflect students' potential. In other words, without a safety net for those 'left behind', it results in endless investments in shadow education as additional tuition seems to be viewed as a means to obtain and maintain a better position. Moreover, the competition for a better position will be worsened with the embracing of the neo-liberal economic principles of education.

The major problems of shadow education include the following: (1) increasing inequality in education, (2) heavy financial burdens, (3) reverse effects on the public school system, and (4) negative impact on children's psyche. Among those problems, the first three have emerged as central issues at the societal level.

In addition to these points, it is noteworthy that it is highly probable that private tuition may affect educational achievement; due to the difference of economic status, and the inequity caused by private tuition may be transferred to the next generation. The South Korean Development Institute (KDI)'s Report in 2009 (Kim, 2009) underlined that education has a 50 % influence on economic inheritance.

Public responses to government education policy in South Korea have suggested overall policy directions and measures to deal with the problem of shadow education, though not explicitly articulated, including: (1) the equalisation of school resources to prevent inequality among schools, (2) the prohibition of illegal private tutoring practices, (3) the enhancement of the quality of the public education system, and (4) the reduction of financial burdens of households spent on private tuition by providing alternative academic assistance to those requiring it.

Education System, National Curriculum and Textbooks

South Korea has maintained a relatively centralised system of education with the national Ministry of Education. The Ministry of Education (MOE) used to play a key role in the management of a centralised South Korean education system (OECD, 1998), and it was recently reorganised as the Ministry of Education, Science and Technology (MEST) in order to deal with policies regarding all educational and scientific study along with formal (K–12) and lifelong education and academic standards. Colleges and universities are directly controlled by the MEST while regional offices are responsible for secondary schools and local councils are in charge of elementary and middle schools. Such an organisational structure has been considered to be positive in influencing students' achievement (Chun & Kum, 2011).

Hongik Ingan (弘益人間: goal of education in South Korea) means education should be beneficial to all human beings. The South Korean education reform of May 1995 encouraged open and lifelong education to provide individuals with equal and easy access to education at any time and place (OECD, 1998). The aim of education is to enable every citizen to fully develop their personality, uphold the ideas of universal fraternity, develop a capability for self-support in life, and to work for the development of a democratic state and for common prosperity of humankind. National education is to teach citizens how to live independently, foster attitudes towards a democratic citizenship, and to enjoy living in harmony with others. Everyone should develop a strong sense of national identity and to respect sovereignty of the nation (Ministry of Education, Science and Technology [MEST], 2011).

The national curriculum of South Korea comprises mandatory subjects and elective subjects (2011). The curriculum for secondary schools consists of seven basic subjects (Korean language, English, social studies and moral education, mathematics, science and technology, physical education, music and arts), the electives, and extracurricular activities; 2011). In high schools, Korean language, mathematics, and English are classified in the basic subject category. The inquiry category comprises social studies (including history and ethics) and science. Physical education, music, and fine arts form another category. The category of culture and life comprises technology, home economics, second foreign language, the learning of Chinese characters, and others. Each school is given autonomy of innovate up to 30 % of the curriculum (2011). High schools with specific purposes have the autonomy to design up to 60 % of school curriculum (2011). As described above, the educational reform emphasised 'selectiveness and concentration of curriculum by students themselves' in order to cater for their own interest and future goals in life (2011).

As for textbooks, Kim (1993) pointed out that South Korean textbooks emphasised concepts-learning at each grade level, with more 'advanced' mathematical problems and fewer pages as compared to American textbooks. Zambo and Hong (1996) noted that South Korean teachers more strongly agreed, compared to their counterparts in the US, that textbooks supplied all they needed to know about problem solving (1996). Thus, we may conclude that, in South Korea, textbooks take on a very important position in education.

School Teachers and Teachers' College

In South Korea, teachers are supposed to supervise students' intellectual, academic and social development, while parents are to respect teachers as trained professionals (Paik, 2001). In addition to classroom teaching, teachers are also in charge of counselling, helping students with college applications and keeping in close touch with parents.

Teachers are generally more respected in South Korea than in other countries (OECD, 1998) and Teachers' Day is widely celebrated (Sorenson, 1994). In schools, student–teacher relationship is characterised as 'warm authoritarianism' or 'demanding respect, but convincing them that they have students' best interests in mind' (Sorenson).

However, due to the excessive competition and recent incidents in schools (for example, violence in schools), there are views that teachers' authority has collapsed, and the respect for teachers has also declined among parents and students

(Cho, 2012). Moon (1993) found that in Grades 7–12, American students show, despite lower achievement, more positive attitude towards school with more positive perception of responsibility for learning, more favourable relationships with their teachers than the South Korean students do (Moon). In addition, the self-efficacy of South Korean teachers was ranked 23rd among 23 OECD countries (OECD, 2010).

In South Korea, 45 universities have colleges of education who have the right to issue teacher certification, and their graduates are eligible for public school placement test. About a third of them (14 colleges, 1,162 faculties) are national universities and the other two thirds are private (31 colleges, 1,200 faculties). Only the top 5 % of students of secondary schools can gain a place in the colleges of education.

Teaching is a highly acknowledged profession by the South Koreans. In a recent survey, teachers or principals of elementary schools were ranked first on the list of South Koreans' preferred jobs for their job security (e.g., retirement at the age of 62). As a result, the supply of teachers largely exceeds the demand for teachers in South Korea (Lee, 2006).

Education Reforms in South Korea

Major Concerns of Education Reform in South Korea

Equality of educational opportunity with an anti-shadow education stance was one of major targets of reform in South Korean education (Lee et. al., 2010), as was discussed in section "Shadow education (Private tuition)".

Anti-shadow education measures implemented over the past five decades are as follows:

- 1968: Interdiction of selection in Middle School Entrance Examination
- 1978: Interdiction of selection in High School Entrance Examination
- 1980: Educational Reform Measure (Restriction of 'shadow education')
- 1980s–1990s: Reorganisation of college entrance examination system and public education system for reducing household expenditure on shadow education.
- 2000–2004: Introduction of educational policies for reducing household expenditure on shadow education by enhancing public education
- 2009–present: Reduction of household expenditure on shadow education by increasing school autonomy

With anti-shadow education policies as one of the government's policy goals, other goals of education reform such as 'the enhancement of public education' were established as well, as listed below (Lee et al., 2010; Ilon, 2011):

- Redefinitions of academic achievement and criteria in the knowledge-based society

- Diversification of educational programmes and expansion of school choice.
- Choice and concentration of school curriculum units catering to students' career paths and interests
- Enhancement of public education
- Increase in autonomy in the college admission system and introduction of 'self-directed learning' as a new category in the screening process
- Changing the role of government from a regulative agency to a cooperative and supportive one
- Lifelong learning accreditation (1995); 922 programmes in 348 organisations (2010)
- Brain Korea 21 (2007); a government funded project to support research-oriented universities with research funds and graduate students' scholarships (90,000 students supported, number of publications tripled in supported universities)
- Middle school (since 1968) and high school equalisation policy (since 1974); to prevent selection processes in middle and high schools

Education Reform of 1995: Responses to Globalisation and Civilian Democracy

President Kim Yong Sam (1993–1998) launched the Presidential Commission on Education Reform (PCER) in 1994. It was to liberalise and decentralise national education, to relieve university entrance competition and to upgrade educational environment and performance to global standards. The reforms were designed on the basis of ideas such as

> (1) the nation state now has to restructure the educational system to reduce its own role in education by employing such reform measures as liberalisation, decentralisation and privatisation, and (2) nevertheless, it has to prepare a well-trained, flexible and versatile workforce by reinforcing primary and secondary education and, at the same time, secure a cadre of highly-trained professionals by improving quality in higher education.

The 5.31 Education Reform (1995), succeeded by presidents Kim Dae Jung and Roh Moo-hyun, put the new terminology into operation. These are, among others, 'open education system', 'orientation towards individual consumer needs (choices)', 'diverse and specialised education', 'autonomy and accountability-based education', and 'cultivating humanity and creativity' and the 'improvement of academic achievement'.

The 5.31 reform faced several criticisms for not being compatible with reality in schools such as the request for the increase of academic achievement and the cultivation of personality and creativity at the same time. In addition, changes of priority from the personality and creativity of Y. S. Kim to the national achievement test of elementary and secondary school students of D. J. Kim gave rise to confusion

(Jeong, 2004). Moreover, the 31 May reform, introducing the concept of the 'consumer', has been criticised for its neo-liberal point of view (Sin, 2003).

Following the 5.31 reform, with the 7th national curriculum, new policies were introduced into schools; such as Open Education, Performance Assessment, and Information Communication Technology Education (Korean Committee of Open Education and Korean Educational Development Institute, 1997). Open education comprised student-centred curriculum, diverse learning activities in and out of school, and the significance of teaching and learning procedure being as important as test scores. Beyond paper and pencil tests, performance assessment has been adopted and required teachers to develop 'diverse' teaching and assessment methods with an extension of traditional classroom teaching to diverse activities such as movies, plays, sports, and animation (Ministry of Education & Human Resources Development [ME & HRD], 2001). Teaching with Information Communication Technology (ICT) was highly recommended (ME & HRD). Then, those policies were introduced as criteria for the assessment of the local education office and schools since 1996. As for university entrance competition, qualitative methods had been imposed (Ministry of Education, 2000).

Education Reforms Since 2000

After the economic crisis of 1997–1998, the issue of 'school (or classroom) collapse' has emerged. The term 'school collapse' defines the situation where the schools cannot operate normally. The school collapse was closely related with poor academic achievement, school violence and lack of communication between students and teachers.

While discussing about school collapse, on-going education reforms have been criticised (Chosun, 1999, 2001). Overriding classrooms, top–down processes, and neglecting the right for 'school choice' were pointed out as the causes of school collapse. Emphasis on the productivity of schooling was also an important issue (Jeong, 2003).

Under these circumstances, new policies were introduced. The National Scholastic Achievement Assessment was developed and administered from 2005. The new test was supposed to evaluate fundamental competence as a citizen, but in reality, it is perceived as assessing scholastic achievement of each elementary and middle school and evaluating the school inspection system. The assessment has been criticised to have intensified competition among schools and distorted the school curriculum.

As to 'school choice,' 'high schools for special purposes', such as science high schools, foreign language schools, autonomous private schools, international schools were established and expanded since 2000. These schools have considerable autonomy in terms of school curriculum management. In addition, 'high school choice for students' belongs to this type of system. Introduction of school choice system, however, confronted the criticism for enlarging the scholastic gap among schools.

Education reforms following the 5.31 reform can be summarised as follows: focusing on open education, educational autonomy; respecting diversity and consumers' needs; introducing nationwide achievement tests; emphasising educational productivity; and opening up the possibility of school choice. However, the priority difference between the former and the latter created confusion to schools and eventually triggered 'school collapse'.

The South Korean Education System Under Scrutiny

Recent Educational Attainment in South Korea: Excellence and Inequality

As mentioned in sections. "The culture, context and tradition of education in South Korea" and "Education reforms in South Korea", South Korean education has undergone many reforms but has its foundational building upon the Confucian tradition; the view of education as positional goods, increased investments in, and demand for, shadow education; respect towards teachers; and a centralised education system and curriculum. The 5.31 reform marked an attempt to make changes in education in South Korea.

The attainment of South Korean education can be discussed in terms of academic achievement and education inequality. Academic achievement can be seen via the high scores obtained at PISA and/or TIMSS and the overall education participation rate. To minimise education inequality is important from the perspective of upholding education justice and to ensure equal distribution of educational opportunities.

International indices showed the following characteristics of South Korean education: at first, South Korea ranked the highest among the OECD countries for tertiary education participant rate of approximately 60 % among adults aged 25–35 in the Year 2008. However, it is rated as an inefficient investment because years of education and GDP per capita was below the curve of efficient production possibility frontier of education. In addition, the index to show how many years of education can increase the growth rate of human capital and GDP reports that the education efficiency has fallen from 0.8 in 1995 to 0.73 in 2000 to 0.33 in 2005.

Nevertheless, the scholastic achievement of South Korea was considered to be excellent as measured by the PISA results. South Korea ranked the highest in all areas of mathematics, science and reading. This achievement was considered to be the result of recent education reforms, the placement of excellent teachers, and long-standing tradition of valuing education. Still, the problems remained for top students' performance (for example, the overall students' performance in reading ranked 2nd while the top students' performance ranked 9th) as well as the relatively

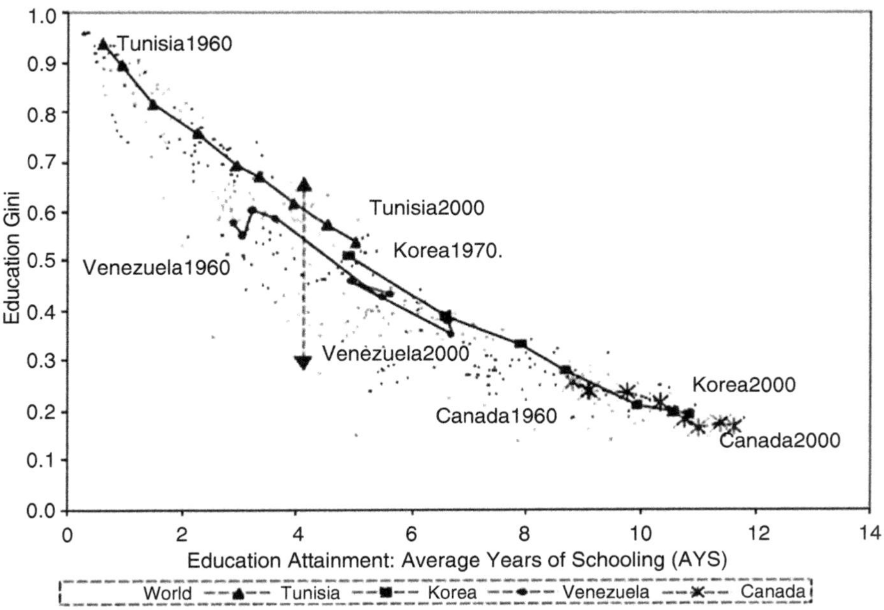

Fig. 8.1 Education Gini index: selected countries and world, 1960–2000 (Barro & Lee, 2000)

poor performance in Science (11th in 2006). The PISA 2009 results have considered South Korea to be the best among OECD countries for its implementation of effective education policy (Hwang, 2001).

An interesting phenomenon has been observed between income level and PISA scores. Comparing PISA scores with human resources development, among countries where new technology development is important (more than $20,000 income per capita), the higher the PISA scores were, the lower GDP per capita was, while among countries with lower than $20,000 income per capita, the higher the PISA scores, the higher the GDP per capita (Kim et al., 2011). This means that PISA scores are irrelevant to the formation of creative human capital; and South Korea's high scores signal that for educational attainment, you need to have at least $ 20,000 national income per capita, but not to exceed it.

To mention the degree of education inequality in South Korea, according to an international analysis, the Education Gini index has a tendency to decrease in proportion to the increase in the average years of education. In South Korea, in the Year 2000, the level of education inequality has been as low as in Canada (see Fig. 8.1). This is due to the increase in the completion rate of higher education as well as the increase of years of education due to the industrialisation and economic growth policies of South Korean society.

However, the exacerbation of South Korean education inequality is confirmed by the mediation of education inequality due to private tuition (see section "Shadow education (Private tuition)"). A recent study compared the education inequality in South Korea with that in the U.S. and concluded that the influence of SES on student achievement has increased over time in South Korea. According to the study (Byun & Kim, 2010), in 1999, one standard deviation difference in the index of SES was associated with an average performance difference of approximately 25 score points. In 2003, it was associated with an average performance difference of approximately 29 score points. In 2007, an average score difference was 32 score points. This tendency was less evident for the United States.

The education inequality is manifested in the cultural differences surrounding how to bring up children between different classes of society. The South Korean middle class considers school records and educational backgrounds to be crucial for success in life. Parents intervene in a child's study very (often overly) actively by continuously checking and systematically managing children's performance at school, motivating them and gathering academic information. Moreover, they try to maintain a good relationship with schools and teachers.

In contrast, those falling in the low-income brackets behave somewhat differently. They think that 'success in life depends on one's capacity' and tend to recognise meritocracy rather than academic background. The parents merely express their wishes and do not strongly intervene in their children's study. They respect their children's opinion and do not impose on them because they accept their children's low achievement, which they considered to be due to their family circumstances.

There is a huge difference in study behaviour in daily life between those in the middle-income bracket compared to the low-income bracket (*The JoongAng Ilbo*, 2011). The students from middle class families spend about 6 h for studying out of regular class (private educational institute and home), while students in the low-income bracket spend only 2 h studying and more than 4 h working in a part-time job.

To summarise, students from low-income families or minority groups in South Korea have poor and unfavourable home and social environment, experience inherent limitations in learning due to 'cultural capital', and have limited reliable social networks. The limitation, in fact, confirms the concept of socioeconomic reproduction, that is, one's educational achievement is determined by the hierarchy of classes which he/she belongs to.

Going All Out to Enter into Prestigious High Schools and Universities

The characteristics of South Korean education mentioned in sections. "The culture, context and tradition of education in South Korea" and "Education reforms in South Korea" – Confucian tradition and education fever of South Korean society which considers education as a course of life and a positional good – makes most students go all out to gain admission to high schools that appears to provide a pathway for entering a college/university with a good reputation, starting from a very young age.

Competition for entering those schools and universities is extremely keen. From early in the morning to late at night, students travel between schools and private tuition institutes in order to achieve good grades and their parents also do their best to assist them. In general, private tuition focuses on the three key subjects: Korean language, English and mathematics. As the Korean proverb goes, 'the best farming is getting your children to study.' In such an environment, students' non-academic experiences are often very limited.

Here is a sample of a day in the life of a high school student. In fact, the routines of elementary and middle school students are almost the same. This daily routine might be very different from that in the other countries. A study reveals that South Korean students study 15,000 h more than U.S. students during the course of 12 years of primary and secondary education.

8:00 a.m.–4:30 p.m. At school

(Class runs for 50 minutes with 10 minutes break in between and a 50 minute lunch break)

(Very often, schools provide extra classes until 6 or 7 pm)

6:00–10:00 p.m. Some students stay at school for self-study

7:00–9:00 p.m. Other students attend private tuition for mostly mathematics and English, or watch EBS (Korean Educational Broadcasting System) for Mathematics and Science instruction.

10:30 p.m.–12 a.m. Students move to the library or continue with private tuition

As mentioned in section "The culture, context and tradition of education in South Korea", this situation places parents under the pressure of excessive private education expenses starting from elementary education. In South Korea, private tuition expenses for elementary and secondary education comprise more than 1 % of GDP (in 2008) and it is the highest level among OECD countries (OECD, 2010). The pattern is the same for secondary education, with more than 2 % of GDP spent on private tuition, which is again the highest level among OECD countries (OECD).

What Happened to Teachers: 'De-pedagogised?'

In sections "Recent educational attainment in South Korea: Excellence and inequality" and "Going all out to enter into prestigious high schools and universities", it has been discussed that students' high achievement and conditions for learning resulted partially from the South Korean educational tradition and their efforts to change. In this section, a change in classroom teaching and learning, with regard to the role of teachers, will be discussed.

In South Korea, the role of teachers as well as the scope of their work have expanded. For instance, the expansion of teachers' work resulting from introducing English in elementary schools after 1997; mastering ICT skills and applying them to their classes as ICT education was introduced after the 5.31 reform; diversifying the evaluation system by introducing performance assessment; and providing after-school programmes, etc. According to one study (Kim, 2004), the number of tasks that teachers needed to handle increased from 126 (6th national curriculum) to 283 (7th national curriculum).

Without supplementary budget or support, the increased workload inevitably fell upon teachers. The economic crisis of 1997–1998 resulted in a budget cut for public schools. As a result, teachers became multifunctional with limited resources as demanded in the 7th national curriculum.

This constraint made teachers unfavourable towards the 7th National Curriculum. Reform policies such as open education and performance assessment were forced on schools and teachers by the government without enough support, and this created serious side effects, and aroused criticism among teachers.

Inconsistency of the reform efforts coupled with the reality faced in schools made teachers increasingly frustrated. For example, the reform required performance assessment using diverse evaluation methods and criteria but the objectivity of scoring was still disputable, as school records were still a very important factor for the college entrance examination. Eventually, performance assessment called for 'objective criteria' applicable to all students in a school.

Moreover, the national level academic assessment as a tool to evaluate teachers and schools moved in the direction of evaluating by means of scores obtained in high-stakes test. Also, under the pretext of protecting students from school violence and bullying, non-academic intervention came in more frequently, which weakened teachers' positions and their expertise.

In conclusion, as students all go out to prepare for the high-stakes tests used for college entrance, school education became standardised; and schools suffered from a rush of non-educational requests from the outside; teachers' rights to devote to students were violated; and the areas where teachers were able to exercise their professionalism were being severely curtailed. In other words, due to the education reforms and the changing environments of South Korean classrooms, South Korean schooling turned out to be 'de-pedagogised'.

Over-Politicised Process in Decision-Making of Educational Policy

As mentioned in the previous sections, the education fever and shadow education industry have resulted in economic inequality and caused a vicious circle. The resolution of education inequality is an ideological issue in South Korean politics. The issues of private tuition, the college entrance examination system and school choices were points of debate between the progressives and the conservatives in recent parliamentary and presidential elections.

In addition, regarding the policy decision on politicised educational issues, public opinion, education-related NGOs' and teachers' roles were greatly affected. One example is that a 6-year teachers' college model proposed after 10 years of research was not approved by the National Assembly not because of logical reasons nor the lack of evidence but because of the lack of a sufficient number of votes.

In fact, without support in votes, even very logical suggestions with evidence-based research cannot survive the policymaking process. For the enactment of education policy, public opinion is more important than the perceived long-term benefits to South Korean education. Thus, in the process of enactment, related and interested political groups can raise their voices. We can conclude that in South Korean education, there is an Over-politicised Process of Education Policy.

Through this process, two teachers' groups played an important role in the decision making of educational policy. One is The Korean Federation of Teachers' Association, which supports the progressive political party, and the other one is The Korean Teachers' Union, which favoured the conservative political party.

Conclusion: Overcoming Barriers and Looking Ahead in South Korean Education

Re-pedagogisation of South Korean Education

The education fever of South Korean society was a main reason for excessive private tuition and a contortion which emphasised self-fulfilment following the logic of the survival of the fittest as well as the liberal market associating with education as positional goods. Nevertheless, thanks to the education fever, South Koreans' students have emerged with high achievement scores in internationally benchmarked tests such as PISA and TIMSS, etc.

Despite several negative aspects caused by the education fever, we have to be reminded that attachment to education and the strong scholastic sprit stemmed from the Confucian tradition of the past and is associated with the original education fever and intrinsic value of education rather than its instrumental value. In South Korean society – the education for one's success to contribute to society (立身揚名), the emphasis on one's introspection (修己), education to seek after the truth (道) and to become a rational being (性), and to reach the Heaven's will (天命) – are the collective root causes of the education fever today. In other words, instead of parents' going all out to help their children to gain entry into good colleges, it is necessary to go back to the traditional values which first brought about an education fever.

In South Korean schools, without a feasibility study or financial support, education reforms are also solely relying on teachers. Also, school violence and private tuition problems made present external parties in the school. In this situation, teachers' expertise cannot be fully appreciated and the de-pedagogisation of teaching and non-pedagogical focus kept expanding.

Under the circumstances, over-politicised South Korean educational policy should also be pedagogised. The over-politicised educational policy means that autonomy and justice in education is violated as the intrinsic value of education is reduced to political area. Based on this analysis, 're-pedagogisation' has to be an urgent issue in the education system of South Korea. Parents and students should broaden their perspectives to look beyond the education fever and to engage in self-reflection while teachers should not be just be allowed to exhibit their expertise in the private confines of their classrooms. Instead, the intrinsic value of education and educational autonomy should be respected in the education policymaking process.

Redefining the Concept of the Teacher: 'Teacher as Practical Researcher and Cultural Mediator'

Discussions on education inequality revealed that schools somewhat reproduce hierarchical differences of students' scholastic achievement, but at the same time, they also help students to improve their scholastic achievement. Educational experiences (learning participation, etc.) in school have a large influence on students' scholastic achievement. Of course, teachers are the core of this achievement. Students spend most of their time in the class with teachers.

There is a general recognition that teachers in South Korean society are knowledge transmitters. This is very different from the image of teachers as masters (師範) in the past. This perception may have resulted from the university admission-oriented school education.

However, teaching, the main task of teachers, should not be limited to simply transmitting knowledge by rote but should focus on generating knowledge of important concepts and theory. And teaching should enable students to critically reflect on their lives and explore new alternatives. Teachers should help disadvantaged and minority students actively participate in meaningful activities so that these students can improve their scholastic achievement and self-esteem. 'Teachers as cultural mediators' should respect, encourage, and empower students, and help free their students from schools' dominant cultures.

The general recognition of teachers should be re-conceptualised. Teachers should no longer simply be knowledge transmitters but be active researchers and cultural mediators in order to realise educational justice and who encourage their students to think critically and creatively. Teachers should be capable of pursuing research on students' cultures, classes, school lives and educational practices; and be able to give advice and encouragement to students based on their professional knowledge; participating in education with students; helping to promote students' self-exploration. In this respect, teachers should be someone superior in personality, intelligence, cultural understanding and morality. These teachers will enable the South Korean education system to truly excel and to fully realise educational justice.

Democratic Organisation, Communication, Leadership in Education Reform

The more education reform progressed, the more schools and teachers were excluded from education; teachers had less opportunities to use their expertise and ended up feeling frustrated. Given this anti-educational situation, South Korean education may not guarantee students' bright futures because the quality of education may not be getting better.

On the other hand, there exists the shortage of financial support but top-down education reform and an absence of communication between key stakeholders in the education system. The lack of understanding about schools and teachers' lives and the lack of a rationale communication system were key factors explaining the eventual failure of education reform.

To pursue education reform, democratic educational organisation and a rational communication system are essential. Democratic education means that teachers and schools play important roles in educational decision-making. To do this, the central administration such as the Ministry of Education should be satisfied with supportive and advisory functions and hand over power to individual schools and the local education authority. Likewise, local education authority, maintaining the function of local education policy direction and enforcement policy, can consider handing over all other functions to individual schools. Also, curriculum and education policymaking can serve to provide a broad outline and specific goals may be set by individual units. In elementary, middle, and high schools, the national curriculum can set common goals, while schools and teachers can further refine these goals for customised to the needs of their students.

The configuration of educational organisations also makes it a rule to become a flexible learning organisation; and, with regard to each educational policymaking, vertical hierarchical relationship should be supported by a horizontal and equal relationship. To do this, individual members should systemically consider the whole education system and compose organisations that allow for rational communication.

For the democratisation of a large-scale and innovative education system, it is important to restore the confidence among educational subjects and consolidate the communication system. A pathway to meet internal demands thorough open conversations and participation on a variety of educational topics and a system to draw public opinions and to reach a consensus are required. Then, various educational issues will be discussed, and different opinions will be explored.

In addition, for the qualitative growth of South Korean education as well as the success of education reform, education leaders should have democratic and professional leadership rather than bureaucratic and authoritative leadership of the past. South Korean educational organisation was highly centralised (refer to section "Education system, national curriculum and textbooks") and South Korean educational leadership was still authoritative. To operate the educational organisation as a democratic learning organisation, educational leaders should take professional responsibility rather than bureaucratic accountability and allow teachers' voices to be heard, and educational targets should be shared with teachers.

The Necessity of 'Participatory Research in Policy Construction'

If the process of policy construction in education was regarded over-politicised, the research to effect policy changes needs to reflect those processes. Through those reflections, suggestions provided by evidence-based research can be successfully implemented. Only then can research-based policy initiatives be translated into practice.

One of these reflections can be the expansion of research interests in policymaking. It means that the present research used to inform policymaking will have more challenges, and be successful in informing policy construction. In other words, it is necessary to expand the concerns (or horizon of the research) to those requiring negotiation among key stakeholders in policy politics.

This expanded horizon will have to deal with two more challenges to activate research-based policy. One is the challenge of knowledge application. This is to strengthen the capacity of educational research and evidence-building. Policy oriented research has to be so contiguously bound to their contexts and to tighten the relationship between research being evidence-based and policy translating into practice. Only then can the culturally and politically-bound context of education research help inform policy formulation that can be successfully translated into practice. The cultural-political reflection for application in policy-oriented research can then contribute to seed pedagogical innovations and educational improvements.

The other challenge is to increase the power of knowledge mediation. The mediation is a way of building the bridge between the created knowledge for policy and the political process for activating policy such as legislation in Parliament. Without this mediation, knowledge creation cannot be empowered. In policy-oriented research, the mediation includes not only translating and widely spreading the newly created knowledge but also cooperating and discussing the issues concerned with stakeholders in the policymaking process. According to Foucault (1971), the mediation of communication of knowledge (or information) is the beginning of social transformation through the concerned discourse.

To sum up, policy-oriented research meeting these two challenges can be defined as 'Participatory Research' in policy construction. Participatory research will turn the horizon of research into expanded and valuable evidence not to be lost in the politics of the policymaking process. Additionally, practitioners may contribute their experiences to the creation of educational knowledge. This will enhance the ability of policy-oriented research to be translated seamlessly into practice.

References

Barro, R. J., & Lee, J. W. (2000). *International data on educational attainment: Updates and implications*. Boston: Center for International Development, Harvard University.

Burt, M., & Park, N. (2008). Education inequality in the Republic of Korea: Measurement and causes. In D. Holsinger & J. Jacob (Eds.), *Inequality in education: Comparative and international perspective* (pp. 261–289). Dordrecht, The Netherlands: Springer.

Byun, S., & Kim, K. (2010). Educational inequality in South Korea: The widening socioeconomic gap in student achievement; Globalisation, changing demographics, and educational challenges in East Asia. *Research in Sociology of Education, 17*, 155–182.

Cho, Y. (2012). *In the age of pain, the hope of education*. Seoul, South Korea: Dream-Pig.

Chosun Ilbo (1999). Crisis of school, crisis of students. *Chosun Ilbo 2nd November* (pp. 3–10), Seoul, South Korea: Chosun Daily.

Chosun Ilbo (2001). The effect of 'Open Education'. *Chosun Ilbo 26th April* (pp. 3–15). Seoul: Chosun Daily.

Chun, Y., & Kum, H. (2011). A study on the determinants of performance in Korean educational organisations. *Korea Journal of Public Administration, 49*(2), 235–266.

Foucault, M. (1971). Order of discourse. *Social Science Information, 10*(2), 7–30.

Hirsh, F. (1977). Social limits to growth. *Economic Analysis and Policy, 7*(1), 61–67.

Hwang, Y. (2001). Why do Korean students study hard? Reflections on Paik's study. *International Journal of Educational Research, 35*, 609–618.

Ilon, L. (2011). *Knowledge mobilisation in Korea: Linkages with economic, social, and political development*. Seoul, South Korea: COE, Seoul National University.

Jeong, G. O. (2003). Starting of the department of Ministry of Education & Human Resource Development. In Korean Educational Development Institute (Ed.), *Korea education review 2002* (pp. 33–48). Seoul, South Korea: KEDI.

Jeong W. K. (2004). Education reform policies and classroom teaching in South Korea. *International Studies in Sociology of Education, 14*(2), 125–145.

Kim, H. (1993). A comparative study between an American and Republic of Korean textbook series coverage of measurement and geometry content in first through eighth grades. *School Science and Mathematics, 93*(3), 123–126.

Kim, H. (2009). *The present and future of inter-generational economic mobility* (Korean Development Institution report). Seoul, South Korea: KDI.

Kim, J. W. (2004). Education reform policies and classroom teaching in South Korea. *International Studies in Sociology of Education, 14*(2), 125–145.

Kim S.J., Ryu, G. K., et. al. (2011). *The necessity of the growth of creative human capital as a growth factor*, Report in Division of Economics 10-05-01(Chapter II-2). Seoul: Division of Economics, Seoul National University.

Korean Committee of Open Education & Korean Educational Development Institute. (1997). *Introduction of open education*. Seoul, South Korea: Educational Science Publishing.

Lee, C. J. (2006). The development of education in Korea: Approaches, achievement and current challenges. Paper presented at World Bank seminar, Singapore.

Lee, C., Lee, H., & Jang, H. (2010). The history of policy responses to shadow education in South Korea: Implications for the next cycle of policy responses. *Asia Pacific Educational Review, 11*, 97–108.

Ministry of Education. (2000). The announcement of ministry of education about the system of entrance to University in 2002. Retrieved from http://hinuri.net/jinhak/2002mundap.html

Ministry of Education & Human Resources Development (ME & HRD). (2001). *Handbook of the major works of ME & HRD*. Seoul, South Korea: Author.

Ministry of Education, Science and Technology (MEST). (2011). *National curriculum for elementary and secondary schools in Korea*. Seoul, South Korea: Author.

Moon, S. B. (1993). *A comparison of Korean and American students' attitudes about school*. Paper presented at the annual meeting of the Mid-South Educational Research Association, New Orleans, LA.
OECD. (1998). *Reviews of national policies for education: Korea* (pp. 89–104). Paris: Author.
OECD. (2010). *PISA 2009 at a glance*. Retrieved from http://dx.doi.org/10.1787/9789264095298-en
Ogbu, J. (1987). Variability in minority school performance: A problem in search of an explanation. *Anthropology & Education Quarterly, 18*(4), 312–334.
Ogbu, J. (1988). Cultural diversity and human development. In Slaughter, D. T. (Eds.), Black children and poverty: A developmental perspective; *New directions for child development* (Vol. 42, pp. 11–28). San Francisco: Jossey-Bass.
Paik, S. (2001). Introduction, background, and international perspectives: Korean history, culture, and education. *International Journal of Educational Research, 35*, 535–607.
Park, N., & Weidman, J. C. (2000). Battlefield for higher education. In J. C. Weidman & N. Park (Eds.), *Higher education in Korea* (pp. 1–94). New York: Garland.
Sin, H. S. (2003). A general review about policy making and enforcement process. In KEDI (Ed.) Korea education review, 2002 (pp. 7–32). Seoul: Korean Educational Development Institute.
Sorenson, C. (1994). Success and education in South Korea. *Comparative Education Review, 38* (1), 10–35.
The JoongAng Ilbo (2011). The difference in daily life between middle-income bracket and low-income bracket, The JoongAng Ilbo, 11th March (pp. 3–9). Seoul: The JoongAng Ilbo Corp.
Zambo, R., & Hong, E. (1996). Korean and American elementary school teachers' beliefs about mathematics problem solving. *School Science and Mathematics, 96*(4), 208–214.

Chapter 9
Effective Teachers for Successful Schools and High Performing Students: The Case of Shanghai

Minxuan Zhang, Jinjie Xu, and Chuangyuan Sun

Snapshot of the Education System in Shanghai

Shanghai is the largest city in China with a population of 23.03 million. This population consists of 14.04 million who are permanent residents with registered households and defined as those possessing bank accounts; and about 8.97 million who are considered part of the so-called 'floating population', meaning that they are not permanent residents and classified as temporary residents (Shanghai Municipal Statistics Bureau [SMSB], 2011). The education system in Shanghai has experienced several stages of development: multiple models which were strongly influenced by the Western model co-existed in the first half of the twentieth century, the period of reconstruction and large-scale expansion took place after the founding of the People's Republic of China in 1949, and, currently, Shanghai is in the process of modernisation and striving to become an international centre for economy, finance, trading and shipping as a global metropolis in the twenty-first century.

Shanghai is the first city in China to have instituted the 9-year compulsory education system – which includes 5 years in a primary school and 4 years in junior secondary – and to have made this uniformed across China. In abiding with the national policy on education, the provision of a high quality education service and promotion of students' all-round development in terms of their moral, intellectual and physical development are carved out as main priorities guiding basic education in Shanghai. Basic education follows a '5-4-3' format: 5 years in a primary school,

M. Zhang (✉)
President, Shanghai Normal University, 100 Guilin Road, Xuhui, Shanghai, China
e-mail: mxzhang@shnu.edu.cn

J. Xu
Center for International and Comparative Education, Shanghai Normal University, 100 Guilin Road, Xuhui, Shanghai, China

C. Sun
Department of Management, Shanghai Open University, 100 Guilin Road, Xuhui, Shanghai, China

S.K. Lee et al. (eds.), *Educational Policy Innovations: Levelling Up and Sustaining Educational Achievement*, Springer Education Innovation Book Series 1,
DOI 10.1007/978-981-4560-08-5_9, © Springer Science+Business Media Singapore 2014

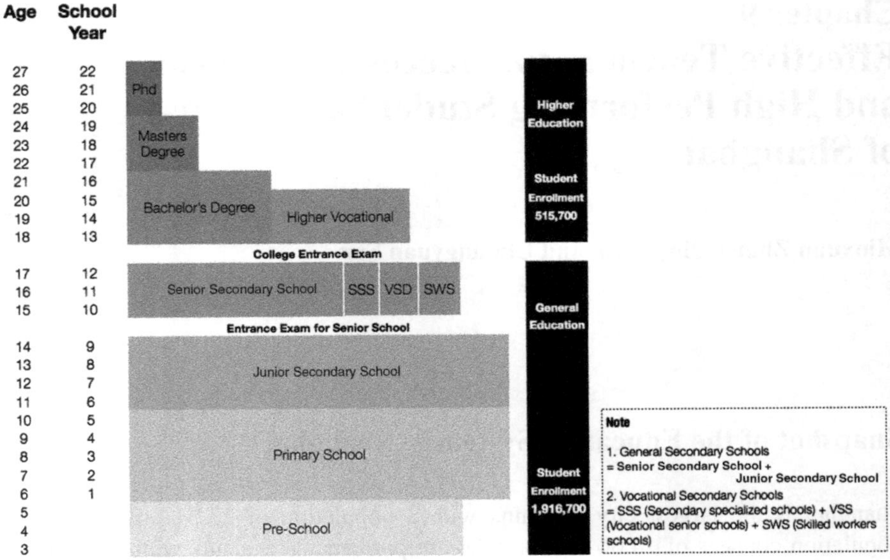

Fig. 9.1 Shanghai's education system

4 years for junior secondary, and 3 years for senior secondary level. There are also schools that offer 12 years of continuous schooling across the different levels of study from primary to senior secondary. Figure 9.1 shows Shanghai's general education system of progression from pre-school all the way to the doctoral levels.

Shanghai's education system has attracted international attention since its students emerged top in reading, mathematics and science on the Programme for International Student Assessment (PISA) tests in 2009. This surprised local educators who felt that several weaknesses and shortcomings within the system still needed fixing. However, to elucidate why Shanghai may be considered as one of the high performing education system (HPES), the answer should lie in the ability of the system to provide a high quality of education and to ensure equity in learning outcomes. The gaps between top-, bottom- and middle-band performers in reading, mathematics and science are relatively small in Shanghai and academic achievement of the bottom-line or tail-end performers is higher than OECD average.

Amongst various factors, an important one behind these achievements is the persistent commitment to developing a high-quality teaching force, with strong support for teacher professional development by governments and schools. The rest of this chapter will therefore focus on how Shanghai has developed and sustained a high quality teaching workforce and the key characteristics and profiles of this workforce from selection, to teacher preparation, to the professional development of teachers (Zhang & Kong, 2012).

The Teaching Workforce in Shanghai

The Shanghai Municipal Government attaches great importance to the building of a high quality of school administration and teaching workforce. Over the last 20 years, the overall teaching quality of primary and secondary schools and kindergartens has been significantly improved. According to the SMSB (2011), by 2010, there are totally 131,604 full-time teachers who are responsible for teaching in basic education, among them 26,724 are from kindergarten, 45,239 from primary school, 50,741 from general junior and senior secondary school and about 8,900 teachers in vocational track, and about 8,900 teach students in the vocational track (including secondary specialised schools, vocational high schools, skilled workers schools and adult secondary specialised schools). Figure 9.2 shows the age breakdown of the teaching workforce in Shanghai; the average age of majority of the teaching workforce ranges from between 31 and 40 years.

Taking 2008 as the year of reference, the ratio of teachers' salaries in Shanghai after 15 years of experience (minimum training) to GDP per capita at the different levels is presented in Table 9.1. The data shows that teachers after 15 years of service, are paid on average higher than the GDP per capita in China, which implies that teaching teachers in Shanghai are relatively well-paid.

Ensuring a Highly Qualified Teaching Workforce

The Teacher Qualification System (TQS), which is mandatory for teacher accreditation, was officially launched on 1 October 2001 in Shanghai. It stipulates the minimum requirements necessary for entering teaching:

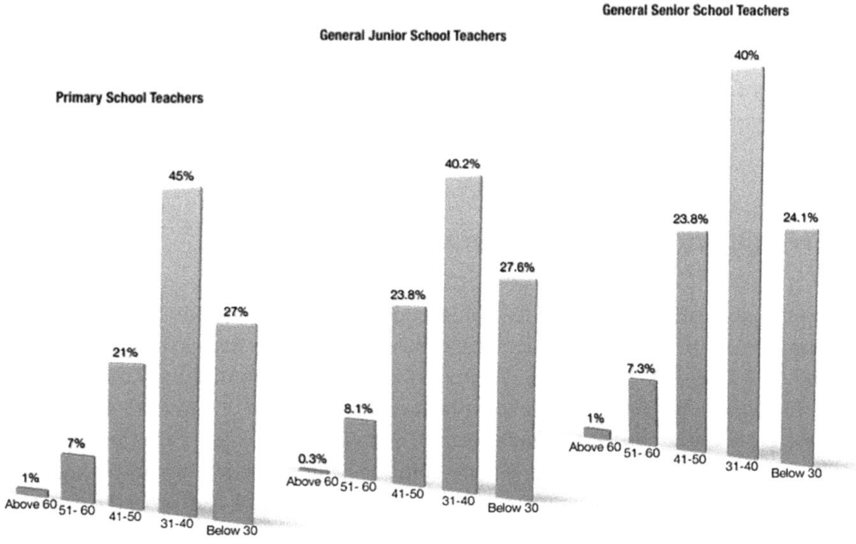

Fig. 9.2 Age breakdown of teachers (Shanghai Municipal Education Commission [SMEC], 2010)

Table 9.1 Ratio of teachers' salaries in Shanghai after 15 years of experience (minimum training) to GDP per capita at the different levels

Types of schools	Ratio
Primary schools	1.39:1
Lower secondary education (General junior schools)	1.71:1
Upper secondary education (General senior schools)	1.75:1

- All teacher candidates should undergo professional training and pass the tests in the following areas of study: pedagogy, educational psychology and teaching methods.
- All teachers in kindergartens or primary schools must hold a level of education minimally higher than the preschool teacher training schools or the teacher training schools (at least senior secondary education).
- Teachers in general junior high schools must possess an educational qualification at least equivalent to or higher than that provided by the teacher training college or other colleges for professional training (at least a Bachelor's degree).
- Teachers in general senior high schools or vocational secondary schools must hold an educational qualification at least equivalent to or higher than a regular university or other universities (at least a Bachelor's degree).
- Fieldwork supervisors in vocational secondary schools hold an educational qualification at least equivalent to or higher than vocational secondary schools (at least a Bachelor's degree).

The purpose of TQS is to ensure that those entering the profession are qualified and it also serves to raise the social standing of teachers. Thanks to the rapid development of higher education in Shanghai and the successful implementation in of TQS since 2001, the percentage of teachers with a Bachelor's degree (or above) in kindergartens, primary schools, and junior high schools has been increasing rapidly. In fact, possessing a Bachelor's degree with some kind of teacher professional training has become the new threshold for all the new entrants to the teaching profession in Shanghai. Figure 9.3 shows the educational qualifications for primary school teachers while Fig. 9.4 shows the qualifications for secondary school teachers.

Improved Quality of the Teaching Workforce

In Shanghai, according to the regulation issued by the Shanghai Municipal Education Committee, primary school teachers can be graded into five different certified levels that indicate their professional status (posts/titles): high/middle school senior teacher, primary school senior teacher, primary school Level I, Level II and Level III – based on their education background and years of work experience. The Shanghai government also awards the title of 'master teacher' to recognise and motivate excellent teachers with high/middle school senior educational

Fig. 9.3 Educational qualifications for primary school teachers (Shanghai Education Committee, 2012)

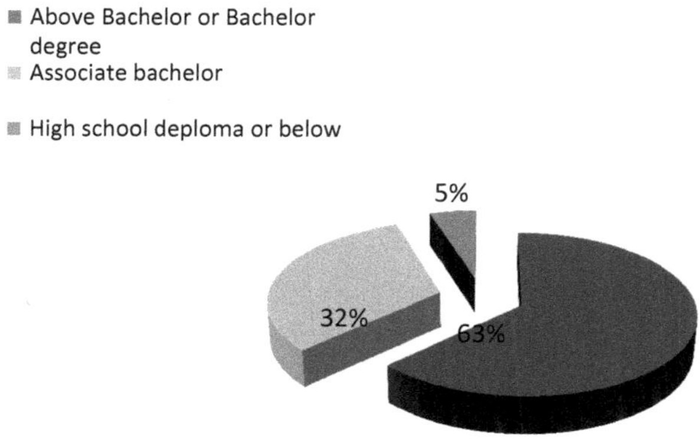

Fig. 9.4 Educational qualifications for secondary school teachers (Shanghai Education Committee, 2012)

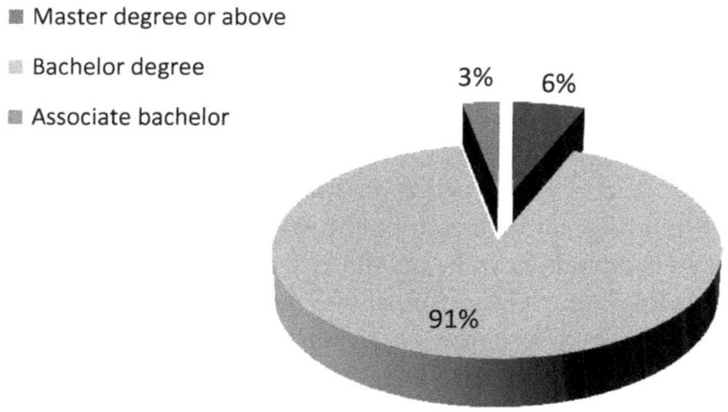

qualifications teaching in the primary and secondary schools. By 2007, there were 584 master teachers in Shanghai and 200 of them are still in service today. There are also 82 'master principals', with 72 % of them in the urban areas, 18 % in the suburban areas, and 10 % in the rural areas. At present, 73 % of master principals are still in office. In 2009, the Shanghai government has appointed 81 master teachers and 40 master principals in primary and high schools. Middle/high school teachers can also be graded by four certified levels (posts/titles): high/middle school senior teacher, high/middle school Level I, Level II and Level III – based on their educational backgrounds and years of working experience (Shen, 2007).

Supportive Teacher–Student Relationship

According to the results from PISA 2009 (OECD, 2010a), the student–teacher ratio in Shanghai is 14.06:1 which is a smaller student–teacher ratio compared to the OECD average of 14.65:1. For key secondary vocational schools, the ratio reaches the highest, which is 24.13:1.

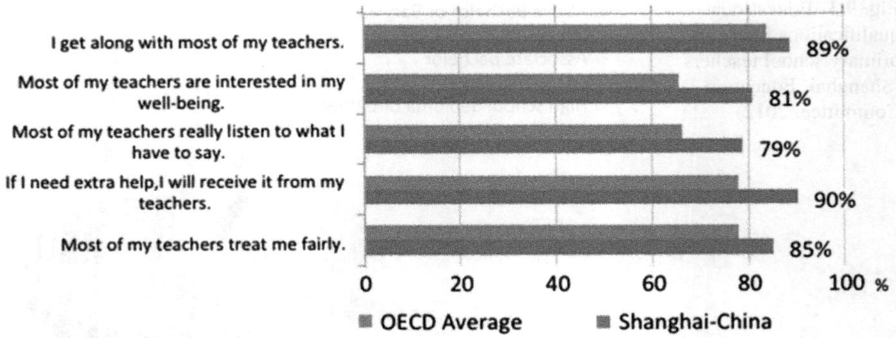

Fig. 9.5 Students' views of teacher-student relations (OECD, 2010a)

Positive teacher–student relations are crucial in establishing an environment that is conducive to learning. Results from PISA suggest that schools with better disciplinary climates, and better teacher–student relationships tend to achieve higher scores in reading. The index of teacher–student relationship in Shanghai based on information from the student surveys is 0.21, which is higher than the OECD average of 0, and is positively correlated to the index of disciplinary climate and reading performance of the students PISA 2009 (OECD, 2010a). PISA 2009 asked students to indicate the extent of their agreement with several statements regarding their relationships with teachers in school. In Shanghai, 89 % of students were reported to agree or strongly agree that they got along with their teachers, 81 % reported that their teachers were concerned about students' well-being, 79 % of students reported that teachers really listened to students' needs, 90 % reported teachers were available if students needed extra help, 85 % of students reported that teachers treated them fairly, as shown in Fig. 9.7. However, principals in Shanghai did not speak highly of their teachers. According to principals, views about how teacher behaviour affected students' learning and the index of teacher-related factors affecting school climate was negative (−0.601), and significantly lower than the OECD average with no correlation to student performance in reading, science and mathematics (Fig. 9.5).

Pre-service Teacher Education

China's teacher education began rather late relative to its national history. The first Normal school, Shanghai Nanyang Normal School, was created only in 1897 by the Qing government, and Shanghai may be considered the birthplace of formal teacher education in China. Pre-service teacher education has been in existence for about a 100 years. The constitution of the Imperial school, issued by the Qing government in 1904, symbolised the establishment of China's first multi-levelled teacher education system. The constitution mandated the provision of two pre-service teacher education programmes: junior normal schools (at secondary school level for

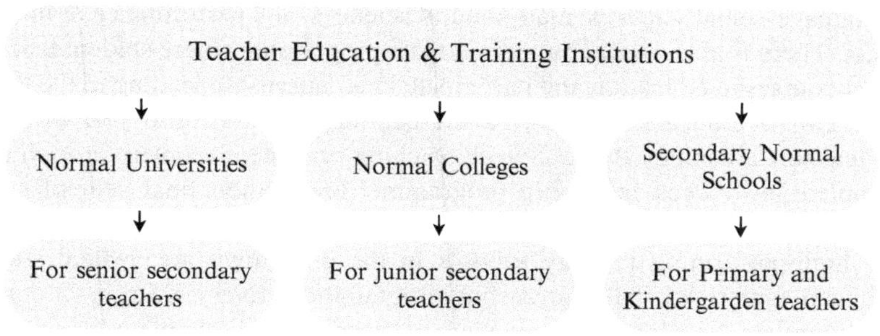

Fig. 9.6 Teacher education system in the early years of the People's Republic of China

preparing primary and kindergarten teachers) and senior normal schools (teachers' colleges or universities for preparing secondary school teachers). After the founding of the People's Republic of China in 1949, China's pre-service teacher education system was reformed, following the Russian model, and a three-tiered teacher education system was established as shown in Fig. 9.6.

In the early 1980s, pre-service teacher education in Shanghai was delivered via three types of institutions:

- Normal colleges and universities, for preparing senior high school secondary teachers;
- Normal colleges, for preparing junior secondary teachers;
- Secondary Normal schools, for preparing primary and kindergarten school teachers.

Since 1995, according to the regulation issued by the Shanghai Municipal Government, secondary teachers' education has been upgraded, and the students in secondary Normal schools were also accordingly upgraded to students of Normal universities. Pre-school teachers' education was incorporated firstly into the Faculty of Pre-school and Special Education within East China Normal University and later incorporated as part of the Faculty of Education, Shanghai Normal University; while primary teachers' education was provided by the Faculty of Education at Shanghai Normal University. After 30 years of development, pre-service teacher education in Shanghai was upgraded to the university level for all categories of teachers, and the selection mechanism had been completely integrated within the university examination system and its structure fully incorporated into the university degree system.

Programme for Preparing Primary School Teachers in the Normal University

Shanghai Normal University prepares primary school teachers within its Faculty of Education. Student teachers study pedagogical courses in one of the three major areas: language-social sciences, math-natural sciences, and performance or fine arts and crafts. There is also a 4-year undergraduate programme where student teachers can select courses in education and participate in an internship leading to the award of a Bachelor of Education (BEd). At the beginning of the third year of study, student teachers are exposed to a 2-week teaching practice placement in each term and complete an 8-week internship programme during their final year of study. Shanghai Normal University has established a collaborative partnership with more than 27 high-performing primary schools in the downtown area where student teachers can undertake their internship programmes. Every year, 6–7 student teachers complete their internships in each of these partner schools.

Programme for Preparing Secondary School Teachers in East China Normal University and Shanghai Normal University

The two normal universities provide academic content in their various academic faculties with pedagogical courses by their education faculties. All the secondary school teachers are trained as subject teachers and student teachers have to offer pedagogical courses. Teacher education programmes in normal universities both for primary and secondary schools include an 8-week teaching practice and a dissertation that must be submitted in order to fulfil the Bachelor's degree requirements. As an international normal university, graduates from East China Normal University usually work for schools in other provinces or regions of East China while graduates from Shanghai Normal University, a local university, normally end up teaching in schools located within Shanghai.

Programme for Teacher Candidates with No Previous Normal University Education Background

In recent years, more and more young graduates from other comprehensive universities and specialised institutions want to enter teaching. For this group of teacher aspirants, the Shanghai Government designed a teacher qualification programme and test. These candidates have to study courses in pedagogy, educational psychology and subject-teaching methodology. Only the candidates who have passed the government-organised Teacher Professional Qualification Test will have the opportunities to teach in the primary or secondary schools. At present, teacher education institutions are designing and trying out a new curriculum in Shanghai aiming at extending the undergraduate programmes to post-graduate and Master's degree levels and building multiple models of pre-service teacher education programmes. These innovations can be classified into three modes as shown in Fig. 9.7.

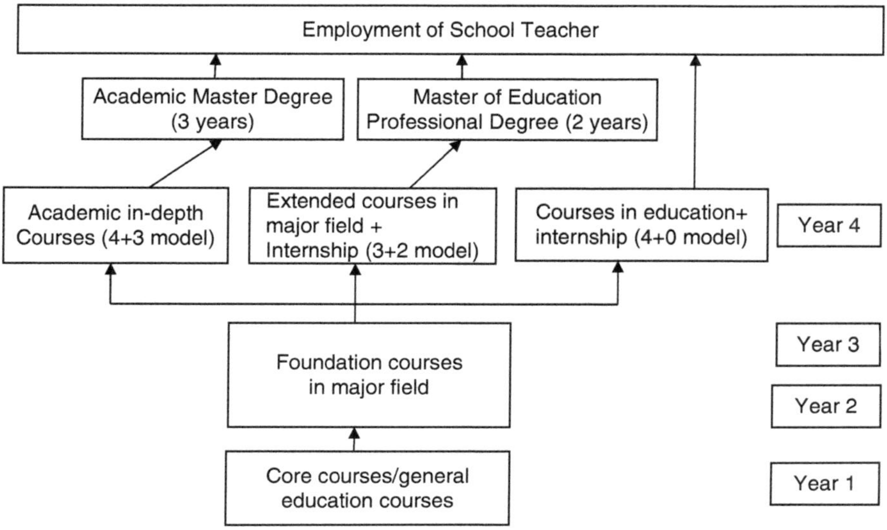

Fig. 9.7 Three models of pre-service teacher's education to be established

To further elucidate, these three modes are:

- '4-year' model: Within 4 years of study, student teachers are required to study courses in education and to complete an internship leading to the award of a BEd. At the beginning of the third year of study, student teacher will undergo a 2-week teaching practice posting in each term and complete an 8-week internship program at the final year of study. After being employed as a teacher, they can also further their studies on a part-time basis.
- '3 + 2' model: After 3 years of study, including those enrolled in programmes leading to a teaching certification or a non-teaching related programme, these students can apply for admission into Master of Education Professional Degree programme for a further 2 years of study. These students can enter into teaching after being screened by the university without the need to pass any additional national teacher certification tests.
- '4 + 3' model: After 4 years of study in their respective disciplines, students can take the national tests in order to be qualified for the academic Master's degree programmes for a further 3 years of study. Those who fail the test can still enter the market workforce (not teaching) with their basic BA or BSc degrees.

Taken together, the three proposed models will create flexible pathways into teaching, and students can have more choices and the system can attract more talented people to join the teaching profession.

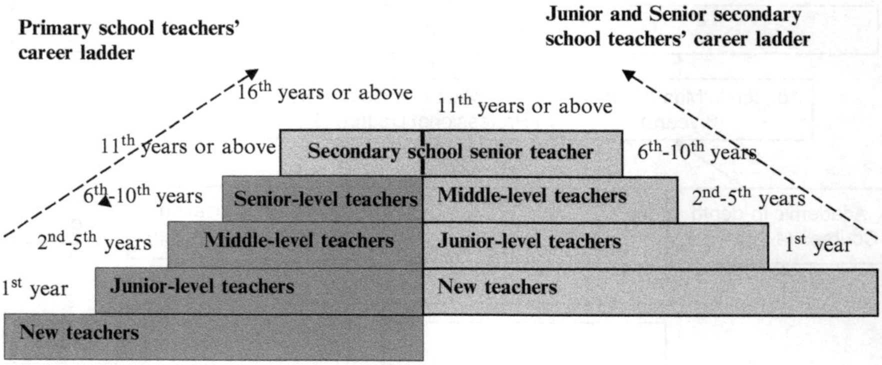

Fig. 9.8 Development for primary and secondary school teachers in Shanghai

Professional Learning and Development

Besides a strong focus on pre-service education, Shanghai also has a systematic and effective in-service training and lifelong professional development network for both school teachers and principals.

Career Pathway for Teachers

As mentioned earlier in this chapter, the minimal educational requirement for entry to teaching profession has already been upgraded in Shanghai. According to the plans laid out by the Shanghai Medium- and Long-term Education Reform and Development Programme (2010–2020), the recruitment of school teachers must be improved and the percentage of teachers with postgraduate degrees must be increased (Shanghai Municipal Government, 2010). Currently, the percentage of junior secondary school teachers with postgraduate degrees is 2.8 %, while the percentage of senior secondary school teachers with postgraduate degrees is 8.3 % (2010). However, these percentages are still much lower compared to those of other developed countries like Austria, Bulgaria, Estonia, Lithuania, Slovakia, Finland, England, Spain, Korea.

According to the Twelfth 5-Year Plan of Shanghai Teaching Staff in basic Education (SMEC, 2004), the percentage of teachers with bachelor's degree and above in kindergartens, primary schools, and junior secondary schools will be increased.

In Shanghai, a teacher's professional development is defined as a process of continuous learning throughout their lifespan as teachers (see Fig. 9.8). Throughout their entire career, teachers can be generally graded along four professional levels as an indication of their professional status: new teachers (1st year), junior-level teachers (2nd–5th years), middle-level teachers (6th–10th years) and senior-level teachers (11th years or above). And primary school teachers can also obtain the professional status of senior-level teachers for junior and senior secondary school teachers. In addition, a higher special-level teacher title 'master teacher' can be given as an honour to the senior secondary school teachers in Shanghai because of their outstanding contributions to education.

Teachers' promotional prospects are primarily determined by professional evaluation, which is largely based on several activities including classroom observation and evaluation, good demonstration lessons, quality of mentorship, performance during the induction programme, among others.

Development Through Continuous Learning

Induction Programme: From Being Qualified to Being Competent

Induction programmes for newly prepared teachers in Shanghai have become increasingly standardised. According to The National Middle- and Long-term Education Reform and Development Programme (2010–2020) and the Shanghai Primary and Secondary School (including kindergarten) Teacher Standardised Training Guidance (Trial), the Shanghai Municipal Education Commission requires each newcomer to pass the evaluation conducted by the different districts before being employed as teachers (Shanghai Education Committee, 2012). After completing a 1-year standardised induction programme, new teachers are subject to performance evaluation conducted jointly by colleges of education in districts, the training school and the prospective schools where new teachers are to be recruited. New teachers who pass the evaluation can obtain a certificate as one of the necessary basis for obtaining teacher qualification. Since June 2011, four districts of Shanghai, namely, Pu Tuo, Chang Ning, Xu Hui and Feng Xian, have begun to implement this standardised training programme for novice teachers and by June 2013, 570 new teachers have been trained in this new programme (2012).

In the Pu Tuo district of Shanghai in 2012, there are 120 new teachers recruited without teaching experience. Based on the requirements for standardised teacher training, these 120 newcomers are incorporated into 14 designated training bases and equipped with 76 excellent mentors according to different disciplines and levels of schooling. The standardised training for new teachers in primary and secondary school in Shanghai comprise four major areas of coverage: professional ethics, class management and personal experience, teaching research, and professional development. New teachers are expected to accomplish the first development stage, and transition from being 'qualified' to becoming 'competent' professionals.

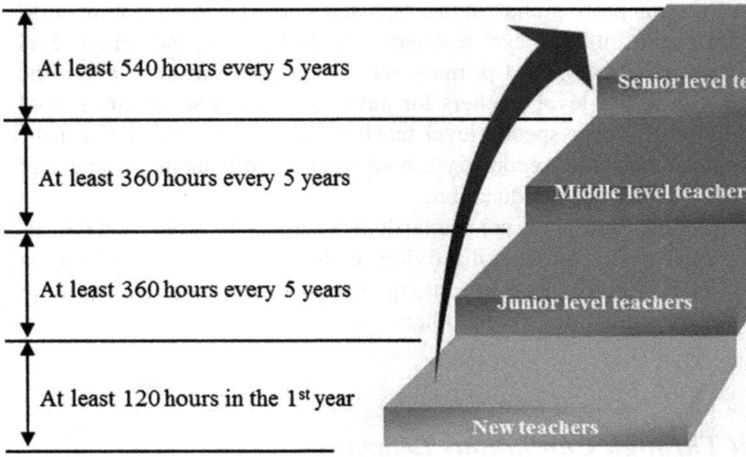

Fig. 9.9 Professional development model in Shanghai

In-Service Training: Project 240 and 540

Since 2002, Shanghai Municipal government released a requirement for in-service training for Shanghai school teachers Shanghai Municipal Education Commission (2007). In concrete, new teachers were set a target of 240 h of training in their first 5 years of teaching, while those who took 540 h over 5 years could apply for senior professional titles. Project 240 and 540 provided Shanghai teachers with institutionalised training opportunities at teacher training colleges to enable new teachers to adapt to their new work and senior teachers to undergo professional development (see Fig. 9.9).

Among 240 h of training a total of 36 learning credits must be completed within 5 years. These credits are distributed into three types of courses: morality and literacy (12 credits), knowledge and skills (14 credits), and practical experience (10 credits). Meanwhile, teachers should attend other courses, such as sharing courses at the municipal level, courses at the district level, and school-based courses among which school-based courses account for 50 % and above (SMEC, 2011b). In addition, senior school teachers are required to finish 18 credits of personalised self-learning courses focused on educational research (SMEC, 2011c).

At present, strong foci are attached to the following five aspects of primary and secondary school teachers' training in Shanghai: (1) to raise teachers' professional standards and to carry out training programmes customised to teachers' needs; (2) to cultivate excellent teachers and talents in the field of basic education; (3) to improve the professional levels of teachers in the rural area and weak schools; (4) to enhance the comprehensive quality of teachers, especially their innovative literacy; (5) to strengthen the quality of the teaching force, especially the training of teacher educators.

Training Providers and Programmes

In shanghai there are at least three major providers for teacher's in-service training and various training programs. The first group is two normal universities, Shanghai Normal University and East China Normal University, which both offer Ph.D. and academic Master degree program for teachers. At meantime they also offer professional D.Ed and MED programs, including curriculum on school management and administration. Every year more than 400 in-service teachers enter to these programs. In addition, government and schools can pay 2/3 tuition fees for the teachers. The second group is city and district education colleges which offer programs for improving teachers' professional ethics or pedagogy. The third category is school-based program which is our focus in next section.

School-based training and professional development activities in Shanghai showcase what is a good lesson and how to develop effective teachers and successful students through teachers' participating in mentoring for new teachers, teaching and research, lesson planning and various kinds of activities.

School-based training and professional development activities includes:

- mentors for new teachers,
- teaching and research groups,
- lesson preparation groups,
- grade groups,
- classroom observation and classroom evaluation,
- task-driven training, and
- vacation training and school visits.

Mentoring for New Teachers

Mentoring for new teachers is a common practice in Shanghai schools, but in fact, mentoring is for all teachers, not just new teachers (Jensen, 2012). Beginning teachers typically have two mentors, one for classroom management and one for subject-specific guidance. Teachers who can be appointed as mentors are usually senior primary and secondary school teachers or teachers with many years of teaching experience at the school, a subject-leader at the District Teacher Training College, or a university researcher being brought into the school. These mentors are usually called 'master teachers' or even 'specialist teachers'. They mentor many teachers across many schools in order to share their experience and expertise.

The mentoring relationship, which lasts 3 or more years, usually begins with a comprehensive diagnosis of new teachers' strengths and weaknesses. The mentor and mentee observe each other's lessons, as well as make public demonstration lessons. Mentees frequently observe mentor lessons and write up reflections based on these observed lessons. Mentors observe mentees' teaching and give immediate feedback on areas for improvement.

Teaching and Research Groups

Teaching and research groups (TRGs), which comprise teachers of the same subject, exist in every school in Shanghai. They are basic units of teaching research and administrative management at the school level. School TRGs are generally divided into different groups according to different subjects, for example, Chinese TRG, Math TRG, Foreign Language TRG and so on. Teachers in these groups collaborate closely with their colleagues and frequently talk about the latest developments in their discipline of teaching, observe classroom teaching and develop new teachers' teaching skills and make specific suggestions for improvement. Peer observation and evaluation of lessons in TRGs are very common today in Shanghai. They have an impact not only on teacher professional learning and development but also student learning and performances.

During actual teaching, teachers may observe each other or may be observed by peers (in the case of a new teaching topic because of curriculum change, for example), by new teachers (so they can learn from more experienced teachers), by senior teachers (for mentoring), or by the school principal (for monitoring or for constructive development purposes). Sometimes, teachers are expected to teach demonstration lessons (called 'public lessons') for a large number of other teachers to observe and comment. This structured organisation of teaching and research in Shanghai is thus not only a means for administration but also a major platform for professional enhancement (OECD, 2010b). TRG activities are usually held twice every month.

Most teachers have become accustomed to teaching and research activities as part of their professional routine. A national survey of Ding Gang's team (2010) shows that of 11,190 teachers, a total of 87.6 % were engaged in teaching and research activities once a week over the past 2 years, 54.4 % participated in the activities once or more every week, and only 2.3 % did not participate. It can be seen that the majority of teachers in schools participated in regular teaching and research activities organised by schools (Ding).

Lesson Preparation Groups

Lesson preparation groups (LPGs) are made up of teachers of the same subject and of the same grade. They are typically smaller versions of teaching and research groups. Group members guide and support each other in lesson planning and design, with a focus on developing new teachers' skills in these areas.

Collective lesson planning is the core task for these groups. It is a kind of problem-based learning and aims at designing classroom teaching plans and solving the teaching problems. These training activities focus on creating collective wisdoms and improving teaching quality. During the collective discussions each week, every member contributes towards understanding the teaching materials, making teaching improvements and preparing for the following week's work.

Lesson plans are thought to help the teacher think through the lesson in advance, resolve problems and difficulties, to provide a structure for a lesson, and to provide a 'map' for teachers to follow and to provide a record of the lesson just taught. The success of a lesson is often thought to be dependent on the effectiveness of lesson plans. LPGs help improve student learning as teachers jointly reflect on diagnosing student learning, lesson design and teacher approaches. Teachers discuss alternative teaching approaches, observe each other's classes, re-examine content, and identify and solve problems in teaching the content (Kennedy, 2005). LPG activities are usually held once every week and then every teacher in the group spends many hours of lesson preparation covering the standard 40–45 min period.

Lesson planning (LP) is not only a task but also an important way to promote the professional development of teachers. TRGs and LPGs play a role in LP capability and classroom teaching skills of teachers, and can thus contribute to the sustainable development of teachers' professional standards. According to research from Chinese scholars such as Ding's team (2010), although 82.2 % of the teachers often prepare lessons individually and independently, TRGs play a major role in the collective preparation of instruction, which 74 % of the teachers sometimes or often used. Classroom group (CG) ranks second place, with 62 % of teachers sometimes or often using it.

Grade Groups

Grade groups are usually composed of all the teachers of the same grade (for example, Grade 6 in a junior secondary school) in Shanghai. It is a middle-level administrative unit of a school. One grade group often contains several classes and all the subject teachers of the classes. The group leader presides a grade meeting and coordinates teaching and management work of all the classes.

Leadership Building

In Shanghai, there are also varieties of training programmes at the municipal, district or school levels to help school principals and leaders to meet the needs of teachers' further professional development and promotion. These training programmes provide:

- training for potential school leaders,
- annual task-driven training for school principals,
- middle-level managers' training,
- principals' training at district level, and
- exemplary city principals' training.

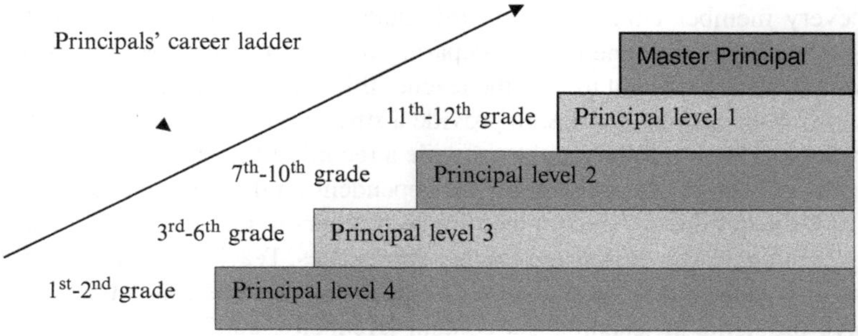

Fig. 9.10 Professional grading of school principals in Shanghai

In Shanghai, every teacher is expected to have leadership training and some of them can be further developed as subject leaders or teaching experts. Since 2005, Shanghai has begun to select and cultivate 1,000 young teacher candidates of various kinds of subjects every year. In every 5 years, when the number reaches 5,000, 10 % of them will be developed into exemplary city teachers and subject leaders – well-known teachers – and 100 of them are trained to be national educators and teaching experts who can master educational theories at home and abroad, possess strong capabilities in teaching and research, and participate in international educational exchanges.

Principals now have more responsibilities for long-term development in schools. They must plan and strategize for future planning of their schools and therefore, they must know how to do strategic planning (Chu & Chen, 2010). The Shanghai Municipal Education Commission has released three phases of programmes in the Well-known Teachers and Principals Training Project in Basic Education, and these have made remarkable achievements since 2005. Since then, Shanghai has selected and cultivated 200 young and middle-aged principals who are highly ambitious and of strong management capabilities and exhibit great potential. Every 5 years, when the number adds up to 1,000, 100 of them are to be developed into the city's well-known principals who are model teachers and can participate in international educational exchanges and corporations; ten principals are further selected to be exemplary nation-wide principals (SMEC, 2004).

Career Pathways for School Leaders

Principals of primary and secondary schools in Shanghai are graded into 4 levels and banded into 12 grades. Each grade lasts about 2 years, but if one principal is appraised to be excellent, he or she can be promoted one grade band a year. Besides, a higher special-level principal title is given as an honour to the first-level principals in Shanghai because of their outstanding contributions to the cause of education. The proportion of senior-level principals in Shanghai is about 30 %, and the proportion of special-level principals is 5 % (SMEC, 2011a; see Fig. 9.10).

Professional Standards for Principals

According to Professional Standards for Principals in Shanghai developed by the Shanghai Municipal Education Commission, professional development for principals can be divided into four periods, namely, role adaptation period, experience accumulation period, professional maturity period and thoughts leading period (SMEC, 2011a). Professional standards for each period involves six aspects as follows:

- Planning school development,
- Creating a culture of educating students,
- Managing curriculum and instruction,
- Leading teachers' development,
- Optimising internal management, and
- Adapting external environment.

In-Service Training for Principals

The State Education Commission (SEC) issued a document entitled "Strengthening the Training for Principals of Elementary and Secondary Schools Nationwide" in 1989. In 1995, the "Training Direction for Principals of Elementary and Secondary Schools" was issued by SEC. Since then, the quality of principal training has improved vastly. School principals' training, especially for young principals, has always been placed at the top of the education agenda in Shanghai. School principals' training in Shanghai involves the following aspects:

- school principals' preparation for undertaking the position – this programme is targeted for the new principals to adapt for the roles and responsibilities undertaken, competence-based, job skills;
- school leader candidate training – this programme is targeted for potential school leaders, not just confined to principals also including vice-principals or other leaders of departments;
- school principals' qualification training;
- exemplary principals' advanced training; and
- excellent school principal professional training.

New principals or principal candidates are required to participate in training of knowledge and skills that are essential for their future positions. The training time must not be less than 120 h. The main objectives for in-service principals' position training are: the learning of new knowledge and skills, and improving their capabilities of management, research and communication skills. The training time within a 5-year period must not be less than 360 h. The aims of exemplary principals' advanced training are to develop them into educational specialists because these principals have already had some knowledge about theories and capabilities of research. The training time must not be less than 200 h. These principals must complete papers or research reports within 5 months (SMEC, 2011a, 2011b, 2011c).

Summary of Lessons from Shanghai

This chapter has detailed how, in a short span of about 30 years, Shanghai has introduced great reforms in order to raise the quality of the teaching force. This starts with the more stringent academic qualifications required at entry point, the more rigorous teacher education programmes with multiple pathways and models designed for different profiles of teacher candidates to the strong in-service professional development system that is financed by the government and the strong systemic coherence between the Shanghai Municipal Commission, the schools and the universities offering teacher education programmes. Carefully organised school-based professional development activities which are highly innovative such as TRGs and LPs coupled with a carefully structured school leadership preparation programme are further measures that ensure that Shanghai maintains its top level league standing in the international arena.

References

Chu, H., & Chen, C. X. (2010, January). *Developing principals in China: Challenges, opportunities, and strategic directions*. Paper presented at the Asia Leadership Roundtable hosted by the Asia Pacific Centre for Leadership and Change, Hong Kong Institute of Education, Hongkong.

Ding, G. (2010). *National survey and policy analysis for teacher professional development in primary and secondary schools*. Shanghai, China: East China Normal University Press.

Jensen, B. (2012). *Catching up: Learning from the best school systems in East Asia*. Melbourne, Australia: Grattan Institute.

Kennedy, M. M. (2005). *Inside teaching: How classroom life undermines reform*. Cambridge, MA: Harvard University Press.

Shanghai Education Committee. (2012, April 10). From 'the qualified' to 'the competent': The first stage of new teachers' development – Practice report from Shanghai standardized training program of novice teachers. *China Education Daily* (p. 1).

Shanghai Municipal Education Commission (SMEC). (2004). *Shanghai well-known teachers and principals' training project in basic education*. Shanghai, China: Author.

Shanghai Municipal Education Commission. (2007). *The eleventh five-year planning outline of Shanghai on basic education teachers' training[R]* (pp. 7–8). Shanghai, China: Shanghai Municipal Education Commission.

Shanghai Municipal Education Commission (SMEC). (2010). *Annual report on education in Shanghai in 2010*. Shanghai, China: Shanghai Educational Publishing House.

Shanghai Municipal Education Commission (SMEC). (2011a). *Teacher professional development programme*. Shanghai, China: Author

Shanghai Municipal Education Commission (SMEC). (2011b). *The twelfth five-year plan of Shanghai teaching staff of basic education*. Shanghai, China: Author.

Shanghai Municipal Education Commission (SMEC). (2011c). *Views on implementation of Shanghai primary and secondary school and kindergarten teachers' training during the 12th five-year plan (trial)*. Shanghai, China: Author.

Shanghai Municipal Government. (2010). *Shanghai medium- and long-term education reform and development programme (2010–2020)*. Shanghai, China: Author.

Shanghai Municipal Statistics Bureau (SMSB). (2011). *Shanghai basic facts 2011*. Shanghai, China: Shanghai Literature and Art Publishing Group.

Shen, X. (2007). *Shanghai education*. Shanghai, China: Shanghai Century Publishing.

Shanghai Education Committee. (2012). *Regulations on subjects of teacher professional qualification test in Shanghai*. Shanghai, China: Author.

OECD. (2010a). *PISA 2009 results: What makes a school successful? Resources, policies and practices* (Vol. 4). Paris: Author.

OECD. (2010b). Shanghai and Hong Kong: Two distinct examples of education reform in China. In OECD (Ed.), *Strong performers and successful reformers in education: Lessons from PISA for the United States* (pp. 83–115). Paris: Author.

Zhang, M., & Kong, L. (2012). An exploration of reasons for Shanghai's success in the OECD Programme for International Student Assessment (PISA) 2009. *Frontiers of Education in China, 7*(1), 124–162.

Chapter 10
Levelling Up and Sustaining Educational Achievement: The Case of Hong Kong

Esther Sui Chu Ho

Introduction

Many studies have attributed the outstanding performance and success of East Asian learners to their cultural model of learning (e.g., Hau & Salili, 1991; Lee, 1996; Li, 2005; Schneider & Lee, 1990; Wong, 2004, 2009). A number of researchers attribute it to the values and aspirations these students share with their parents (Schneider & Lee, 1990; Shon & Ja, 1982; Yao, 1985); to these students' motivation for socioeconomic advancement or self-perfection through education (Lee, 1996; Salili, Chiu, & Lai, 2001; Sue & Okazaki, 1990); to the learning activities at home (Chen & Stevenson, 1989; Schneider & Lee, 1990); to the interactions these students have with their teachers and classmates in school (Hau & Salili, 1991; Schneider & Lee, 1990); and to school leadership and teacher participation (Mourshed, Chijioke & Barber, 2010; OECD, 2010b). These analyses seem to provide a very encouraging picture of the education in East Asian societies. Nevertheless, Ho (2006) pointed out the existence of challenges despite these findings such as high participation (of the mind) but low engagement (of the heart), doing well academically but feeling bad emotionally, achieving high academic scores but low in terms of the practices within these societies (Ho, 2009).

The Hong Kong education system has always been a hybridisation of the West and the East (Morris & Adamson, 2010). Its schooling system is influenced by the legacies of the Chinese tradition and the British colonialism. At the system level, its outstanding performance could be a product of the dynamic interaction between decentralisation and centralisation policy. Its outstanding performance of mathematics and science since the 1990s (Martin et al., 2000; Mullis et al., 2000) and

E.S.C. Ho (✉)
Faculty of Education, The Chinese University of Hong Kong, Rm 209, Ho Tim Building, Shatin, New Territories, Hong Kong
e-mail: estherho@cuhk.edu.hk

S.K. Lee et al. (eds.), *Educational Policy Innovations: Levelling Up and Sustaining Educational Achievement*, Springer Education Innovation Book Series 1,
DOI 10.1007/978-981-4560-08-5_10,

reading since the 2000s (Ho et al., 2003) in Trends in International Mathematics and Science Study (TIMSS), Progress in International Reading Literacy Study (PIRLS) and Programme for International Student Assessment (PISA) supported the perception that Hong Kong's basic education system had moved from good to great in terms of cognitive measures implemented since the 1990s (Mourshed et al., 2010).

In this chapter, it is argued that as lifelong learning and all-round development of students are set to be the ultimate goals of current education reforms in Hong Kong, searching for a balance between cognitive and non-cognitive abilities as well as hard versus soft skills is essential. The middle way of decentralisation to empower teachers and to involve parents and careful planning of various centralised and standards-based assessments at different levels of the schooling system is a promising avenue in the next wave of reform.

Social-Cultural-Political-Economic Context of Hong Kong

Hong Kong, a Special Administrative Region (SAR) of the People's Republic of China (PRC), is a city of 1,104 km^2, located on the south coast of China. Hong Kong is one of the most densely populated areas in the world. In 2011, its population was over seven million with approximately 93 % of ethnic Chinese, most of whom are immigrants from China. The remaining 7 % are immigrants from India, Pakistan and Nepal, and foreign domestic helpers from the Philippines, Indonesia and Thailand. Moreover, some immigrants are British, Americans, Australians and Japanese, largely employed in the commercial, financial and educational sectors (Census and Statistics Department, 2012).

Hong Kong is a micro-polity with no natural resources except for its deep harbour. It developed over the past 150 years from a fishing port when British settlement began in 1841, to a manufacturing hub during the 1960s–1970s, and to an international financial centre since 1980s. After the handover to PRC in 1997, the economic development of Hong Kong went through another transformation cycle. Policy agreements, such as 'The Mainland and Hong Kong Closer Economic Partnership Arrangement' (CEPA), were signed after 1997 and these brought new business opportunities to Hong Kong. Consequently, Hong Kong's economy flourished and its per capita gross domestic product (GDP per capita) rose to US $34,400 in 2011 (Information Services Department, 2011).

Hong Kong is a meeting point where Chinese and Western cultures co-exist and is hybridised in a unique form. For instance, education reform in Hong Kong has drawn together expertise from both the Eastern and Western worlds. As Hong Kong returned to PRC's government from British in 1997, it was mutually agreed that the principle of 'One Country, Two Systems' and that Hong Kong's previous capitalist system and lifestyle should remain unchanged for the next 50 years.

Hong Kong Education Reform

In 1999, Hong Kong embarked on a major systemic education reform to prepare its children for the transition to a knowledge economy in a globalised labour market. Over the past decade, growing evidence suggested a strong link between educational development and economic growth. Hanushek and Woessmann (2007) conducted a secondary analysis using data from TIMSS and PISA to examine the role of educational quality in economic growth. They found that the test-score measure features a statistically significant effect on the growth of real GDP per capita in 1960–2000 even after controlling for the initial level of GDP per capita and for students' years of schooling. They affirmed that the supply of skilled labour is related to the pattern of education attainment within a nation. These findings have given policymakers solid empirical evidence to import new education reform policies and programmes in the Asia-Pacific region during the 1990s (Cheng, 1999, 2003).

In 2000, the Education Commission (EC) recommended reforming the education system, with the objectives of constructing a system conducive to "lifelong learning and all-round development" (p. 4) of students. The scope of the reform extends to curricula, assessment mechanisms, school-based management (SBM), parental involvement, student-centred learning, reading to learn, learning to learn, ICT in education, language education, professional development, student admission systems as well as increasing post-secondary education opportunities and so on (Education Bureau [EDB], 2007). Yet, these reform policies have not always received a ready acceptance among teachers and other practitioners at the school level (Cheng & Walker, 2008). In fact, there is a unique way that certain reform processes worked (e.g., reading to learn reform task, teacher participation in SBM) while others did not (e.g., lowering the pressure of tests and public examinations) for lifelong learning and all-round development of students in Hong Kong.

In response to the general public's concerns about whether the Hong Kong education reform works, policymakers claimed that Hong Kong is on the right track (Education Commission [EC], 2000). The evidence always cited by the policymakers is that Hong Kong students ranked top 10 in reading, mathematical and scientific literacy in the PISA, PIRLS and TIMSS studies since the 2000s. These outstanding performances are always used to justify the comprehensive reform of 2000s.

Accomplishments and Challenges of Hong Kong Education System

Hong Kong has participated in PISA since the first cycle in 2002, which provided a set of baseline indicators as the education reform process had just started. In a recent survey of PISA 2009, Hong Kong 15-year-old students again stood amongst the top tier among 65 countries and regions (Ho, 2012b; Ho et al., 2003, 2005, 2008).

In particular, Hong Kong students ranked fourth in reading and third in both mathematics and science in 2009. Regarding equality in education, the impact of students' socioeconomic status (SES) on their performances remains very small and changes little when compared with the first PISA survey in Hong Kong. The percentage of variance in student performance between schools, an important indicator of academic segregation among schools, was once larger than the OECD average in the first two cycles of PISA but is now getting smaller and closer to the OECD average. This is related to the reform of the streaming policy of Secondary 1 students, where the school bands are reduced from 5 to 3.[1] Taken together, these changes suggest that the basic education of Hong Kong is moving towards a quality education with equality.

However, several major challenges still exist and emerge. For instance, although the impact of students' SES including the occupation and education level of their parents has relatively small impact on their performance, significant gender differences are still evident in the performance of both mathematics and reading. Specifically, boys outperform girls by 14 points in mathematics and girls outperform boys by 33 points in reading, both differences being statistically significant in 2009. Also, the performance of immigrant students who were born outside Hong Kong was significantly poorer than that of the locally born students, the difference being 30–40 points. Moreover, perhaps as a result of school banding being reduced from 5 to 3, the between-school variance has been reduced but the within-school variance of student performance has increased significantly, suggesting that increased diversity of students within schools. As such, how secondary school teachers should equip themselves, and what kinds of support the education authority should provide for schools in order to cater for the widened learning difference of students within schools would be a timely agenda.

Review of Factors Related to the Accomplishments or Challenges

Various student and parent factors have been identified to consistently have a significant impact on students' literacy performance across the previous four cycles of PISA (Ho, 2012b). At the student level, students' reading engagement is consistently related to their reading, mathematics and science performance in Hong Kong since the first cycle of PISA. As defined in PISA 2009, engagement in reading refers to three aspects: reading enjoyment, reading diversity, and reading online. Findings

[1] In Hong Kong, primary school graduates are categorised into different bands according to their academic performance, with Band 1 students having the highest priority in being allocated into their first choice of secondary school while lower-banding students having lower priorities. To reduce the labeling effect on schools and students, the number of allocation bands has been reduced from 5 to 3 starting from 2001.

in PISA 2009 show that Hong Kong students' extent of reading engagement is significantly higher when compared with that of PISA 2000+. This can be attributed to the fact that 'reading to learn' is set to be one of the four key tasks of education reform since 2000s, and that extra resources have been provided for schools to buys books in the classroom and school library and structured daily reading time has been reserved in the timetable to get students in the habit of reading.

At the parental engagement level, parents in Hong Kong do not participate much in school-based decision-making but are highly involved in home-based and learning-focused activities (Ho et al., 2003, 2005, 2008). Results from multilevel analysis suggested the strong impact that parental involvement and investment on students' reading, mathematical and scientific literacy performance. Results show consistent findings as follows: (1) students' reading performance was significantly related to parental investment in reading materials and their early involvement for nurturing children's reading habits (Ho et al., 2003); (2) students' mathematical literacy was significantly related to parental investment in educational and cultural resources and computer facilities at home (Ho et al., 2005); and (3) students' scientific literacy and self-efficacy towards science were significantly associated with parental investment in cultural resources and organising science learning enrichment activities[2] from an early age (Ho et al., 2008). Clearly, parents and the community need to ensure such early learning opportunities are equally available for both boys and girls, and for children of all socio-cultural-economic backgrounds so that the financial and geographic dislocation do not mitigate against future reading, mathematical and scientific literacies (Ho, 2010; Yore, Anderson, & Chiu, 2010).

At the systemic level, several recent reports examine how the world's most improved school systems keep getting better. The 2010 McKinsey Report (Mourshed et al., 2010), entitled *How the World's Most Improved School Systems Keep Getting Better*, identified 13 school systems as 'sustained improvers' and seven school systems as having a 'promising start', based on a university scale of student outcomes computed by the reading, mathematics and science achievement scores from PISA 2000 to PISA 2006. Among these 20 school systems, Hong Kong, Singapore, South Korea, Ontario, Canada and Saxony, Germany were identified to have sustained improvement in their school system, having moved from being 'good to great'. The Report further pointed out that systems, which have moved from 'good to great', shared common interventions – that is, they ensured teaching autonomy and school leadership as a full-fledged profession. In addition, OECD (2010a) suggested that "most successful school systems grant greater autonomy to individual schools to design curricula and establish assessment policies" (p. 15).

In the case of Hong Kong, evidence from PISA 2003 supported that school decentralisation, especially teacher participation, is the essential contributor to the

[2] Moreover, activities that could be provided at an early age (e.g., watching TV programmes about science, reading books on scientific discovery, watching, reading or listening to science fictions) were found to be highly effective activities for promoting children's science achievement and self-efficacy (Ho et al., 2008).

high performance of Hong Kong (Ho, 2006). While the management of schooling is decentralised by providing schools with a platform and supporting them with resources, the government centralises the assessment of outcomes by establishing a multilevel accountability system including performance assessment and public examinations of students as well as internal and external evaluations of schools (Ho, 2012a). As a challenge, schools are pushed to take a professional stand, exercise professional autonomy in the process of schooling; but at the same time, are held accountable for the improvement of learning outcomes of their respective student bodies.

To understand more deeply how the balance of decentralisation – centralisation policy works for or against the school system in Hong Kong, the following sections will first explore why the Hong Kong government has advocated the different models of decentralisation, and how the different forms of school decentralisation have emerged globally and locally. Finally, the nature and impact of school decentralisation in Hong Kong will be examined.

Global and Local Perspectives of Educational Decentralisation

Global Phenomena of Decentralisation and Centralisation in Education

Decentralisation is the transfer of authority from a higher governmental level to a lower organisational level (Brown, 1990; McGinn & Street, 1986). The main rationale behind decentralisation is that people at the lower level of a hierarchy are most knowledgeable about their own needs and problems. It is believed that, under decentralisation, people can have more control and input into their own lives (Brown, 1990; Chapman, 1973). In the educational setting, decentralisation was seen to be a major policy to increase efficiency, flexibility, accountability, and responsiveness for economic development in both developed and developing countries (Cheng, 1994, 2000; Hannaway & Carnoy, 1993; Hanson, 1991; Ho, 2003; Kim, 2000; Suzuki, 2000).

In the field of education, school-based management (SBM) is a major avenue of decentralisation that has been adopted since 1960s around the world. Whether it is under the banner of school autonomy or teacher empowerment, SBM has been on the education reform agenda for decades. Reformers of the 1980s called for changing schools, imitating business efforts to redesign workplaces and involve employees in 'participatory decision-making'. SBM typically involves the creation of a school governance body – comprising teachers, parents, or community members/agencies – that, through legislative action, are empowered to make decisions in the following areas: organisational goals, budgeting, staffing, and curriculum and instruction.

Decentralisation in the Education Sector in Hong Kong

The Hong Kong school system has a high degree of decentralisation in terms of the dominance of government-funded but privately managed 'aided schools'. In 2012, there are only about 6 % of government schools in Hong Kong. The government has been subsidising school-sponsoring bodies (SSBs), mainly churches, charitable organisations and other local associations or agencies, to run the aided-schools which comprised 70 % of schools in Hong Kong.[3]

In addition, with the 2000 Education Reform (EC, 2000) which aims to provide choice for parents and to address the diversified needs of students, the amount of private schools, directly subsidised schools, and international schools had increased substantially to 24 % during the past 10 years. This dominance of privately managed 'aided schools' in Hong Kong is quite unique even among the East Asian societies which is related to the philosophy of 'positive non-intervention' and the notion of 'small government, great market' of the Hong Kong SAR government.

In March 1991, the Government published a booklet entitled *The School Management Initiative*: *Setting the Framework for Quality in Hong Kong Schools* (Education and Manpower Branch & Education Department [EMB & ED], 1991) With this SMI initiative, a reform was initiated by the British colonial administration in the early 1990s, and pushed further with the name of SBM by the Hong Kong, SAR government after the return of Hong Kong to China. Nonetheless, both before and after 1997, there was no popular demand both from the education sector and the public for a change in the governance of school education and its management. As mentioned by Tsang (1995), cost savings in public spending is not the main reason, which pushed the government to initiate the decentralisation reform. Public expenditure on education in 1991–1992 was 21.5 % of the total public expenditure. It rose to 24.2 % in 1997–1998, remained around 22–23 % between 1998 and 2001, and kept at about 23 % until 2012. So why did the government push forward the reform with a new name?

As stated explicitly in the SMI document, the main objective of SMI was to improve the system of accountability and to provide better school services by a comprehensive programme of managerial and financial changes, which is consistent with the basic principal of the Public Sector Reform. Therefore, the main motive behind the Government's decentralisation policy was to increase school accountability and tighten its control in the aided-school sector by delegating authority not only to school-sponsoring bodies but also to parents, teachers and community members. As Leung (2001) puts it, the primary objective of the reform was first to re-regulate the aided-school sector by a redefinition of the roles of various stakeholders. Critics argued that SBM in Hong Kong was packaged under a

---

[3] The sponsoring bodies abide by a Code of Aid, a kind of contractual agreement with the government. The 'aided schools' are near the US concept of charter schools, except that the Code of Aid governs operational procedures rather than performance.

political cover of 'decentralisation' of authority to the school level in order to encourage 'school initiative', 'school effectiveness', 'teacher empowerment' and 'parental participation in management' (2001).

When the SMI scheme was launched in 1992, it only received lukewarm support from schools. As late as 1997, 6 years after its implementation, only about 30 % of the schools in Hong Kong had joined the programme (EC, 1997). However, the policy was firmly pushed by the government under the new name of SBM in 1997. In 1997, the *Education Commission Report No. 7* (Education Commission) recommended that SBM – in the spirit of SMI – would be implemented in all schools by 2000. With regard to the management structure, it recommended that schools implement the SMI structures, such as the formal procedures for setting school goals, school profiles, budgeting, development plans and means for evaluating progress and staff appraisal. Nevertheless, schools were given the flexibility in deciding the governance structure. Since schools were given flexibility in deciding their own governance structures, there was no strong objection to the mandatory implementation of SBM scheme in all schools. Many schools have adopted a two-tier structure in school management, that is, the School Executive Committee (SEC), which comprised teacher and parent representatives, was subject and answerable to a higher level of authority, the School Management Committee (SMC).

In December 1998, the Director of Education appointed the Advisory Committee on School-Based Management (ACSBM) to recommend on the governance structure and accountability framework for the SBM scheme. It published the SBM consultative document in 2000 (Education Department [ED], 2000), which recommended that all schools adopt a government structure, that is, SMC, which aimed to devolve power to 'all stakeholders', including the representatives of School-Sponsoring Bodies (SSB), principals, teachers, parents and community members. The teacher associations and parent groups welcomed the proposal to introduce teacher and parent representatives into SMC. However, SSBs, especially the Christian organisations and the Catholic Board of Education, expressed strong reservations about this one-tier governance structure. Under the new governance structure, SSBs would no longer be entrusted with full responsibilities and control of school management. Instead, as the incorporated bodies, SMCs rather than SSBs would be the legal entities entrusted with the power to make decisions.

The main challenge is the lack of trust between the sponsoring bodies of aided schools and the government. Throughout the reform process, the government maintained an upper hand as it had public support. Its proposal to enhance transparency, public accountability and participation of all key stakeholders would surely win the support of teachers, parents and public at large.

In July 2004, the Education (Amendment) Ordinance was passed by the Legislative Council. Under the Amendment Ordinance, sponsoring bodies of all aided schools are required to submit a draft constitution of its Incorporated Management Committee (IMC) and a list of proposed managers to the Permanent Secretary for Education and Manpower on or before 1 July 2009 in order to set up IMC to manage the school. It also stipulates that the composition of IMC shall include: (1) managers nominated by the sponsoring body, constituting at most 60 % of the total number of managers; (2) the principal; (3) one or more teacher manager(s); (4) one or more parent manager(s); (5) one or more alumni manager(s); and (6) one or more independent manager(s). It was suggested that the transition period would be 5 years to allow more time for SSBs to put in place the new governance structure. In 2012, the establishment of IMC became mandatory. The effect of this unique form of SBM model on school process and outcomes are to be investigated in the future.

Nature and Impact of School Decentralisation in Hong Kong

Main Actors in School Decentralisation

Schleicher (2012) stated that Hong Kong's success in PISA can be attributed to 'one system, many actors' and the influential role of parents. As he put it,

> With the majority of schools run by private entities, the government has few levers for direct intervention and parents have a powerful influence on schools, both through their choice of schools (though still banded) and through local control. They sit on school management committees, parent-teacher associations and on home-school cooperation committees.

To learn from the case of Hong Kong, it is important to examine to what extent parents, teachers, school management boards, and other actors are actually involved in different decision areas (see Fig. 10.1).

Evidence from PISA 2009 showed the extent of involvement of five major actors in four decision areas: staffing, budgeting, instruction and assessment. Results from Fig. 10.1 indicated that the School Management Board (SMB) appeared to have the highest level of involvement in the decision making of staffing (87 %) and

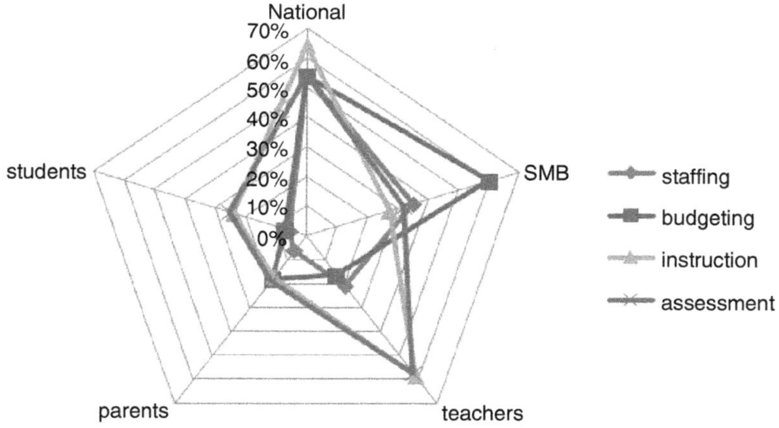

Fig. 10.1 Decentralisation to different stakeholders of Hong Kong in PISA 2009

Table 10.1 Comparison of level of involvement of different actors in the four decision areas (Hong Kong vs PISA 2009 average)

	Decisions areas	National (%)	SMB (%)	Teachers (%)	Parents (%)	Students (%)
Hong Kong	Staffing	40	87	9	0	0
	Budgeting	57	96	29	11	5
	Instruction	68	25	71	27	18
	Assessment	40	29	67	23	17
PISA 2009 average	Staffing	54	35	21	6	5
	Budgeting	54	60	16	18	7
	Instruction	65	27	58	17	24
	Assessment	54	32	57	19	25

budgeting (96 %). Teachers were more likely to be involved in decision making of instruction (71 %) and assessment (67 %). All these percentages of PISA 2009 are higher than the respective percentages in PISA 2000.

As shown in Table 10.1, parental involvement is much less than teacher and SMB involvement both in Hong Kong and in the other participating countries/ regions in PISA 2009 in almost all decision areas. While Hong Kong parents are not used to intervening in school activities as do parents in many Western societies, they still have certain influence over schools, either through their choice of schools or through their participation in school Parent Teacher Association (PTAs) and SMCs (Ho, 2010).

Major Forms of School Decentralisation

In PISA 2009, two indices were constructed to measure the extent of teacher participation and principal participation in 12 decision-making items. The 12 - decision-making items were measured in the principal questionnaire, covering the areas of: appointing teachers, dismissing teachers, establishing teachers' starting salary, determining teachers' salary increases, formulating school budgets, allocating budgets within the school, establishing student disciplinary policies, establishing student assessment policies, approving students for admission into schools, choosing textbooks, determining course content, and deciding courses to offer. Each item asked the principals who has the main responsibility for the different types of decisions regarding the management of the school. The response category could be 'principal' or 'teachers'. Choosing 'not a main responsibility of the school' was given a score of 0, and choosing others was given a score of 1. Scores were then summed across the 12 items for principal participation and teacher participation.

Cluster analysis is used to identify the possible forms of SBM based on these two indices (see Table 10.2).

Table 10.2 Results of cluster analysis

Z score	1	2	3	4
Principal participation	−.922	.923	−.436	1.036
Teacher participation	−.985	.057	.455	1.610

Table 10.3 Cluster distribution in PISA 2009

Four clusters	Number of schools	Percentage of schools (%)
1. Centralised	5,799	34
2. Principal-driven	5,142	30
3. Teacher-driven	3,955	23
4. Shared	2,249	13
Total	17,145	100

Table 10.3 shows the results from the cluster analysis, which identifies four forms of school decentralisation: (1) highly centralised model; (2) principal-driven model; (3) teacher-driven model and (4) shared model.

Table 10.4 shows the forms of school decentralisation in four East Asian countries/regions, Finland, the United States and the PISA 2009 average. Results of PISA average indicated that centralised model still dominates (36.5 % in 2009, 38.6 % in 2000+), and this is followed by teacher-driven model (increased to 27.9 % in 2009 from 21.5 % in 2000+), the principal-driven model (decreased to 19.7 % in 2009 from 29.2 % in 2000), and the shared model (increased to 16.0 % in 2009 from 10.7 % in 2000). Moreover, of the 65 countries/regions, it is difficult to find any country/region, which is managed by a single model, though some countries are dominated by a particular model in their education system.

Among the four East Asian countries/regions, Hong Kong, which was dominated by the principal-driven model in 2000 (Ho, 2006), has shifted to a shared model in 2009. Schools in South Korea and Japan were dominated by the centralised model in 2000. In 2009, Japan remains similar but South Korea has changed from mainly a centralised model to a balanced mix of centralised and teacher-driven models. Shanghai and Singapore participated in PISA for the first time in 2009 and therefore only their results of 2009 are shown. Shanghai is dominated by the teacher-driven model but Singapore is a balanced mix of all the four forms of decentralisation models. Finland is consistently dominated by a teacher-driven model, yet in 2009 it also blended its model with other forms of decentralisation. For the United States, it was dominated by the principal-driven model in 2000 but has shifted to a mix of principal-driven and shared models in 2009.

Impact of School Decentralisation on Student Outcomes

Data on teacher participation was collected from every cycle of the PISA studies. It was found that the degree of teacher participation increased from the international

Table 10.4 Forms of decentralisation in selected countries/regions (Ho, 2006)[a]

	PISA 2009				PISA 2000			
Forms of Decentralisation	Centralised (%)	Principal-driven (%)	Teacher-driven (%)	Shared (%)	Centralised (%)	Principal-driven (%)	Teacher-driven (%)	Shared (%)
Hong Kong, SAR	2.6	2.0	8.6	86.8	10.9	44.8	33.0	11.3
Japan	56.5	16.7	19.4	7.5	62.9	14.5	16.4	6.3
South Korea	38.9	5.7	39.5	15.9	62.6	13.3	23.4	0.7
Shanghai, China	9.9	15.1	53.3	21.7	m	m	m	m
Singapore	22.8	32.7	26.3	18.1	m	m	m	m
Finland	16.3	15.3	59.6	8.9	7.1	2.1	87.5	3.2
United States	7.9	38.2	12.7	41.2	3.8	55.5	10.8	29.9
PISA average	36.5	19.7	27.9	16.0	38.6	29.2	21.5	10.7

[a]Findings of 2000+ is from Ho's (2006) article
m = 'missing' since both Shanghai & Singapore didn't participate in PISA2000(+)

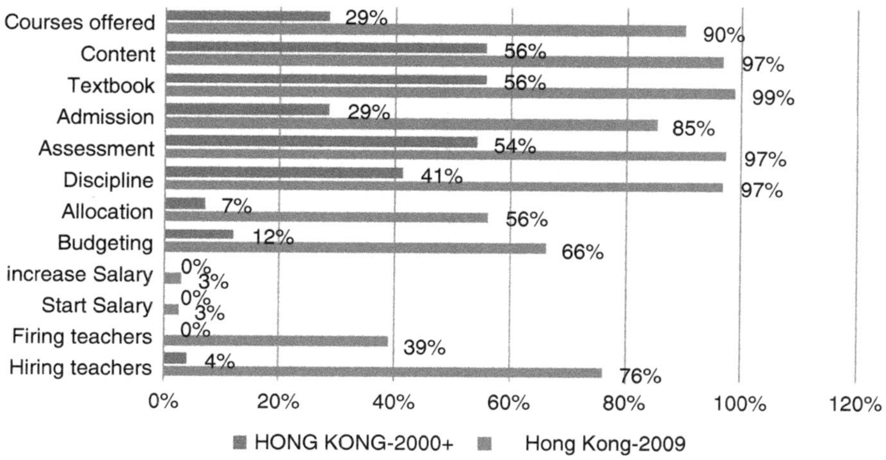

Fig. 10.2 Teacher participation in decision-making in Hong Kong 2000–2009 (Fok et al., 2009)

scale of −0.05 in 2002, 0.29 in 2003, to 2.02 in 2009 (Ho et al., 2005). The index of teacher participation of Hong Kong is top among the 65 participating countries and regions. To have a more accurate estimation of teacher participation over the past 10 years, we need to analyse the percentage of teacher participation in the 12 decision items.

Results from Fig. 10.2 indicate that teacher participation enhanced from 2000 to 2009 in all the 12 decision items. The percentage increase ranged from 3 % in establishing starting salary to 72 % in hiring teachers. In fact, over the past 10 years of SBM, teacher participation increased mainly in three main decision areas: (1) instruction, which includes deciding courses to offer, course content and textbook; (2) student affairs, which include admission, assessment and discipline; (3) budgeting, which includes allocation of resources and budgeting. These three areas are more directly related to the curriculum and students' learning.

These findings are consistent with previous review of the success of curriculum reform in mathematics. In reviewing the Mathematics curriculum reform of Hong Kong in the period of the 1940s–1980s, Fok, Wong, Tang, Ngan, and Wong (2009) noted that the Education Bureau had adopted various effective decentralised strategies in curriculum reform while centrally controlling the development (2009). The experience of success of Mathematics Education reform in Hong Kong suggested that reform using centralised top–down approach must accept voices from the bottom–up, especially those from professional associations so as to close the gap between policy and implementation (Fok et al., 2009; Morris & Scott, 2003).

Overall, researchers attribute the success of Hong Kong's basic education to the balance between various decentralised strategies under the government's centrally-controlled educational development (Fok et al., 2009; Jensen, 2012). However, Fok et al. noted that some teachers are reluctant to take on greater responsibilities that are outside their usual sphere of interest and competence in teaching. They are not willing to participate in administrative work that takes up their time and energy but are willing to be involved in areas that are directly related to teaching.

Regarding the impact of school decentralisation on student outcomes, Ho (2006) used multi-level analysis to analyse data from the second cycle of the Programme for International Student Assessment (PISA 2003). She found that the Hong Kong index of school autonomy (0.58) was well above the OECD average, while that of teacher participation was slightly above the OECD average (0.29). Yet, the study found that teacher participation is more important than school autonomy for students' mathematics performance in Hong Kong. In addition, the effect of teacher participation on students' performance is mediated by four major school climatic factors – sense of belonging, disciplinary climate, students' morale and student behaviour – in Hong Kong's secondary schools.

Quality Assurance Mechanism and Accountability System Under the SBM in Hong Kong

While allowing schools to have greater management autonomy, the Hong Kong Government has to make sure that schools are held accountable for the results of their decisions. Quality Assurance Inspection (QAI) was introduced in 1997 by the Education Department (ED) in the Education Commission Report No. 7 (EC, 1997). QAI in Hong Kong serves as a mechanism for external quality assurance to highlight the strengths and weaknesses of each school and to give a direction for improvement through the external inspections (ED, 2002). In 2003, QAI was renamed as the External School Review (ESR). In addition, Hong Kong benchmarks students' learning outcomes with the various kinds of international and national/regional assessments so as to capture the different kinds of student competencies attained at different levels of the system.

Review of the Multi-level Student Learning Assessment in Hong Kong

As shown in Fig. 10.3, at the international level, Hong Kong has participated in a number of international assessment studies including PIRLS (reading achievement at Primary Grade 4), TIMSS (mathematics and science at Primary Grade 4 and Secondary Grade 2), ICCS (civics of Secondary Grade 3) and PISA (reading, mathematics, and science of students of age 15).

At the local level, Hong Kong has the Territory-wide System Assessment (TSA), a national/regional assessment for all students at P3, P6 and S3, and the new local public examination, Hong Kong Diploma of Secondary Education (HKDSE)

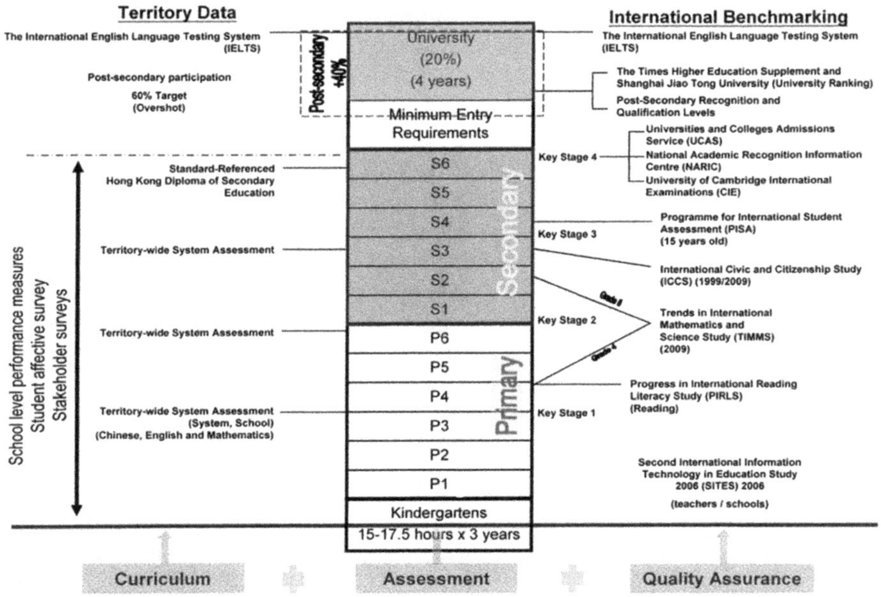

Fig. 10.3 Multi-level monitoring system of Hong Kong (Ho, 2012a)

Examination, which has just been implemented in 2012 for S6, the final year of the New Senior Secondary System. School-based Assessment (SBA) has also been integrated into most of the 2012 examination subjects, so that teacher assessment at the classroom level can cover a wider range of curricular outcomes that cannot be assessed in public examinations.

At the school level, under the current ESR policy, all schools are to conduct a student survey and stakeholder survey for parents, teachers and school administrators. Over 20 performance indicators are generated from these surveys. In addition, the Education Bureau of the Hong Kong Government constructs value-added measures of academic performance of schools based on their public examination results. Results of all these academic and non-academic indicators have been reported to schools annually since the Year 2000.

Challenge on Multi-level Assessments of Hong Kong

Building on the strengths of international assessments, national/regional assessments, SBA and public examination, Hong Kong has a very comprehensive mechanism to monitor school quality, in terms of both cognitive and non-cognitive outcomes, at different stages of schooling. However, although lifelong learning and all-round development of students are the ultimate goals of the current reform, there is still a large gap between the rhetoric and the reality in the use of assessment results.

For instance, although Hong Kong is putting more emphasis on non-cognitive aspects of students' performance in its performance indicators, academic performance is still the most important selection criteria for undergraduate admission. Even though students may score high in academic assessment, employers complain that some of them are of 'high scores with low calibre', that is, high achievers do not necessarily have sufficient problem-solving competency and communication skills.

School based assessment (SBA) is an important policy for the promotion of 'assessment for learning' by using assessments in a positive and formative way to understand students' strengths and weaknesses. However, when SBA becomes an integral part of the high-stake public examinations as in the case of Hong Kong, it must be administered by schools under strict directions regarding the substance of the assessment tasks, the condition of implementation and its scoring specification (Hill, 2010). A moderation process is usually employed to adjust the score of SBA before it can be combined with the public examination score, which is still very controversial at the moment in Hong Kong.

Overall, Hong Kong is still struggling to build a balanced system of assessment of learning (AOL) and assessment for learning (AFL). AOL is used for reporting, selection and accountability whereas AFL is used for educational improvements (James, 2010). The unique context of school choice policy in Hong Kong might heighten inter-school competition and rivalry, which bring about negative effects. That is, many principals will have to function like chief executives of large corporate organisations, requiring more managerial and marketing skills to deal with the increasing organisational complexities which often take principals and teachers away from a focus on teaching and learning. In sum, principals and teachers are facing a constant daily struggle to balance administrative accountability, client accountability and professional accountability.

Concluding Remarks

Is Hong Kong basic education really improving and successful under the current educational reform? It might be true that Hong Kong has moved from 'good to great' in terms of 'cognitive achievement' (Mourshed et al., 2010). However, the aim of education should not be merely raising knowledgeable and talented people, but also be nurturing people with integrity who care about social justice and the wider interests of the society.

Therefore, whether Hong Kong and other East Asian societies such as Shanghai, Singapore, South Korea and Japan can be claimed to be strong performers depends on how we define success and how we assess success. In fact, students from these East Asian societies share similar strengths in terms of high academic achievement, high aspirations, and good discipline in school. Yet they also share common weaknesses of low self-concept, high test anxiety and disengaged learning climate. This is the 'primary cognitive habitus' of East Asian societies basically nurtured by the similar Confucian culture (Ho, 2009).

Even if we accept using the cognitive outcomes of reading, mathematics and science as the basic criteria to judge the success of a schooling system, one might not be able to attribute the success to the current education reform. According to the 2010 Mckinsey Report (Mourshed et al., 2010), Hong Kong exhibited improvement even prior to the 1995 TIMSS. Therefore, the outstanding performance should not be an outcome of the education reforms launched after the handover in 1997. However, it should be fair to say that Hong Kong reform is on the right track and that reading performance and reading habits of students did improve substantially after the handover in 1997.

In search of the success factors beyond the current education reform, the present chapter argues that the dynamic interaction between decentralisation of SBM and centralisation policy of multilevel assessment might be the key contributors. Decentralisation policy provides flexibility for schools to make decisions in allocating resources and to diversify and innovate teaching and learning processes. This allows the government to decrease its involvement in direct policy implementation but to increase the autonomy of school leaders and teachers and involvement of parents to make changes at the school level to better serve the students.

The major challenge of school decentralisation in Hong Kong in the 1990s is that authority might not be shared at the school level. For instance, in PISA 2000+, Hong Kong had a relatively high level of school autonomy but teacher participation was still below the OECD average in the PISA studies. These results indicated that power delegated to schools might not be shared with teachers. The principal could become the 'little emperor/empress', as described by the SMI document (EMB & ED, 1991). Successful school decentralisation needs time and resources to involve teachers and other stakeholders. In the 10 years after SMI was revised into SBM, teacher participation enhanced gradually as reflected in PISA 2009, especially in the areas of instruction and assessment. Further analysis indicates that the SBM manifests itself in different forms – shared, teacher-driven, principal-driven or centralised forms. From an international perspective, the shared form of SBM shows the strongest association with students' learning outcomes, which is followed by teacher- and principal-driven models, and the centralised model is the worst model.

On the one hand, evidence from PISA studies indicated that the decentralised model of school governance appears to be most efficient in mobilising different actors and resources for students' learning. On the other hand, centralisation may be good for providing more equal learning opportunities for all children especially at the basic education level. Centralisation through standardisation of teaching facilities and learning outcomes might be important for enhancing not only equality of opportunity but also equality of outcomes (Ho, 2012a). As centralisation or standardisation of basic competence might provide equality, understanding the various forms of assessment in different countries might be the first step for the establishment of a comprehensive monitoring system.

To improve the quality and equality of education, further investigations are needed to study how strong performing countries utilise assessment results in informing stakeholders, in supporting decision-making in instruction, and in monitoring teachers, principals and schools. Assessments, as used tactically in high performing education systems, could be cost-effective tools to drive educational improvement.

Over the years, major international assessment projects such as PISA, TIMSS and PIRLS have an important impact on education systems worldwide. They have influenced the development of national assessment policies and practices in many countries, as well as pedagogy, teacher training and funding in some countries (Ho, 2012b). Yet, caution needs to be taken to avoid the techniques originally tailored for these international assessment exercises to dominate local assessment practices.

For future research, Hong Kong needs longitudinal surveys and in-depth case studies to examine the complex interaction and balance of the current centralisation–decentralisation policy and its possible impact on school practices and culture. These studies will be useful for educators, researchers and policy makers to better understand how the SBM framework coupled with multilevel assessments can lead to changes in the school system, including both positive ones and undesirable side-effects.

References

Brown, D. J. (1990). *Decentralization and school-based management*. London: Taylor & Francis.

Census and Statistics Department. (2012). *2011 population census: Summary results*. Hong Kong, China: Government Logistics Department.

Chapman, R. (1973). Decentralization: Another perspective. *Comparative Education, 9*(3), 127–134.

Chen, C., & Stevenson, H. W. (1989). Homework: A cross-cultural examination. *Child Development, 60*(3), 551–561.

Cheng, K. M. (1994). The changing legitimacy in a decentralizing system: The state and education development in China. *International Journal of Educational Development, 14*(3), 265–269.

Cheng, Y. C. (1999). The pursuit of school effectiveness and educational quality in Hong Kong. *School Effectiveness and School Improvement, 10*(1), 10–30.

Cheng, Y. C. (2000). Educational change and development in Hong Kong: Effectiveness, quality, and relevance. In Y. C. Cheng & T. Townsend (Eds.), *Educational change and development in the Asia-Pacific region: Challenges for the future* (pp. 17–56). Lisse, The Netherlands: Swets & Zeitlinger.

Cheng, Y. C. (2003). Trends in educational reforms in the Asia-Pacific region. In J. Keeves & R. Watanabe (Eds.), *The handbook on educational research in the Asia-Pacific region* (pp. 3–16). Dordrecht, The Netherlands: Kluwer.

Cheng, Y. C., & Walker, J. A. (2008). When reform hits reality: The bottle-neck effect in Hong Kong primary schools. *School Leadership and Management, 28*(5), 467–483.

Education and Manpower Branch & Education Department (EMB & ED). (1991). *The school management initiative: Setting the framework for quality in Hong Kong schools*. Hong Kong, China: The Government Printer.

Education Bureau (EDB). (2007). *Education reform highlights*. Retrieved from http://www.edb.gov.hk/index.aspx?nodeID=88&langno=1

Education Department (ED). (2000). *Transforming schools into dynamic and accountable professional learning communities: School-based management consultation document*. Hong Kong, China: Advisory Committee on School-based Management.

Education Department (ED). (2002). *Performance indicators for Hong Kong schools: Evidence of performance*. Hong Kong, China: Quality Assurance Division, Education Department.

Election Commission (EC). (1997). *Education Commission report no. 7*. Hong Kong, China: The Government Printer.

Election Commission (EC). (2000). *Progress report on the education reform (4): Learning for life, learning through life*. Hong Kong, China: The Government Printer.

Fok, P. K., Wong, N. Y., Tang, K. C., Ngan, M. Y., & Wong, K. L. (2009). 鑑古識今:從課程發展策略的視角看課程改革 [Learning from the past: To review curriculum reform from the perspective of curriculum development strategies]. *Hong Kong Teachers' Centre Journal, 8*, 73–85.

Hannaway, J., & Carnoy, M. (1993). *Decentralization and school improvement: Can we fulfill the promise?* San Francisco: Jossey-Bass.

Hanson, M. E. (1991). *School-based management and educational reform: Cases in the USA and Spain* (ERIC Document Reproduction Service No. ED 336 832). http://search.proquest.com/eric/docview/62895055/abstract/14103088D3F612F4FAF/1?accountid=10371

Hanushek, E. A., & Woessmann, L. (2007). *The role of education quality for economic growth* (Policy Research Working Paper No. 4122). Washington, DC: World Bank.

Hau, K. T., & Salili, F. (1991). Structure and semantic differential placement of specific causes: Academic causal attributions by Chinese students in Hong Kong. *International Journal of Psychology, 26*(2), 175–193.

Hill, P. (2010). *Asia-Pacific secondary education system review series no. 1: Examination systems*. Bangkok, Thailand: UNESCO.

Ho, S. C. (2003). Teachers' views on educational decentralization and parental involvement in an Asian educational system: The Hong Kong case. *International Studies in Educational Administration, 31*(3), 58–75.

Ho, S. C. (2006). Educational decentralization in three Asian societies: Japan, Korea and Hong Kong. *Journal of Educational Administration, 44*(6), 590–603.

Ho, S. C. (2009). Characteristics of East Asian learners: What we learned from PISA? *Educational Research Journal, 24*(2), 327–348.

Ho, S. C. (2010). Family influences on science learning among Hong Kong adolescents: What we learned from PISA? *International Journal of Science and Mathematics Education, 8*(3), 409–428.

Ho, S. C. (2012a). *Asia-Pacific education system review series no. 5: Student learning assessment*. Bangkok, Thailand: UNESCO.

Ho, S. C. (2012b). *Multilevel analysis of the PISA data: Insights for policy and practice*. Hong Kong, China: Hong Kong Institute of Educational Research, The Chinese University of Hong Kong.

Ho, S. C., Chun, K. W., Yip, D. Y., Wong, K. M., Chiu, M. M., Sze, M. M., et al. (2003). *The first HK PISA report: Monitoring the quality and equality of education in Hong Kong from an international perspective*. Hong Kong, China: HKPISA Centre, The Chinese University of Hong Kong.

Ho, S. C., Wong, K. M., Yip, D. Y., Chun, K. W., Law, H. Y., Sze, M. M., et al. (2005). *The second HKPISA report: Monitoring the quality and equality of education in Hong Kong from an international perspective*. Hong Kong, China: HKPISA Centre, The Chinese University of Hong Kong.

Ho, S. C., Yip, D. Y., Cheung, S. P., Lau, K. L., Wong, K. L., Lo, N. K., et al. (2008). *The third HKPISA report: Monitoring the quality and equality of education in Hong Kong from an international perspective*. Hong Kong, China: HKPISA Centre, The Chinese University of Hong Kong.

Information Services Department. (2011). *Hong Kong 2011*. Hong Kong, China: Government Logistics Department.

James, M. (2010). Educational assessment: Overview. In E. Baker, B. McGaw, & P. Peterson (Eds.), *International encyclopaedia of education* (3rd ed., Vol. 3, pp. 161–171). Oxford, UK: Elsevier.
Jensen, B. (2012). *Catching up: Learning from the best school systems in East Asia*. Melbourne, Australia: Grattan Institute.
Kim, Y. H. (2000). Recent changes and developments in Korean school education. In Y. C. Cheng & T. Townsend (Eds.), *Educational change and development in the Asia-Pacific region: Challenges for the future* (pp. 83–106). Lisse, The Netherlands: Swets & Zeitlinger.
Lee, W. O. (1996). The cultural context for Chinese learners: Conceptions of learning in the Confucian tradition. In D. A. Watkins & J. B. Biggs (Eds.), *The Chinese learner: Cultural, psychological and contextual influences* (pp. 25–41). Hong Kong, China/Melbourne, Australia: Comparative Education Research Centre, The University of Hong Kong/Australian Council for Educational Research.
Leung, J. Y. H. (2001). The politics of decentralization: A case study of school management reform in Hong Kong. *Education and Society, 19*(3), 17–36.
Li, J. (2005). A Chinese cultural model of learning. In L. Fan, N. Y. Wong, J. Cai, & S. Li (Eds.), *How Chinese learn mathematics: Perspectives from insiders* (pp. 124–156). Singapore/River Edge, NJ: World Scientific.
Martin, M. O., Mullis, I. V. S., Gonzalez, E. J., Gregory, K. D., Smith, T. A., Chrostowski, S. J., et al. (2000). *TIMSS 1999 international science report: Findings from IEA's repeat of the third international mathematics and science study at the eighth grade*. Chestnut Hill, MA: Boston College.
McGinn, N., & Street, S. (1986). Educational decentralization: Weak state or strong state? *Comparative Education Review, 30*(4), 471–490.
Morris, P., & Adamson, B. (2010). *Curriculum, schooling and society in Hong Kong*. Hong Kong, China: Hong Kong University Press.
Morris, P., & Scott, I. (2003). Educational reform and policy implementation in Hong Kong. *Journal of Education Policy, 18*(1), 71–84.
Mourshed, M., Chijioke, C., & Barber, M. (2010). *How the world's most improved school systems keep getting better*. London: McKinsey & Company.
Mullis, I. V. S., Martin, M. O., Gonzalez, E. J., Gregory, K. D., Garden, R. A., O'Connor, K. M., et al. (2000). *TIMSS 1999 international mathematics report: Findings from IEA's repeat of the third international mathematics and science study at the eighth grade*. Chestnut Hill, MA: Boston College.
OECD. (2010a). *PISA 2009 results: Executive summary*. Paris: Author.
OECD. (2010b). Shanghai and Hong Kong: Two distinct examples of education reform in China. In OECD (Ed.), *Strong performers and successful reformers in education: Lessons from PISA for the United States* (pp. 83–115). Paris: Author.
Salili, F., Chiu, C. Y., & Lai, S. (2001). The influence of culture and context on student's motivational orientation and performance. In F. Salili, C. Y. Chiu, & Y. Y. Hong (Eds.), *Students motivation: The culture and context of learning* (pp. 221–247). New York: Plenum.
Schleicher, A. (2012, May 23). *Hong Kong's Success in PISA – One system, many actors* [Web blog post]. Retrieved from http://oecdeducationtoday.blogspot.hk/2012/05/hong-kongs-success-in-and-pisa-one.html
Schneider, B., & Lee, Y. (1990). A model for academic success: The school and home environment of East Asian students. *Anthropology & Education Quarterly, 21*(4), 358–377.
Shon, S. P., & Ja, D. Y. (1982). Asian families. In M. McGoldrick, J. K. Pearce, & J. Giordano (Eds.), *Ethnicity and family therapy* (pp. 208–228). New York: Guilford.
Sue, S., & Okazaki, S. (1990). Asian – American educational achievements: A phenomenon in search of an explanation. *The American Psychologist, 45*(8), 913–920.
Suzuki, S. (2000). Japanese education of the 21st century: Educational issues, policy choice, and perspectives. In Y. C. Cheng & T. Townsend (Eds.), *Educational change and development in the Asia-Pacific region: Challenges for the future* (pp. 57–82). Lisse, The Netherlands: Swets & Zeitlinger.

Tsang, D. (1995). Public sector reform: Key issues and future directions. In J. C. Y. Lee & A. B. L. Cheung (Eds.), *Public sector reform in Hong Kong: Key concepts, progress-to-date and future directions* (pp. 3–14). Hong Kong, China: Chinese University Press.

Wong, N. Y. (2004). The CHC learner's phenomenon: Its implications on mathematics education. In L. Fan, N. Y. Wong, J. Cai, & S. Li (Eds.), *How Chinese learn mathematics: Perspectives from insiders* (pp. 503–534). Singapore/River Edge, NJ: World Scientific.

Wong, N. Y. (2009). Exemplary mathematics lessons: What lessons we can learn from them? *ZDM – The International Journal on Mathematics Education, 41*, 379–384.

Yao, E. L. (1985). A comparison of family characteristics of Asian-American and Anglo-American high achievers. *International Journal of Comparative Sociology, 26*(3–4), 198–208.

Yore, L. D., Anderson, J. O., & Chiu, M. H. (2010). Moving PISA results into the policy arena: Perspectives on knowledge transfer for future considerations and preparations. *International Journal of Science and Mathematics Education, 8*(3), 593–609.

Chapter 11
Perspectives on High Performing Education Systems in Finland, Hong Kong, China, South Korea and Singapore: What Lessons for the U.S.?

A. Lin Goodwin

Introduction

The notion of sharing and learning across international borders is becoming accepted and commonplace; there seems to be widespread (and growing) agreement that the intractable problems of the world are not unique to particular nations, but actually represent mutually perplexing concerns that require the collective expertise and thinking of the global community. Indeed, a particularly stubborn issue in one context is likely to have been similarly experienced in several other settings, but perhaps addressed differently and with different levels of success and outcome. Thus, there is a growing desire to learn from international peers and colleagues, especially those seen as high achieving or demonstrating strong improvement. It should come as no surprise then, that in education there has been increasing movement towards international benchmarking and comparisons in an effort to claim 'world class' standards, schools, and educators (Levin, 2012). As countries seek to grow their economies and jostle for resources and status on the world stage, most have turned a keen eye on a reform of the teaching profession given education as the accepted route towards upward social mobility, and teachers as the accepted key to quality schooling (Chetty, Friedman, & Rockoff, 2011).

In 2011, an International Summit on the Teaching Profession was held in New York City (NYC), the first-ever international summit on the teaching profession (Stewart, 2012). The summit brought together representatives from 16 countries for the purpose of putting "a spotlight on the importance of the teaching profession, and to begin to share the world's best policies and practices in developing a high-quality profession" (p. 3). There is particular interest in "look[ing] at high performing countries, Finland, Singapore and others" (Duncan, 2012) that consistently score well in international assessments such as PISA (Programme of International

A.L. Goodwin (✉)
Teachers College, Columbia University, 525 West 120th St., New York, NY 10027, USA
e-mail: alg25@tc.columbia.edu

S.K. Lee et al. (eds.), *Educational Policy Innovations: Levelling Up and Sustaining Educational Achievement*, Springer Education Innovation Book Series 1,
DOI 10.1007/978-981-4560-08-5_11,

Student Achievement). The success of the first summit led to a second a year later, again in NYC, this time attended by 23 countries, each of which shared its experiences and policies in relation to teacher preparation for the twenty-first century, teacher supply versus teacher demand, and the development of school leaders. The exchange of innovations, challenges, strategies and practices helps to "show where some of the successes and failures have been [and can] help to design new approaches, informed by the world's best practices" (Stewart, 2011, p. 26). This international conversation about the quality of teachers and teaching promises to be an enduring one, with the Netherlands hosting a third summit in March 2013.

Openness on the part of the U.S. to learning from international peers has been fuelled by America's lacklustre performance on international assessments, and a decline from first to fourteenth in terms of college graduation rates (Duncan, 2012). There is deep concern in the U.S. that the country is falling behind its peers across the globe, and that drastic reforms in education and in teaching are desperately needed to rectify this crisis. The international summits, hosted by the U.S. in collaboration with other organisations and agencies, are concrete indicators of America's current interest in lessons from other countries, particularly those that have achieved top scores on international achievement assessments such as PISA and TIMSS (Trends in International Mathematics and Science Study). One example is Finland, which consistently achieves high(est) rankings in international comparisons; other noteworthy examples include several Asian countries such as Shanghai, China, South Korea and Singapore. While each of these nations could surely offer much advice in the way of particular practice or national initiative, and each has its own unique story to tell in terms of its journey and struggle towards higher levels of achievement and excellence, the reality is that context matters and no one idea or strategy can be carte blanche imported from one country to another without losing something in the translation. So, the question is, if there are lessons to be learnt by one site from another, what might those be? What insights are powerful enough to transcend the practicalities, realities and limitations of implementation, culture, human capital, resource distribution, and local norms to support intellectual trade across countries?

In this chapter, I intend to address that question by focusing on the level of principle – big ideas or basic, fundamental lessons that we all need to heed if we intend to do right by all our children and attain the world-class teaching profession and education system to which every country aspires, but few have yet to fully realise. My focus will be on lessons that the United States might do well to adopt from these four high performing education systems, specifically Hong Kong, SAR, Finland, South Korea and Singapore, even while I would argue that these lessons are ones that have universal application and sit at the heart of meaningful education reform and excellent teaching. I will conclude with some thoughts about lessons the U.S. might do well to unlearn – as well as relearn – if its goal is to benefit from the example of high performing nations.

Lesson One: Teaching as a High Quality Profession – Attracting, Retaining and Sustaining Quality

All prevailing discussions about high quality education and strong achievement point to teacher quality as essential – the equation is fairly simple: quality teachers equals quality teaching equals quality results. If the objective is to have quality teachers in the system, it seems reasonable then to first recruit the best and the brightest to teaching, and then ensure that these strong candidates receive the best, most rigorous and relevant preparation designed to fully equip them to enact quality teaching in twenty-first century classrooms. U.S. Secretary of Education Duncan has consistently pointed out that, highly ranked countries such as Finland and Singapore recruit teachers "from the top third and sometimes the top 10 % of their graduating classes. They are getting the most committed talent, the super stars to come into education" (Duncan, 2012). Indeed, in South Korea, Singapore and Finland, teaching is perceived as a career of choice, one to which many young people aspire (Low, 2012) but not all can achieve given stringent requirements for entry and strong competition for a limited number of spots (Goodwin, 2012; Sahlberg, 2012). In South Korea, "the top 5 % of secondary students aspire to be teachers" (Cho, 2012, p. 24) and teaching is ranked "as their top career choice" (p. 24) by South Koreans. Teachers in Finland are selected from the top percentage of graduates and "in 2010, 6,600 applicants vied for 660 primary school training slots" (Taylor, 2011). Singapore similarly selects teacher candidates from the top third of graduates and "although teachers are in great demand. . .many people [are] unsuccessful in gaining admission to NIE (National Institute of Education)" (Ministry of Education [MOE], 2009).

Recruiting the most capable does require some monetary incentives, even while those who choose teaching consistently state that salary is not the most important factor in their decision to teach (Goodwin, Genishi, Asher, & Woo, 1997; Panisoara, 2008; Richardson & Watt, 2006; Sahlberg, 2011). Teacher salaries in Finland "are competitive compared to other professions" (Center on International Education Benchmarking, 2012), versus teachers in the U.S. who earn anywhere from 67 to 72 % of the salaries commanded by other college-educated workers (Organisation for Economic Co-operation and Development [OECD], 2012). In Singapore, teacher salaries were significantly upgraded by the government in 1996 so that they are now "commensurate with salaries for new graduates entering other fields that require equivalent preparation and study, such as engineering, law and business" (Goodwin, 2012, p. 27). In both Singapore and Finland, teacher candidates' university tuition is covered by the government, plus they receive salaries or stipends to support them during their preparation (Darling-Hammond & Lieberman, 2012; Goh & Lee, 2008). While undergoing preparation, Singapore teachers also receive benefits such as medical coverage, funding for materials, other equipment such as a laptop loan; once on the job as teachers of record, they are then eligible for additional compensation or bonuses for performance or increased responsibilities (Goodwin, 2012). In contrast, prospective teachers in the U.S. typically fund their own education and often graduate with substantial debt even as they enter a profession that does not pay well. "Perversely…there are currently greater subsidies for candidates entering teaching through alternate routes where they train on the job, than there are for candidates that choose to enter pre-service programmes that would prepare them before they enter" (Darling-Hammond & Lieberman, p. 153), which reinforces implicitly the message that teaching does not require specific know-how and encourages prospective teachers to short-change their own professional preparation for the sake of economics.

Still, as stated earlier, for teaching to be seen (and structured) as a high quality profession requires much more than generous levels of compensation. Potential recruits are drawn to teaching because they perceive it to be worthwhile and meaningful work that is well respected and highly valued by society. In Finland, teaching is "a most admired future career" (Sahlberg, 2012, p. 15), and seen as a 'top job' for the following reasons: it allows teachers to "fulfil their moral missions"; teacher education is "sufficiently competitive and demanding to attract talented young high school graduates"; and Finnish teachers not only earn above average salaries, but they can "climb the salary ladder as their teaching experience grows" (Sahlberg, 2011, pp. 76–77). Teachers are "highly revered by South Koreans…and highly respected by society" (Cho, 2012, p. 24); in Singapore, teachers are a clear national priority and are consistently featured in political speeches, public media, and national priorities as valuable and critical to the success and growth of the nation (Goodwin, 2012; Yip, Eng, & Yap, 1997). Thus, teaching is upheld as a high status career, one that only the best can enter.

But recruiting the best is not sufficient. Teaching as a high quality profession also ensures that its members are treated as autonomous, thinking professionals who can be depended upon to meet high standards of practice because they have undergone rigorous and extensive preparation. If teaching is to be a high quality profession, it must also insist that its members continually stay abreast of research and developments in the field, and must therefore provide the support and on-going professional development members need to enrich and deepen their knowledge and expertise. All three countries insist that teachers are formally prepared by universities and meet high standards for graduation. Indeed, a key reform strategy in the case of each was to move teacher preparation into the university, in contrast to the U.S. where reform legislation such as Race to the Top (U.S. Department of Education, 2009) and the proposed G.R.E.A.T. (Growing Excellent Achievement Training) Act (112th Congress First Session, n.d.) actually shifts teacher education away from universities to any number of 'providers'. Unlike the U.S., one cannot enter a government-funded or public school in South Korea, Singapore or Finland without this preparation; in Hong Kong, as of 2004, all teachers are required to be "professionally trained and degree holders" (Education Bureau, Hong Kong, SAR, 2008). This stands in stark contrast to the multiple alternate pathways available to U.S. teacher candidates, some of which completely bypass any preparation whatsoever in favour of a multi-choice, paper-pencil test, or recruit new teachers directly to the classroom where they learn on the job – and on students (Goodwin & Kosnik, 2013). Rather than multiple pathways, the one pathway is rigorous, university-based teacher preparation, a curriculum that is comprehensive, extensive, research-based and grounded in theory as well as practice (Goodwin, 2012; Sahlberg, 2011; Weingarten, 2011). Again this is directly opposite to trends in the U.S. where not only are alternate pathways into teaching proliferating, but alternate, non-university providers have received substantial (federal and private) funding to operate teacher training facilities, many of which have adopted an almost exclusively site-specific, practice-based apprenticeship approach that eschews advanced study, research or theory (Goodwin & Kosnik, 2013).

Not so in Finland where all teachers are required to have Master's degrees, while in Singapore, the goal is for 20 % of teachers to attain Master's degrees by 2020, double the current number (MOE, 2012). Singapore especially has implemented a variety of policies designed to enhance teacher quality including an entitlement of 100 h of paid professional development per teacher as part of their teaching hours, mentors assigned to every new teacher, and a variety of instructional, professional and personal supports provided through the Academy of Singapore Teachers, including support for further study, tools and instructional materials, on-line support and mentoring, and opportunities for reflection and renewal (Goodwin, 2012). In Finland, while professional development opportunities are undergoing further strengthening, teachers are afforded 2 h a week for 'pedagogical reflection' and work with colleagues on planning and curriculum development (Sahlberg, 2011; Taylor, 2011). Many Finnish teachers also possess or pursue doctoral study while teaching.

Lessons from Singapore and Finland make clear that any particular input is not a criterion by which teaching should be judged or conceptualised as a high quality profession; similarly, simply adding or subtracting – that is, manipulating inputs – cannot make a difference in academic achievement or success. Rather, it is more meaningful to focus holistically on the nature of teachers' work, and on the ways in which teachers as professionals are defined and supported. To illustrate this, one can examine a particular input that is perceived in the U.S. to be a key factor in student performance – the length of teaching hours in a school day or year. Among Americans, there exists a pervasive and common misperception that teachers in most countries put in more hours than their U.S. peers because school attendance policies supposedly require students around the globe, particularly those in high performing countries, to spend more hours in school than those mandated by U.S. states. The logic is that more instructional time results in improved achievement. However, OECD data directly contradict this misconception and indicate that teachers in the U.S. actually work far more hours than their counterparts in Singapore, South Korea and Finland, as well as teachers in many developed – and developing – countries (OECD, 2012). We see that "a typical middle-school teacher in Finland teaches less than 600 h annually...In the United States, by contrast, a teacher at the same level devotes 1,080 h to teaching over 180 school days" (Sahlberg, 2012, p. 17). These data refute Secretary of Education Duncan's declaration that the U.S. is at a "competitive disadvantage...because the United States has shorter school years than other countries such as India and China" (Streitfeld, 2009), and call into question the increasing number of schools that have extended their instructional day and year (Hull & Newport, 2011). In fact, five states recently announced that they would be adding a minimum of 300 more hours to their school year (Lederman, 2012) despite an absence of data indicating that more has resulted in better. The example of Finland, in particular, tells us that less can evidently be more, and that it is how teachers use their time that matters, not how much time they are required to put in. Finnish teachers are trusted to be thoughtful professionals who use their time not just for instruction, but also to make important decisions about curriculum, student learning, and assessment (Sahlberg, 2011); this is evidence of "Finland's respect for teacher autonomy" and the "recognition of teachers as high functioning performers with the ability to shoulder accountability" (Niemi, p. 21). Somehow, the U.S. might be wise to pay attention to this philosophy and practice given that "Finland scores near the top of every international assessment" (Lederman).

Lesson Two: Teachers as Professionals at the Centre of Educational Reform, Improvement and Accountability

It would surprise most Americans to know that teachers in Finland not only teach about half the time required of American teachers, they "do not need to be present at school if they do not have classes" (Sahlberg, 2012, p. 17). However, Sahlberg is quick to point out that this does not mean Finnish teachers work less hard than teachers elsewhere, but instead that part of their work is "devoted to school improvement and work with community" (p. 17). This notion of teachers as professionals who are essential if not key to school improvement and reform is emblematic of the high performing systems that the U.S. uses as benchmarks for success (OECD, 2011). In Finland, high quality teachers have "enabled schools to have an increasingly active role in curriculum planning, evaluating education outcomes, and leading overall school improvement" (p. 129). There is a high level of trust between educators and the community, and so "there is no achievement testing, probation or inspectorate to monitor teacher performance" (Niemi, 2012, p. 21). Rather, teacher accountability rests in the hands of educators themselves, all of whom exhibit a strong sense of ownership for the welfare of all students, and share a clear and public understanding that the learning and achievement of students is the professional responsibility of teachers. In fact, educational reform depends on the research of teachers, not just in Finland, but in Hong Kong and Singapore as well. Finnish teachers "are encouraged to contribute to the knowledge base on effective teaching practices throughout their career" (OECD, p. 237) while the Chinese "method for improving their education system over time relies on research performed by teachers" (p. 237). In Singapore and China, many teachers engage in action research as a way to examine and improve upon practice. The use of lesson study as an instructional and school improvement strategy is apparent in dozens of schools across both countries, and brings teachers together, during school time, to observe one another's lessons for the purpose of closely examining practice and researching better ways of reaching students and strengthening teaching. Lesson study is also a method whereby senior teachers mentor and support their novice colleagues. In this way, "the practice of individual teachers is open to inspection by the other teachers in the school, and the quality of teachers' practice is seen as a matter for all the teachers in the school to be concerned about" (p. 242).

Teachers as professionals are expected – and do exercise the right – to uphold standards of excellence and quality within their own profession. A personal example of this is a visit I made recently to a school in Beijing – one that my Chinese hosts characterised as ordinary, that is, not a special school serving the children of the elite. It was indeed a lovely school, filled with positive energy and bustling with activity. My observations of the school saw numerous spaces for children to have quiet time or gather themselves, there were little libraries everywhere, and classrooms were joyful and busy even while they were crowded with 40+ students per room. When speaking with the principal about teacher quality, I asked about the issue of weak teachers and about teacher evaluations. The principal informed me that the teachers in the school were in charge of teacher assessment, that she as principal does not play a key role. This was quite a revelation to me, and underscored the important part senior teachers play in teacher and school quality. Moreover, the principal informed me, after not quite understanding what I was asking about what happens to weak teachers, that weak teachers are supported and guided until they are no longer weak. This was very far from current notions of (punitive) teacher evaluation in the U.S., but was in keeping with the groups of teachers I saw planning together, going over lesson plans and talking together in teachers rooms clustered by subject. In the U.S., teacher evaluation is a top–down process that seeks to measure teachers according to the test scores they produce. Despite the fact that learning cannot be – and should not be – measured by a test score from a standardised test administered at a particular point in time during a school year, schools and teachers are being publicly judged and ranked according to these numbers, a practice that has the support of current administration and the Secretary of Education.

Early in 2012, the NYC schools publicly released thousands of individual Teacher Data Reports (TDRs), ranking teachers according to standardised test scores over the previous 5 years. TDRs were derived using Value-Added Modelling (VAM), a statistical technique that "calculates a teacher's effectiveness in improving student performance on standardised tests – based on past test scores" (Zhao, 2012), whereby the value-added – or not – is a comparison of where students scored against where they were expected to score. These scores were released despite the fact that VAM cannot take into account the many factors that influence achievement and despite the mounting evidence about the 'highly unstable' nature of value-added models of teacher effectiveness, so much so that "most researchers have concluded that VAM is not appropriate as a primary measure for evaluating individual teachers" (Haertel, Rothstein, Amrein-Beardsley, & Darling-Hammond, 2011, p. 5). The expert opinions of scholars and psychometricians alike have not changed the opinion of policymakers who continue to insist on the use of VAM to measure and rank teachers. In NYC, teachers who scored poorly were not only named, but some had their pictures plastered on the front pages of newspapers and were hounded by reporters who camped outside their homes, schools and the homes of their relatives. Each teacher was 'exonerated' in that one taught consistently highly performing students so the 'value' she was able to add could not be significant; the other taught a very small group of recent immigrants, most of whom did not speak English as a first language, some of whom had only been in the U.S. for 6 months, so the value she added could not be measured by VAM. This approach in the U.S. to identifying quality teachers and driving educational reform originated in large part with *No Child Left Behind*, legislation that requires annual testing in Grades 3–8 in math and literacy and put in place sanctions for schools that did not make adequate yearly progress. This 'punitive law' assumes

> that reporting test scores to the public would be an effective lever for school reform. . .that shaming schools that were unable to lift test scores every year. . .would lead to higher scores. . .that low scores are caused by lazy teachers and lazy principals who need to be threatened with the loss of their jobs. (Ravitch, 2010, p. 110)

At the 2013 international summit, the General Secretary for Education International, which is a global federation of teachers' unions, agreed with Ravitch, stating that public shaming of teachers and other such punishing strategies are "the wrong drivers for reform" because they are "considered invalid and disrespectful by teachers and. . .destroy morale" (Stewart, 2012, p. 4).

We see then that current and emerging U.S. policy around teacher evaluation and accountability is rife with sticks but short on carrots. As accountability is reduced to the ability to raise standardised test scores, teachers have been positioned as the problem and obstacle to reform. High stakes decisions – hinging on test results – not just about students but about the very lives of teachers, principals and schools, have resulted in survival behaviour on the part of educators that has not always been professional or even ethical, but is indicative of a climate of fear in the U.S. There is mounting evidence that states have lowered proficiency scores, tests have been dumbed down, and teachers and principals have engaged in widespread cheating; all in an effort to boost test scores and avoid harsh and demeaning sanctions (Ravitch, 2010). Clearly teachers are not being perceived or treated as professionals, while they, in turn, are reacting in self-preserving ways that do not always have the interest of students at the core.

Accountability in Hong Kong, SAR is quite different. Instead of being seen as separate, something to be imposed on teachers to ensure quality, accountability "is built into the system as social expectations, as fundamental in school leadership, as well as an essential part of teachers' professionalism. It is not about procedures and indicators" (OECD, 2011, p. 108). Indeed, the past decade of system-wide, comprehensive education reform in Hong Kong has consistently included teachers as decision-makers and actors; senior teachers were key participants in the numerous retreats, debates, training sessions and seminars which have resulted in deep and significant changes in schooling, teaching and learning (OECD, 2011).

School-based assessments are now an important component of examinations, an indication of teachers' professional autonomy (Poon & Wong, 2008). Likewise, in Finland, "learning and curriculum design decisions are part of the local school's jurisdiction" (Niemi, 2012, p. 21), and accountability is seen as a professional responsibility. The Finns take assessment very seriously but "do not assess for school accountability purposes" (OECD, p. 127); instead, teachers "do an enormous amount of diagnostic or formative assessment at the classroom level" (p. 127) for the purpose of continuous improvement of teaching and learning.

In Singapore, test data are consistently and carefully analysed, not for the purpose of calling out individual teachers or threatening schools with closure, but for the purpose of identifying problems, suggesting the re-distribution of resources and the use of appropriate supports and interventions. Educational reform deliberately involves practitioners through national conversations where ideas, issues and new policies are discussed and debated. For example, the Minister of Education's public address in September 2012 outlining new directions for schools and teachers (Heng, 2012) was followed by scores of conversation groups across the island, deliberately structured to engage teachers, university faculty, Ministry of Education personnel and other educators or stakeholders in the deliberate review of his plans. In addition, the newly formed Academy of Singapore Teachers (AST), as a "dedicated organisation focusing on teacher professionalism and the professional development of teachers" (Academy of Singapore Teachers [AST], 2012), exemplifies teacher accountability and ownership for renewal and improvement. AST brings together teachers at all levels – beginning, senior, master, principal-master, subject-specific – for the purpose of professional development and support, designed and delivered by practitioners. In keeping with the prevailing focus of education on building capacity and enhancing ability (Goodwin, 2012), among teachers as well as students, "young teachers are continuously assessed for their leadership potential and given opportunities to demonstrate and learn" (OECD, 2011, p. 240). Also, teachers have the opportunity to try out a variety of roles and positions within the Ministry, the National Institute of Education (NIE) and other schools through a 2–3 year period of secondment. This ensures that teachers' voices, perspectives and skills are routinely integrated into curriculum and policy development as well as teacher preparation.

Lesson Three: A Warm Lunch for Every Student – Ensuring a Basic Level of Care for All

The care and welfare of learners cannot be minimised when it comes to achieving positive educational results and high academic performance. The lesson here is simple yet profound – when children's basic needs are neglected, learning suffers. There are ample data that poverty and poor health have a significant and detrimental impact on a child's ability to learn (Basch, 2010; Brooks-Gunn & Duncan, 1997;

National Institutes of Health, 2012); in America, this is evident in the stubborn achievement gap that reveals a correlation between socioeconomic status and achievement. Unacceptable millions of children in the U.S. live in poverty, and millions more are considered low income (Wight, Chau, & Aratani, 2012). In a study of 35 'economically advanced' countries, the U.S. ranked second to last in terms of child poverty rates, lower only than Romania (23.1 % vs. 25.5 %); Finland ranked second from the top in terms of lowest child poverty rates (5.3 %; UNICEF, 2012). "Failure to protect children from poverty is one of the most costly mistakes a society can make" (p. 1), as witnessed by the finding that "17 % of the variation in student performance in the United States is explained by students' socio-economic background" (OECD, 2011, p. 33). Shamefully, nearly eight million U.S. children are without health insurance and "in 2009, nearly one in four households with children struggled to afford the food they needed" (Children's Defense Fund, 2012). Moreover, 1.6 million children are homeless, a figure that is growing, and among industrialised countries, the U.S. ranks the highest in terms of homeless women and children (National Center on Family Homelessness, 2011).

U.S. history tells us that schools and teachers have consistently been a convenient scapegoat when the country falls behind international competitors. While educators and education systems share in the problem – as well as any solutions – in terms of national well-being, they cannot be held responsible for the lack of basic care afforded all the nation's children, basic care of needs that are fundamental to learning readiness and psychological as well as physical wellness. In Finland, every student receives a daily warm lunch regardless of need or family background. Says Professor Hannele Niemi of the University of Helsinki,

> Warm school lunches are symbolic of our deep-seated value of taking care of the physical needs of all our learners. We provide for the essential human needs of ensuring inclusion and equity for all, and learning thrives because of these favourable conditions. (2012, p. 20)

These strongly held "societal values about what all children need and deserve" (OECD, 2011, p. 119) have been in place since the start of a reform movement that began in the 1900s and transformed Finland's educational system from poor to exceptional. This commitment resulted in Finnish schools that also offer a full range of health and counselling services, regardless of income level (OECD, 2011; Sahlberg, 2011), ensuring that learners are cared for as whole human beings. In the U.S., school funding formulas are determined in large part by local taxation, which means that wealthier communities enjoy 'wealthier' schools, not just in terms of materials, resources and physical plant, but also in terms of the depth and richness of the curriculum, and the quality, credentials, expertise and experience of teachers. In contrast,

> Spending patterns in many of the world's successful education systems are markedly different from those in the United States. These countries invest money where the challenges are greatest, rather than making the resources that are devoted to schools dependent on the wealth of the local communities in which schools are located, and they put in place incentives and support systems that attract the most talented school teachers into the most difficult classrooms. (OECD, 2011, p. 53)

In Singapore, extra resources are earmarked for struggling students, plus there is a deliberate focus on 'levelling up' so that lower performing schools are advantaged over schools that serve high performers. The Ministry of Education is now moving to a 'needs-based' approach to resource allocation to ensure that "low-progress students" and "low-enrolment schools" receive the support they require to increase achievement and positive outcomes (Heng, 2012).

However, any notion of resources must go beyond physical materials to conceptions of learners as diverse and capable, as well as opportunities to learn. In Hong Kong, China, Singapore and Finland, "parents, teachers and the public at large tend to share the belief that all students are capable of achieving high standards and need to do so" (OECD, 2011, p. 232). Finnish classrooms are inclusive and integrated so students are not segregated by ability and serve all students well regardless of background or income as evidenced by a 93 % high school graduation rate (Taylor, 2011). Both Singapore and Finland offer excellent technical and vocation education, nurturing different proclivities and capacities and providing multiple pathways to success. A particularly illustrative example from Singapore is the North Light School, a choice school that serves youth who have experienced multiple failures with/in other schools and at least two failed attempts in the Primary School Leaving Examination (PSLE). These arguably "lowest-progress students" are actually taught by "among Singapore's most qualified" teachers (*Edvantage*, 2012), who choose to work at the school.

Lessons to Unlearn, Lessons to Relearn

The Global Education Reform Movement or GERM is a set of strategies that have been shared and exchanged across several countries worldwide, most notably the U.S., U.K., and Australia. GERM, driven by economic and corporate interests as well as models, emphasises competition, standardisation, prescribed curriculum and test-based accountability (Sahlberg, 2011). This movement is more than apparent in the U.S. where there has been a significant narrowing of the curriculum to an almost exclusive focus on literacy and mathematics, heavy corporate involvement (and increasing control) in curriculum decision-making and education reform through massive and targeted funding, high-stakes testing with an attendant reward (and punishment) structure designed to elevate test scores as the indicator of learning (read achievement), bureaucratic or punitive accountability mechanisms instead of professional ones, the use of market strategies to address educational issues or questions, the ranking and sorting of students, their teachers and their schools, and the reification of market forces to drive and shape educational reform.

Yet, there is certainly little evidence that GERM has produced the kinds of quality results the U.S. is striving to attain; in fact, GERM strategies represent lessons the U.S. apparently needs to unlearn if it is interested in following in the footsteps of some of its highest-achieving international peers, all of whom reject, through their practices, this pathway towards education reform. Moreover, it is ironic that many of the strategies and activities that high performing countries now routinely employ to improve teaching and learning are ones developed or long practised by U.S. educators. Yet, these same practices – such as pedagogical content knowledge; action research; professional learning communities; progressive, child-centred practice; authentic assessment; and so on – are ones that the U.S. seems to have discarded in favour of quick fixes, teaching scripts, top down reform, and standardisation. These practices emphasise teachers as professionals and decision-makers, all learners as diverse but capable of success, accountability as a professional responsibility, and reform as a process done with, not on, teachers and schools. They represent lessons that the U.S. would be wise to re-visit so as to relearn ways of thinking about, and supporting, teaching and learning that place educators, students and their families at the centre of educational change, and perceives education as much more than an instrument of economic growth and international competitiveness. This brings the discussion to the final lesson that the U.S. would be well served to learn: that of placing values and fundamental beliefs about caring for children at the centre of education and educational improvement. High-performing countries such as Finland and Singapore demonstrate this deep value in the way they provide basic services for all children – and citizens – so that hunger, (poor) health and poverty do not interfere with learning, the choices they make in terms of resource allocation, and the support they provide to teachers and students that focuses on the whole person, not simply academic achievement measured in the most narrow ways. A particularly illustrative example of values at the centre of education is Singapore's TE21 model (A Teacher Education Model for the Twenty-First Century; National Institute of Education [NIE], 2009). Recently unveiled by NIE, TE21 is the latest national roadmap for teacher preparation and education for the next 5 years. It not only reconfirms values as the core for teacher knowledge and skill as indicated in the previous roadmap, but actually further deepens and expands values as the anchor for what all teachers in Singapore should know and be able to do. These values focus on the development of people and professionals as the avenue towards excellence and achievement and emphasise learner-centeredness, teacher identity, and service to the profession and community (2009). They are a reminder to all countries, not only the United States, that education is neither an industry, nor a corporation, but a perplexing, complicated, challenging and ultimately always a deeply human endeavour.

References

112th Congress First Session. (n.d.). *The growing education achievement training academies for teachers and principals act*. Retrieved from http://www.newschools.org/wp/wp-content/uploads/GREAT-Act-6-21-11.pdf

Academy of Singapore Teachers (AST). (2012). *About AST*. Retrieved from http://www.academyofsingaporeteachers.moe.gov.sg/about-ast

Basch, C. E. (2010). *Healthier students are better learners: A missing link in efforts to close the achievement gap. Equity Matters: Research Review No. 6.* New York: The Campaign for Educational Equity.
Brooks-Gunn, J., & Duncan, G. J. (1997). The effects of poverty on children. *Children and Poverty, 7*(2), 55–71.
Center on International Education Benchmarking. (2012). *Teacher and principal quality.* Retrieved from http://www.ncee.org/programs-affiliates/center-on-international-education-benchmarking/top-performing-countries/finland-overview/finland-teacher-and-principal-quality
Chetty, R., Friedman, J., & Rockoff, J. (2011). *The long-term impacts of teachers: Teacher value-added and student outcomes in adulthood* (National Bureau of Economic Research Working Paper # 17699). Cambridge, MA: National Bureau of Economic Research. Retrieved from http://www.nber.org/papers/w17699
Children's Defense Fund. (2012). *Children's health.* Retrieved from http://www.childrensdefense.org/policy-priorities/childrens-health
Cho, Y. D. (2012). Staying on top in internationally benchmarked tests: South Korea's secrets shared. In E. L. Low (Ed.), *Portraits of top-performing education systems* (CJ Koh professorial lecture series, pp. 23–27). Singapore: Office of Education Research, National Institute of Education, NTU.
Darling-Hammond, L., & Lieberman, A. (2012). Teacher education around the world: What can we learn from international practice? In L. Darling-Hammond & A. Lieberman (Eds.), *Teacher education around the world* (pp. 151–169). New York: Taylor & Francis.
Duncan, A. (2012, October 22). ED mailbag: Arne answers your questions. *Homeroom* [web blog]. Retrieved from http://www.ed.gov/blog/2012/10/ed-mailbag-arne-answers-your-questions
Education Bureau, Hong Kong, SAR. (2008). *Teachers' development.* Retrieved from http://www.edb.gov.hk/index.aspx?nodeID=269&langno=1
Edvantage. (2012). *NorthLight staff among S'pore's most qualified.* Retrieved from http://www.edvantage.com.sg/edvantage/news/schoolnews/990198/NorthLight_staff_among_S_pore_s_most_qualified.html
Goh, C. B., & Lee, S. K. (2008). Making teacher education responsive and relevant. In S. K. Lee, C. B. Goh, B. Federiksen, & J. P. Tan (Eds.), *Toward a better future; Education and training for economic development in Singapore since 1965* (pp. 96–113). Washington, DC: The World Bank.
Goodwin, A. L. (2012). Quality teachers, Singapore style. In L. Darling-Hammond & A. Lieberman (Eds.), *Teacher Education around the World* (pp. 22–43). New York: Taylor & Francis.
Goodwin, A. L., Genishi, C., Asher, N., & Woo, K. (1997). Voices from the margins: Asian American teachers' experiences in the profession. In D. M. Byrd & D. J. McIntyre (Eds.), *Research on the education of our nation's teachers: Teacher education yearbook V* (pp. 219–241). Thousand Oaks, CA: Corwin Press.
Goodwin, A. L., & Kosnik, C. (2013). Quality Teacher Educators = Quality Teachers? Conceptualizing essential domains of knowledge for those who teach teachers. *Teacher Development.*
Haertel, E., Rothstein, J., Amrein-Beardsley, A., & Darling-Hammond, L. (2011). *Getting teacher evaluation right.* Retrieved from http://edpolicy.stanford.edu/sites/default/files/publications/getting-teacher-evaluation-right-challenge-policy-makers.pdf
Heng, S. K. (2012, September 12). *Keynote address, Ministry of Education work plan seminar.* Retrieved from http://www.moe.gov.sg/media/speeches/2012/09/12/keynote-address-by-mr-heng-swee-keat-at-wps-2012.php
Hull, J., & Newport, M. (2011). *Time in school: How does the U.S. compare?* Retrieved from http://www.centerforpubliceducation.org/Main-Menu/Organizing-a-school/Time-in-school-How-does-the-US-compare

Lederman, J. (2012, December 2). Class time increases in five states in an effort to improve U.S. public education. *Huffington Post*. Retrieved from http://www.huffingtonpost.com/2012/12/02/class-time-increases-in-5_n_2229411.html

Levin, H. (2012). More than just test scores. *Prospects, 42*(3), 269–284.

Low, E. L. (Ed.). (2012). *Portraits of top-performing education systems* (CJ Koh professorial lecture series). Singapore: Office of Education Research, National Institute of Education, NTU.

Ministry of Education (MOE), Singapore. (2009). *Teaching as a career*. Retrieved from http://www.moe.gov.sg/careers/teach/faqs

Ministry of Education (MOE), Singapore. (2012). *New 'teacher' framework to enhance the quality of the teaching force*. Retrieved from http://www.moe.gov.sg/media/press/2011/03/new-teach-framework-to-enhance-quality-teaching-force.php

National Center on Family Homelessness. (2011, December). *The characteristics and needs of families experiencing homelessness*. Retrieved from http://www.familyhomelessness.org/media/306.pdf

National Institute of Education. (2009). *TE21*: *A teacher education model for the 21st century*. Singapore: National Institute of Education, NTU. Retrieved from http://www.nie.edu.sg/files/about-nie/TE21%20online%20version.pdf

National Institutes of Health. (2012, August 28). Stresses of poverty may impair learning ability in young children. *NIH News*. Retrieved from http://www.nih.gov/news/health/aug2012/nichd-28.htm

Niemi, H. (2012). Ensuring quality teaching and learning: Lessons learned from Finland. In E. L. Low (Ed.), *Portraits of top-performing education systems* (CJ Koh professorial lecture series, pp. 20–22). Singapore: Office of Education Research, National Institute of Education, NTU.

Organisation for Economic Co-operation and Development (OECD). (2011). *Strong performers and successful reformers in education*: *Lessons from PISA for the United States*. Paris: Author. Retrieved from http://dx.doi.org/10.1787/9789264096660-en

Organisation for Economic Co-operation and Development (OECD). (2012). *Education at a glance, 2012*: *OECD indicators*. Retrieved from https://www.oecd.org/edu/EAG%202012_e-book_EN_200912.pdf

Panisoara, I.-O. (2008). *Motivation for teaching career*. Retrieved from http://www.fpse.ro/index.php?option=com_content&task=view&id=802&Itemid=236

Poon, A. Y. K., & Wong, Y.-C. (2008). Policy changes and impact of the education reform in Hong Kong. *Journal of Taiwan Normal University, 53*(3), 47–65.

Ravitch, D. (2010). *The death and life of the great American school system*. New York: Basic Books.

Richardson, P. W., & Watt, H. M. G. (2006). Who chooses teaching and why? Profiling characteristics and motivations across three Australian universities. *Asia-Pacific Journal of Teach Education, 34*(1), 27–56.

Sahlberg, P. (2011). *Finnish lessons: What can the world learn from educational change in Finland?* New York: Teachers College Press.

Sahlberg, P. (2012). The most wanted: Teachers and teacher education in Finland. In L. Darling-Hammond & A. Lieberman (Eds.), *Teacher Education around the World* (p. 1721). New York: Taylor & Francis.

Stewart, V. (2011). *Improving teacher quality around the world: The international summit on the teaching profession*. New York: Asia Society.

Stewart, V. (2012). *Teaching and learning for the twenty-first century: The 2012 international summit on the teaching profession*. New York: Asia Society.

Streitfeld, R. (2009, February 27). Education chief favours longer school year. *CNN Politics*. Retrieved from http://edition.cnn.com/2009/POLITICS"/02/27/education.school.year/index.html

Taylor, A. (2011, December 14). 26 amazing facts about Finland's unorthodox education system. *Business Insider International*. Retrieved from http://www.businessinsider.com/finland-education-school-2011-12?op=1

U.S. Department of Education. (2009). *Race to the top program executive summary*. Retrieved from http://www2.ed.gov/programs/racetothetop/executive-summary.pdf

UNICEF. (2012). *Measuring child poverty: New league tables of child poverty in the world's richest countries* (Innocenti Report Card 10). Florence, Italy: UNICEF Innocenti Research Centre.

Weingarten, R. (2011). The role of teachers in school improvement: Lessons from the field. *Harvard Law and Policy Review, 6*, 9–38.

Wight, V. R., Chau, M., & Aratani, Y. (2012). *Who are America's poor children*? New York: National Center for Children in Poverty. Retrieved from http://www.nccp.org/publications/pub_912.html

Yip, J. S. K., Eng, S. P., & Yap, J. Y. C. (1997). 25 years of education reform. In J. Tan, S. Gopinathan, & W. K. Ho (Eds.), *Education in Singapore: A book of readings* (pp. 3–32). Singapore: Prentice-Hall.

Zhao, E. (2012, April 25). New York City teacher ratings: Teacher data reports publicly released amid controversy. *Huffington Post*. Retrieved from http://www.huffingtonpost.com/news/new-york-teacher-evaluations

Chapter 12
Sustainable, Large-Scale Education Renewal: The Case of Ontario

Ben Levin

Introduction

Governments across the world are attempting to change their public education systems in ways that support higher levels of achievement and, in many cases, reduced inequities in educational outcomes. However, many of these efforts have been accompanied by significant conflict as educators feel they are being blamed for ills not of their making, and being forced into what they regard as undesirable practices. *No Child Left Behind* (NCLB) in the United States is a striking example. It would be difficult to argue with its goals of high levels of achievement and reduced inequity. Yet from the outset, NCLB has been dogged by controversy and opposition, with significant doubt as to whether the strategy could possibly lead to the desired result. A substantial amount of energy and attention at all levels – teachers, schools, districts, and states – is being diverted from fostering better education to struggles over the desirability of the policy and some of the negative effects it is creating (Allington, 2002; Coles, 2003). Similar examples could be cited from many other countries (e.g., Fielding, 2001).

Scholars of change in education have contended that this climate of conflict is not inevitable. A growing body of knowledge suggests that it is possible to have large-scale education reform that does make a difference for students, does generate public support, and does engage teachers and other education staff in a positive way. The work of researchers such as Elmore (2004), Fullan (2007), Hargreaves (Hargreaves & Fink, 2006), Hopkins (2006), and McLaughlin (McLaughlin & Mitra, 2001) give clear indications of what is required for this to happen. As Levin and Fullan (2008) put it:

B. Levin (✉)
Ontario Institute for Studies in Education, University of Toronto,
252 Bloor Street West, M5S 1V6 Toronto, ON, Canada
e-mail: blevin@oise.utoronto.ca

S.K. Lee et al. (eds.), *Educational Policy Innovations: Levelling Up and Sustaining Educational Achievement*, Springer Education Innovation Book Series 1,
DOI 10.1007/978-981-4560-08-5_12,

> The central lesson of large-scale educational change that is now evident is the following: Large-scale, sustained improvement in student outcomes requires a sustained effort to change school and classroom practices, not just structures such as governance and accountability. The heart of improvement lies in changing teaching and learning practices in thousands and thousands of classrooms, and this requires focused and sustained effort by all parts of the education system and its partners. (p. 291)

This paper, written by someone who was a senior manager responsible for this strategy, describes the last 4 years as the province of Ontario, Canada has been engaged in just that work, moving from a system that was in constant conflict to one that is generating improved results for students and positive energy among educators. That effort has been informed by growing knowledge about effective change and improved outcomes in education (Levin & Fullan, 2008). Ontario's change process is focused on a few key goals while still paying attention to a broad range of student outcomes. The overall approach is respectful of professional knowledge and practice. Change strategies are comprehensive with an emphasis on professional capacity-building, strong leadership, targeted resources, and effective engagement of parents and the broader community. A substantial effort has been made to make main elements of change coherent and aligned at the provincial, district and school level. Key partners – the provincial Ministry of Education, school boards, schools, and provincial and local organisations of teachers, principals, and other partners – work together even though they do not agree on every aspect of the changes. The Ontario strategy is an example of large-scale change that is effective and sustainable.

Context: The Ontario Education System

Ontario has about two million children in its publicly funded education system, which is organised into four sets of locally elected school boards with overlapping boundaries, reflecting Canada's constitutional requirement for public support of minority language and Catholic schools. Thirty-one English public school boards serve about 1.3 million students; 29 English Catholic boards serve about 560,000 students; 8 French Catholic boards have some 60,000 students; and 4 French public boards have 13,000 students. School boards range in size from a few hundred students to about 250,000 students in the Toronto District School Board – one of the largest in North America. In total, there are nearly 5,000 schools extending across a huge geographic area – Ontario is 412,000 mile^2, or about the size of the combined states of North and South Carolina, Tennessee, Mississippi, Alabama, Florida, Georgia and Louisiana, or somewhat larger than France, Germany, Denmark, Belgium and the Netherlands put together. The provincial government provides 100 % of the funding to school boards using a formula that is always controversial, but attempts to allocate money on a combination of per pupil or school amounts and elements that recognise differing needs across the province (Levin & Naylor, 2007).

Although the six largest urban districts have about a third of all the students in the province, many Ontario schools are small, with the average elementary school enrolling about 350 students and the average secondary school having fewer than 1,000. Ontario also has a very diverse enrolment, with 27 % of the population born outside of Canada (1/3 of whom have arrived in the last 10 years), and 20 % visible minorities. The Toronto area, which has nearly 40 % of the Province's population, is one of the most diverse urban areas in the world and receives more than 125,000 new immigrants each year. Ontario's 120,000 teachers are organised in four unions that roughly correspond to the four school systems. Most of the 70,000 support staff – caretakers, secretaries, maintenance staff, education assistants and professional support workers such as social workers – are also unionised.

Education in Ontario has all the challenges one might anticipate – large urban areas and very remote rural areas; significant urban and rural poverty levels; high levels of population diversity and many English as a Second Language (ESL) students; areas with sharply dropping enrolment; and others with rapid growth.

From the early 1990s, for about a decade education in Ontario was troubled (see Gidney, 1999). Two successive governments introduced measures that deeply offended teachers, including reductions in staffing levels and increased workloads. These led to substantial labour disruption including many strikes and sustained 'work to rule' campaigns as well as lower morale and higher teacher turnover. In the late 1990s, the entire governance system was changed, including a reduction in the number of local school districts from about 140 to 70, removal of taxation powers from local districts coupled with 100 % provincial financing, and removal of school principals from the teacher unions. Funding was cut significantly in the late 1990s, leading to the reduction or elimination of many programmes and services, often with the worst consequences for the most vulnerable students, such as recent immigrants. At the same time, many programme changes were introduced including compulsory pencil-and-paper tests for new teachers, compulsory professional development requirements for all teachers, a more intensive programme of teacher evaluation, and new and supposedly more rigorous curricula in every grade and subject. Perhaps most importantly, the government was vigorously critical of schools and teachers in public, including broadcasting television ads that portrayed teachers as overpaid and underworked. Years of this environment led to significant public dissatisfaction, increasing private school enrolment, and poor morale among teachers. In short, nobody was happy with the state of public education (Leithwood, Fullan, & Watson, 2003; Hargreaves, 2003).

Education was a main issue in the 2003 provincial election. The Liberal opposition won the election with the renewal of public education one of its highest priorities and an ambitious set of policy commitments around improving education. A Premier and ministers with a deep commitment to public education brought strong political leadership to this file. Indeed, one of the implications of the Ontario case that does not get sufficient attention in the research literature is the necessity of strong and effective political leadership. Schools are public institutions subject to direction through political processes, which means that advocates of education reform must pay attention to political dynamics as the means through which improvement takes place (Levin, 2007). The government understood clearly that public education can only thrive if citizens have confidence in the public school system, so that they continue to be willing to send their children and provide their tax support.

The New Strategy

The Ontario education strategy that began late in 2003 has two main components and a variety of ancillary elements, almost all of which were part of the government's 2003 election campaign. These priorities were carefully developed by the Liberal Party while it was in opposition through intensive discussion with many stakeholder groups unhappy with the policies of the previous government and also through analysis of efforts in other jurisdictions, notably England.

The crafting of the platform reflected the political reality that to generate public attention, policy goals have to be few in number and relatively simple in expression (Levin, 2005). The two most important goals were the commitment to improve elementary school literacy and numeracy outcomes – including a significant reduction in class sizes in the primary grades – and the commitment to increase high school graduation rates. These priorities were chosen because of public concern about student performance in the province (Livingstone & Hart, 2005). Elementary literacy and numeracy skills as measured by curriculum-linked provincial tests had been roughly static over the previous several years (Education Quality and Accountability Office [EQAO], 2006), while high school graduation rates were actually decreasing following major changes to the high school program and curriculum in the late 1990s (King, Warren, Boyer, & Chin, 2005). The strategies supporting each of these goals will be described more fully a little later.

These core priorities were complemented by a range of other commitments. Some of these ancillary initiatives, such as strengthening school leadership or changing curricula, were necessary to support the key goals. Other initiatives, including provincial support for the negotiation of 4-year collective agreements with all Ontario's teachers, were essential so that all parties could focus on improving student outcomes instead of being consumed by labour issues. Still other initiatives, such as attention to safe schools and healthy schools, sustain public support for improved outcomes by letting people know that the basic needs of students are also being attended to. I will return at the end of this article to the problem of managing all these initiatives simultaneously. However, it is important to note that even where there is a strong focus on a small number of key goals, the ancillary and potentially distracting issues still require attention. Indeed, one of the problems with much of the literature on school change is the lack of attention to the challenge of combining a focus on teaching and learning with the necessity of managing a complex and diverse set of other issues in a volatile and highly political environment (see Levin, 2005; Levin & Fullan, 2008).

Literacy and Numeracy

Ontario's Literacy and Numeracy Strategy is aimed at improving literacy and numeracy skills for elementary school students, which improved only marginally in the 5 years prior to 2003 (Literacy and Numeracy Secretariat, 2007). The goal was to have at least 75 % of Grade 6 students able to read, write, and do mathematics at the expected level by the spring of 2008 – a 4-year time frame. While 75 % represents a substantial gain from the approximately 55 % of students who met this standard in 2003, the reality is that the public would not accept – and the education system cannot be satisfied with – a situation in which even one in four students fails to develop key skills that they need to participate fully in society.

The Literacy and Numeracy Strategy has focused on creating meaningful and sustainable change in teaching and learning practices in Ontario's 4,000 elementary schools (Literacy and Numeracy Secretariat, 2007). The main elements of the strategy include:

- creating a dedicated Literacy and Numeracy Secretariat staffed by outstanding educators from around the province to lead and guide the overall initiative;
- engaging school and district leaders to strengthen their focus on literacy and numeracy by setting ambitious but achievable targets and plans for gains in student achievement;
- developing leadership teams for literacy and numeracy – including teachers and administrators – in every school board and every elementary school;
- providing extensive professional development for educators to improve literacy and numeracy instructional practices, including adding two professional development days to the school calendar;
- changing the provincial testing programme in Grades 3 and 6 to take less time and to provide earlier and more useful information on student performance to schools and teachers;
- adding nearly 5,000 more new teaching positions to reduce class sizes from junior kindergarten (age 4) to Grade 3 to a maximum of 20 students in at least 90 % of classrooms by fall 2007, and providing support to teachers to adopt instructional practices that make effective use of these smaller classes;
- adding about 2,000 specialist teachers to enrich teaching in areas such as art, music and physical education while also providing more preparation and professional learning time for classroom teachers;
- providing high quality resource materials to teachers, including new curricula, curriculum exemplars and sample lesson plans;
- targeting attention to key underperforming groups, including some minority students, ESL students, students in special education, Aboriginal students and boys;
- implementing a voluntary 'turnaround' programme that provides additional support and expert advice for schools facing the most significant challenges in improving achievement;

- supporting research to find, understand and share effective practices in Ontario schools; and
- supporting important ancillary practices such as an expansion of tutoring (often by students in faculties of education) and a fuller engagement of parents and communities.

Increasing High School Graduation Rates

As of 2003–2004 only about 60 % of Ontario students were graduating from high school in the normal 4 years, and only about 70 % were graduating even after taking an extra year (King et al., 2005). These are clearly unacceptable levels in a knowledge society and are well below those of other Canadian provinces and many other comparable countries (OECD, 2005). Ontario's strategy to improve high school graduation rates has much in common with the Literacy and Numeracy Strategy but also some elements that take account of the specific challenges facing high school education. The province has set a target of having at least 85 % of entering Grade 9 students graduate from high school in a timely way by 2010.

Key components of the high school graduation strategy (Zegarac, 2007) include:

- engaging school and board leaders to strengthen their focus on student success by setting ambitious but achievable targets and plans for increases in credit attainment and graduation rates;
- developing leadership teams to support greater success in every school board and every high school, including a dedicated Student Success Leader in every district;
- creating and funding 'student success teacher' positions in every high school to act as champions for success for all students while also reducing class sizes in areas of greatest need. One of the most important elements of the strategy is to ensure that every student in high school is well known to and supported by at least one adult on staff;
- supporting effective use of data in schools and districts to track students' progress and intervene early where problems are occurring;
- building stronger transition models between elementary and secondary schools and paying attention to good transitions into high school for Grade 9 students;
- providing extensive professional development for educators to improve student success, including adding two professional development days to the school calendar;
- developing a focus on and resources for literacy and numeracy in all areas of the high school curriculum;
- expanding programme options through more co-operative education, credits for appropriate external learning, and dual credit programmes with colleges and universities;

- creating a 'high skills major' that allows school boards to work with employers and community groups to create packages of courses leading to real employment and further learning;
- passing legislation to authorise the strategy and also requiring students to be in a learning situation (school, college, apprenticeship, work with training, and so forth) until high school graduation or age 18;
- revising curricula in some key areas such as mathematics and career education;
- supporting research to find, understand and share effective practices across schools and districts;
- supporting important ancillary practices such as an expansion of tutoring and a fuller engagement of parents and communities.

Another noteworthy feature of the high school success strategy is the creation of a Student Success Commission, with representatives of the teacher federations (unions), principals and superintendents to support effective implementation of the strategy in schools. This collaborative effort of school boards, teacher unions and the Ministry represents an important new approach to dealing cooperatively and in advance with issues so as to prevent disputes at the local level.

Sustaining Elements

Both of these strategies share the key principles mentioned at the start of this paper – respectful, comprehensive, coherent, and aligned. These are the elements that are intended to make the changes significant and sustainable.

Respect for Staff and for Professional Knowledge

The Ontario focus on student outcomes rests on the belief that educators in Ontario schools are committed professionals who have enormous skill and knowledge to contribute to school improvement. The Ontario change strategy shows its respect for professionals in a variety of ways. In addition to those elements already mentioned:

- The public statements of the government and ministry are supportive of public education and the work of educators and support staff.
- The government abolished some policy elements, (such as paper-and-pencil testing of new teachers) which were seen by teachers as punitive, and replaced them with policies (such as induction for new teachers and changes to teacher performance appraisal) that are seen as supportive of professionalism. Staffing levels have increased despite declining enrolment, while teacher workload has been reduced and preparation time increased.

- The strategies build on successful practices in Ontario schools and involve extensive sharing of good practice. Almost everything that is happening at the provincial level draws on good practices that were already underway in schools somewhere in the province. Every effort is made to acknowledge publicly the good work of schools and districts.
- The strategies involve job-embedded capacity-building led by respected Ontario educators as well as experts from other places. There are many opportunities for teacher learning at all levels, from schools to families of schools to boards to provincial activities.

Ontario is supporting the development of learning communities in schools and boards through the creation of leadership teams in schools and boards, and the emphasis on sharing good practice.

Comprehensiveness

The Ontario strategy, while centred on a few key student outcomes, is not limited to those. The focus on literacy and numeracy in elementary schools is complemented by strong support for other curricular areas such as physical activity and the arts, both of which have been expanded in the last 3 years. The strategy explicitly rejects narrow views of teaching and curriculum.

The Ontario theory of improvement recognises schools as ecologies. Michael Fullan has played a key role in shaping the government's program, including his ideas about needing to pay attention to all elements of schooling simultaneously (Fullan, 2006, 2007). Thus the strategy gives attention to building capacity among teachers, to improving leadership, to involving parents, to changing policies and to adding resources – all at the same time. It is also important to pay attention to the issues that could turn into huge distractions – such as having collective agreements in place with teachers and support staff, dealing with safety issues such as bullying, and ensuring that school buildings are in good repair. There has been new action in each of these areas. The effort to be comprehensive, however, creates the challenge of overload, discussed a little later.

Coherence and Alignment Through Partnership

The nature of politics is that government directions can change quickly. Sustainable improvement in schools therefore requires real commitment and participation by all the partners – teachers, administrators, boards and the broader community. The Ontario approach builds on Fullan's (2006) "trilevel solution", in which governments, school districts and schools work together on common approaches and strategies. An explicit part of the strategy involves building strong relationships and close connections with boards, schools and other organisations. For example, the staff of the Literacy and Numeracy Secretariat work very closely with school district leaders to ensure that provincial and board strategies are aligned and complementary. At the secondary level, student success leaders in each board, funded by the Ministry, play an important role in ensuring greater alignment. This is a collaborative, not a top–down, approach to coherence.

The Ministry of Education has put in place several new mechanisms for consultation with partners on virtually all programmes and policies. There is a Partnership Table, which brings the Minister of Education together with all the major stakeholders on a regular basis. The Minister and senior ministry staff meet regularly with the main provincial organisations, including teachers, principals and superintendents. Parent and student organisations also play an important role in policy development and implementation.

The Ministry has worked hard to build positive relationships with school boards through greater consultation and more on-going communication. When boards and the Ministry fight in public, for example, over funding levels, the whole public education system suffers because citizens who pay the bill get a negative message about the system's ability to provide quality education.

Given the problems created in Ontario education over the previous decade because of conflict with teachers and support staff, the government took particular steps to involve teachers and their organisations in the development of policies and programs. In 2005 then Minister Gerard Kennedy played a vital role personally in ensuring that 4-year collective agreements were put in place for all teachers across the province, assuring a peaceful labour climate without strikes, lockouts or other withdrawals of service. These agreements not only gave teachers and students a multi-year assurance of stability, but also provided for increased preparation time and reduced workload through adding thousands of new teaching positions to the system.

Teacher organisations are also extensively involved in policy development and the teacher organisations have been provided with substantial funds to support their important role in professional development. Steps have also been taken to work more closely with support staff groups and to recognise their need for involvement and for professional development, although this is more difficult because of the variability in support staff roles and organisation.

Principals also play a vital role in the Ontario strategy, since they are widely recognised as playing key roles in school improvement. Ontario principals were forcibly removed from the teacher unions in the late 1990s, creating some very difficult relationship issues. In 2005, the Ministry issued a paper on the role of the principal that proposed a number of steps that are now underway to support principals in focusing on leading improvement in student outcomes. Professional development for principals has been expanded, and efforts are being made to improve some of their key working conditions, though the job of principal remains challenging.

The success of these efforts can be seen in the much more positive public positions being taken by stakeholder groups in Ontario, including school boards and teacher unions. Of course, differences and issues remain, but the overall tone of discussion has changed dramatically for the better.

Changing the very negative and combative public discourse around education in order to build public confidence was itself an important policy goal of the government. However, the efforts to build and sustain strong partnerships all take place within the common emphasis on improving student outcomes. They therefore have a common value core, and a strong focus on building capacity (Elmore, 2004) everywhere in the system to support students' success more effectively. In the end, people will support public education if they believe it is delivering good results for the province's children and young people.

Targeted Additional Resources

The government has recognised that significant education renewal does require resources. From 2003 to 2007, funding for public education increased by 24 %, which means 28 % on a per pupil basis. As with the dialogue measures, however, these funds have been allocated judiciously to support the student achievement agenda. The largest single portion has gone to salary increases for staff so that schools can attract and retain good people. Another very significant amount has been used to expand staffing in key areas, such as smaller classes in primary grades, student success teachers in high schools, specialist teachers in elementary schools to provide increased preparation time and professional development for teachers, more support staff in key areas, significant renovations and repairs to aging buildings, anti-bullying programmes and the various other elements of the strategies. Additional funding has also gone to small and isolated schools to expand the services they can offer. The point has never been simply to provide more funds, but has always focused on resources to support better outcomes for students.

Testing and Accountability

Ontario has provincial testing of all students in mathematics and language (English or French) in Grades 3 and 6 as well as mathematics in Grade 9. There are no provincial high school exit examinations (as there are in most other provinces) but there is a grade 10 literacy requirement that students must pass, either through success on a provincial test or success in a school course, in order to graduate from high school.

While these tests were quite controversial when initiated by a previous government a decade ago, they are less so today for five reasons:

- The tests have very substantial public support as shown in repeated opinion polling (Livingstone & Hart, 2005). Ontario citizens and taxpayers believe some form of provincial testing is important.
- The tests are strongly linked to Ontario curricula and support a high-skill, effective pedagogy model. Indeed, student performance in 2006 was weakest in areas such as inference and comprehension (Education Quality and Accountability Office [EQAO], 2006), putting increased emphasis on higher order skills. Ontario teachers and Ontario policy are in agreement that a 'test preparation' approach is both inappropriate and ineffective.
- Schools are increasingly, with support from the Ministry, using the test results and their own local data to support their own planning for improvement.
- The tests have been streamlined to take less time while also providing earlier and more useful feedback to schools and teachers.
- While the results of the tests are public, the Ministry discourages school to school comparisons. In releasing results, the testing agency (Education Quality and Accountability Office) focuses on success stories and on recognising the excellent work being done in many schools.

Ontario has also adopted a broader strategy for public accountability, in which the Province and school districts are encouraged to report publicly on a variety of indicators of student progress. For example, the Ministry issues an annual report that provides information about all 72 school districts on eight key indicators (http://www.edu.gov.on.ca/eng/bpr). All of this is intended to foster and support public confidence in the quality of public education.

Political Leadership

It is important to mention again – though space here does not permit a full discussion – the vital role of strong political leadership across the education system. Change in Ontario has been driven by provincial politicians – the Premier and three successive ministers of education, each of whom has helped advance the same agenda. Schools and districts have been able to focus on the same priorities for 4 years. Sustainable change has also been supported by many other political actors, including elected school boards and the leadership of provincial organisations including trustees, parents, teachers, students and administrators. This consensus has not been forced by the provincial government, but has been carefully built through the kinds of measures just discussed. Differences naturally remain among the parties, and can sometimes be heated. But in an atmosphere of increasing trust it is more common for all parties to attempt to work out differences through discussion and compromise rather than through public battles. This political work of building consensus and trust must be an essential element in any programme of education reform (Hubbard, Stein, & Mehan, 2006).

Results So Far

The two main strategies are relatively new. The Literacy and Numeracy Secretariat only began operation early in 2005, and the most important elements of the Student Success Strategy only came into place later in 2005. However, neither started from zero but built on work already underway in a number of school boards. Because of this foundation, the Literacy and Numeracy Secretariat was able in less than 2 school years to have a substantial impact on teaching practices and on students' results. Results on Ontario's provincial assessment have improved substantially and broadly in each of the last 3 years. Overall about 10 % more students, or 15,000 per grade, are now achieving the provincial standard (Literacy and Numeracy Secretariat, 2007; full results are available at http://www.e-qao.com). The number of schools with very low performance has fallen by three-fourths (Literacy and Numeracy Secretariat). The system as a whole is half way towards the target of 75 %, though that target itself is not an end-point. Nor are these results just a matter of test taking. Gains on tests only matter if they represent real improvements in students' skills, and teachers across the province confirm that we are seeing real skill improvements for students, not just increases in test results.[1]

The indicators for high school improvement are also positive. Graduation rates have begun to rise – from 68 to 73 % in 2005–2006 (Zegarac, 2007). Results on the provincial grade 10 literacy test – not a particular focus of the changes – improved substantially in 2005 and 2006 (full results at http://www.eqao.com). Credit accumulation in Grades 9 and 10, which so strongly predicts graduation, is also improving so there should be further significant improvements in graduation rates in the next few years.

Just as importantly, there is a level of energy and enthusiasm in Ontario schools that has not been seen for quite some time. Fewer young teachers are leaving the profession and fewer teachers are choosing early retirement – tangible indicators of improved teacher morale.[2] Thousands of teachers are participating voluntarily in summer professional development programmes offered by the teacher unions and school districts. More teachers are giving positive responses to surveys of their level of satisfaction with their work (Ontario College of Teachers, 2006).

[1] This claim is based on the author's visits to more than 100 schools across Ontario as well as conversations with leaders in all districts and all major stakeholder organisations. All Ontario education leaders will acknowledge the very significant improvement in teacher morale since 2003.

[2] The Ministry of Education spent an additional $30 million on salaries for teachers in each of 2005–2006 and 2006–2007 because the number of teachers actually retiring fell significantly below the projections based on teacher age profiles and previous years' retirement patterns. That is, many fewer teachers retired in each year than had been anticipated.

Challenges

No change of this magnitude occurs without challenges. Four are particularly important to note. First, 2 or 3 years of improvement are only a start. Much remains to be done. For example, although achievement levels are increasing, some groups, such as students in special education or recent immigrants or Aboriginal students, remain far behind (Literacy and Numeracy Secretariat, 2007). Substantial effort has been invested in areas such as improving the physical condition of buildings and improving services to high need students, but nobody would claim that these challenges have yet been fully met.

Second, despite improved morale, Ontario educators are feeling that they are being asked to address many initiatives all at the same time (Ontario College of Teachers, 2006). Even though most people are positive about the elements of change, putting them all together has brought stress – though of a more positive variety than was experienced a few years ago during all the labour disruption. Many teachers, and especially principals, feel overloaded, yet sustainability depends on people seeing the long-term task as feasible as well as challenging. One might describe the situation as being a bit like eating all the Halloween candies at once; each one tastes good but too many at one time does not produce a happy result.

This situation is slowly improving as there are fewer new initiatives and more focus on deeper implementation of those already underway. Capacity-building and support provide more depth and experience so also reduce the stress of the new. Nonetheless, at all levels of the system there is still a need for more alignment and coherence, and fewer distracting issues. Although Ontario districts vary greatly in size and infrastructure, this does not appear to be a critical factor; districts of widely different sizes are showing progress (Campbell & Fullan, 2006).

A third challenge has to do with resources. As noted, the government has increased funding for public education by 24 % since the fall of 2003. Health and Education are the only areas of provincial spending to grow significantly over the past few years. However, schools and boards still face financial pressures in matching resources to demands. All partners will need to continue to work hard to ensure that resources are used as productively as possible. In addition to new resources, this means re-examining current allocations of staff and funds to assess whether these actually are the most effective ways to use resources in support of students. In many areas – from transportation to special education to professional development to use of substitute teachers – there may be opportunities to improve efficiency. The allocation of resources is an important area for more research and more effective application of existing research knowledge. For example, practices such as retaining students in grade or keeping students for a fifth year of high school effectively reduce the resources available for more effective strategies such as early intervention for success (Allington 2002). Effective use of research evidence and data will be critical in this effort to learn more about practices that are more effective, and share that knowledge more widely.

Managing resources will never be easy. In a field like education there will always be more demands for additional services than can be supported. Priority choices can be hard, and intensely political, which makes it all the more important for everyone to make a concerted effort to share what is known about how resource allocations support good outcomes for every students.

Finally, the Ontario approach poses challenges around the balance between support for and criticism of change. Even the strongest supporters of the Ontario strategy would admit that not everything is perfect; there have been bumps on the road and there remain areas of tension and insufficient progress. Governments do tend to try to focus on success and play down problems. Criticism based on evidence plays an important role in helping to identify areas for further improvement. That is why the Ministry of Education is funding credible third parties to undertake public evaluations of its major strategies, with initial results available in the early fall of 2007.

In his post-war novel, *Billiards at Half-past Nine*, Boll (1959) makes the point that it is much quicker and easier to destroy something than it is to build it. This is certainly true of large-scale change in education. The accomplishments in Ontario remain fragile. If government policy were to change significantly, or if other issues were to occur that refocused attention on areas of conflict, the gains of the last few years could largely disappear. There are always groups, including political opposition groups and elements within each of the stakeholder organisations that are looking for increased conflict; that is simply a reality of politics. In that sense, sustainable improvement, like many other human goods, requires constant and relentless attention and reinforcement. It can never be taken for granted but has to be recreated continually.

The challenge is to balance reasonable and necessary criticism with recognition of the danger that too much negativity may undermine the good work and strengthen the hand of those who want to attack public education. In any change effort, it is important to find the right balance of pressure to do better and support for those who are trying hard to do the right thing. This is true for all parties, including researchers, stakeholder groups and system leaders.

Conclusion

The current strategy in Ontario is intended to create an atmosphere of "positive pressure" (Fullan, 2007) that creates the conditions for people at all levels to invest the energy and commitment necessary for the hard and rewarding work of continuous reform. Positive pressure provides resources, increases expectations, furnishes data on an on-going basis connected to further reform, avoids unfair comparisons among schools and interprets results based on multi-year trends. Success is celebrated, blame avoided, and lack of improvement is addressed in a transparent and supportive manner.

Change researchers have argued that there is a body of knowledge that can support effective and satisfying improvement in public education. The Ontario case is an example of large-scale change in education that is respectful of educators, fair to students and communities, and based on the best available knowledge. It is not perfect and remains vulnerable should the political situation change significantly. However, this case does show that when many of the right elements are brought together, both better results for students and higher satisfaction for educators can ensue.

Acknowledgments This article was first published on 18 July 2007 in *The Journal of Educational Change*, *8*, 323–336. The author acknowledges that this paper was written by an insider with a deep commitment to the changes being made in Ontario. Space precludes detailed description of or evidence on many elements of the strategy. More details, including data on outcomes and strategies, can be found on the website of the Ontario Ministry of Education – http://www.edu.gov.on.ca. The author acknowledges the intellectual contribution to the strategy and to the ideas in this paper from many colleagues in the Ministry, but particularly from Michael Fullan and Avis Glaze. However, the paper represents his personal perspective only and should not be interpreted as the official position of the Ontario government or Ministry of Education.

References

Allington, R. (2002). *Big brother and the national reading curriculum: How ideology trumped evidence*. Portsmouth, UK: Heinemann.

Boll, H. (1959). *Billiards at half-past nine*. London: Penguin.

Campbell, C., & Fullan, M. (2006). *Unlocking potential for learning: effective district-wide strategies to raise student achievement in literacy and numeracy*. Toronto, Canada: Queen's Printer. Retrieved from http://www.edu.gov.on.ca/eng/literacynumeracy/inspire/research/ProjectReport_full.Pdf

Coles, G. (2003). *Reading the naked truth: Literacy, legislation and lies*. Portsmouth, UK: Heinemann.

Education Quality and Accountability Office (EQAO). (2006). *The grades 3, 6, and 9, provincial report, 2005–2006: English-Language Schools*. Retrieved from http://www.eqao.com/pdf_E/06/06P031E.pdf

Elmore, R. (2004). *School reform from the inside out*. Cambridge, MA: Harvard University Press.

Fielding, M. (Ed.). (2001). *Taking education really seriously: Four years of hard labour*. London: Routledge Falmer.

Fullan, M. (2006). *Turnaround leadership*. Thousand Oaks, CA/Toronto, Canada: Corwin & Ontario Principals Council.

Fullan, M. (2007). *The new meaning of educational change* (4th ed.). New York: Teachers College Press.

Gidney, R. (1999). *From Hope to Harris: The reshaping of Ontario's schools*. Toronto, Canada: University of Toronto Press.

Hargreaves, A. (2003). *Teaching in the knowledge society*. New York: Teachers College Press.

Hargreaves, A., & Fink, D. (2006). *Sustainable leadership*. San Francisco: Wiley.

Hopkins, D. (2006). *Every school a great school: Meeting the challenge of large scale, long term educational reform*. London: Specialist Schools Trust.

Hubbard, L., Stein, M., & Mehan, H. (2006). *Reform as learning*. New York: Routledge.

King, A. J. C., Warren, W. K., Boyer, J. C., & Chin, P. (2005). *Double cohort study* (Phase 4 report). Retrieved from Ontario Ministry of Education website: http://www.edu.gov.on.ca/eng/policyfunding/reports.html

Leithwood, K., Fullan, M., & Watson, N. (2003). *The schools we need*. Toronto, Canada: OISE/University of Toronto Press.

Levin, B. (2005). *Governing education*. Toronto, Canada: University of Toronto Press.

Levin, B. (2007). Inevitable tensions in managing large-scale public service reform. In M. Wallace, M. Fertig, & E. Schneller (Eds.), *Managing change in the public services* (pp. 136–150). Oxford, UK: Blackwell.

Levin, B., & Fullan, M. (2008). Learning about system renewal. *Educational Management Administration & Leadership, 36*(2), 289–303.

Levin, B., & Naylor, N. (2007). Using resources effectively in education. In J. Burger, P. Klinck & C. Webber (Eds.), *A general theory of everything in education*. Dordrecht, The Netherlands: Kluwer.

Literacy and Numeracy Secretariat. (2007). *Making it happen*. Toronto, Canada: Ontario Ministry of Education. Retrieved from http://www.edu.gov.on.ca/eng/literacynumeracy/makeithappen.pdf

Livingstone, D., & Hart, E. (2005). *Public attitudes towards education in Ontario, 2004*. Toronto, Canada: OISE.

McLaughlin, M., & Mitra, D. (2001). Theory-based change and change-based theory: Going deeper, going broader. *Journal of Educational Change, 2*, 301–323.

OECD. (2005). *Education at a glance*. Paris: Author.

Ontario College of Teachers. (2006). *State of the teaching profession 2006: Annual Survey* (A COMPAS report). Retrieved from Ontario College of Teachers website: http://www.oct.ca/~/media/A5A448A2183E491AAAF5B3B7AD815558.ashx

Zegarac, G. (2007, April 11). *Secondary school reform in Ontario and the role of research, evaluation and indicator data*. Paper presented to the American Educational Research Association, Chicago, IL.

Chapter 13
Comparative Analysis of High Performing Education Systems: Teachers, Teaching and Teacher Education as Factors of Success

Wing On Lee

Introduction: PISA Fevers and Education Miracles

Today, we are living in a globalised world with an active turnover of information about education performance, which is available for immediate analysis with transparency. We are also living in a world in which multiple agencies can participate in defining educational achievements, such as international research organisations, consultancy companies and non-governmental organisations. We are, thus, living in a world that is keen to contemplate what counts as success and define success factors, from diverse perspectives. Our joint efforts in offering our lens to look at successful experiences will be essential and helpful for the global community to identify success factors that could be useful for developing the education agenda in their respective nations.

But in addition to these Asian miracles, Finland has also created a 'Finnish miracle', being ranked top consistently in many of these studies, including the most recently released International Association for the Evaluation of Educational Achievement's (IEA) International Civic and Citizenship Education Study (ICCS) Report (Schultz, Ainley, Fraillon, Kerr, & Losito, 2010). It is, therefore, intriguing to investigate if these high performing education systems (HPES) in Asia are more Finn-like or Finland is more Asian. Another factor common to these HPES is the value that the society holds for education. The consistent success of this small number of jurisdictions has also raised an intriguing question as these relatively smaller states are ranked high in contrast to the many larger participating countries that have tended to be ranked middle to lower in the international benchmarked tests. This leads to the question: If 'small is indeed beautiful', would the size of a country impact the effectiveness of governing the average success of students nationwide?

W.O. Lee (✉)
Office of Education Research, National Institute of Education, 1 Nanyang Walk, Singapore 637616, Singapore
e-mail: wingon.lee@nie.edu.sg

S.K. Lee et al. (eds.), *Educational Policy Innovations: Levelling Up and Sustaining Educational Achievement*, Springer Education Innovation Book Series 1,
DOI 10.1007/978-981-4560-08-5_13,

The 'PISA fever' went viral across nations as Education Ministers, high-level policymakers, researchers, administrators and educators investigated how these HPES continually better themselves to equip their students with twenty-first century skills. International meetings were staged and subsequent publications were penned to appraise what and how HPES have done to raise the bar (e.g., Ministry of Education [MOE], Singapore, 2009). Schools visits, meetings, summits, roundtables, reports and publications also highlighted the immerse importance of providing high quality education for all, coherence throughout the systems (policies and work systems) and a quality teaching workforce.

Phenomenal International Summits on High Performing Education Systems

Among the various factors of success that has been surfaced for discussion, factors that have attracted the greatest attention are teacher, teaching and teacher education. The prestige of the teaching profession has been elevated and the Asia Society organised the International Summit on the Teaching Profession, "Improving Teacher Quality around the World" in New York, US in March 2011 to engage countries in a discussion about outstanding practices for recruiting, preparing, developing, supporting, retaining, evaluating and compensating world-class teachers. Three months later, the 14th OECD Japan seminar, "Strong Performers, Successful Reformers in Education", was held in Tokyo, where high-level policymakers, administrators, researchers and educators gathered to uncover the design and implementation of educational reform and programs that underpin success in countries that have shown consistently strong student learning performance or that have seen rapid improvement in recent years. Down-under, the Grattan Institute convened a roundtable that brought together educators from Australia and four of the world's top five school systems: Shanghai, Hong Kong, Singapore and South Korea to analyse the success of the four outstanding systems and the lessons it provided for Australia and other countries.

These meetings subsequently led to the release of reports and publications including *Improving Teacher Quality around the World: The International Summit on the Teaching Profession* (Asia Society, 2011), *Surpassing Shanghai: An Agenda for American Education Built on the World's Leading Systems* (Tucker, 2011), *Catching Up: Learning from the Best School Systems in East Asia* (Jensen, Hunter, Sonnermann, & Burns, 2012), and *A World-class Education: Learning from International Models of Excellence and Innovation* (Stewart, 2012). The interest in learning from HPES has led to the publication of two McKinsey reports in 2007 and 2010 respectively. The first McKinsey report (Barber & Mourshed, 2007) acknowledges of the quality of teachers and teacher education as key contributors to the quality of the of education system – with the clarion call that the performance of an education system can only be as high as the quality of its teachers.

This implies that education policy needs to converge its policies to attract its finest students of each cohort into the teaching profession. There appears to be some truth as the successful jurisdictions do attract top performers into teacher education, for example, the top 5–10 % in Finland and South Korea and the top 10–30 % in Singapore and Hong Kong SAR.

While the first McKinsey report attempts to tease out lessons from the top 10 education systems, the ambition of the second McKinsey report (Mourshed, Chijioke, & Barber, 2010) was to further confine itself to the lessons from the top five education systems, and it adapted James Collins' concept of 'good to great' into a systemic analysis, also adding a new category called 'great to excellent'. As mentioned, the second report also began to look at the leadership of the education system as a possible factor, in terms of the leaders staying in office for at least 7 years. This implies a need for determination, commitment and persistence in implementing education reform agendas in the respective jurisdictions.

In addition to the McKinsey reports, the OECD published a report entitled *Strong Performers and Successful Performers in Education: Lessons from PISA for the United States* (2011) following the publication of the PISA results. Obviously, this was a study commissioned by the US. The Foreword of the report particularly noted Obama's endeavour in launching one of the world's most ambitious education reform agendas, namely the 'Race to the Top' initiative. For the US, the middle ranking obtained in the PISA 2010 has created today's 'Sputnik' crisis, another call for emergency since the last emergency call by 'A Nation at Risk' in 1983 (National Commission on Excellence in Education, 1983), raising a question whether the US is 'still a nation at risk'.

The publications provided constructive suggestions about how legacy systems could improve by abandoning policies and practices that have shown insignificant progress and investing their resources. The publications also raised evidence to justify the influence of cultural differences, Confucian values, rote learning, size (of system and classes) and expenditure on high achievement and equity through a closer examination and comparison of these systems. These findings have indicated that all education systems are capable of performing and levelling up, and not just systems that have inherited the 'right' conditions.

The Growing Significance of Teachers as a Human Factor for National Development

For a long time, education development has been influenced by human capital theories that focused on manpower forecasting, and education attainments that would indicate the language and numeracy skills plus training in certain disciplines and the level of attainment that may indicate the human capital quality which would further indicate the competitiveness of a certain country. Associated with these foci are such concerns as rates of return for education investment; efficiency and effectiveness of the education system; the school that delivers the training for the students, and, thus, quality assurance of the schools in terms of effectiveness and efficiency, as well as quality management from the perspectives of total quality management for a learning organisation; and the value add of the schools in bringing up students' learning outcomes by the end of schooling, as compared to students' level of knowledge and skills at the point of entry. The conventional concern of educational development, strongly affected by human capital theories, was very much focused on system issues such as qualifications, finance and management, and the measurement of added values. The concerns now are very much system data and factors, rather than human factors (such as teachers and leaders). The discourse began to change when social capital theories began to emerge and gain recognition. Unlike human capital theories that focus on the system factors, social capital theories focus on human factors, such as human relationships, values, and the social fabrics such as collaboration, cooperation and the collectivity that would emphasise social cohesion and social network. The social capital theories argue that human capitals cannot function without social lubrication to make the system factors work (Heffron, 1997; Montgomery, 1997; Putnam, 1995). Diverse, intangible and ambiguous as it may be, the social capital notion has gained momentum and increased attention, and the human factors are increasingly seen as being important in development studies.

The McKinsey Report 2007 (Barber & Mourshed, 2007) basically summarised the predicament of the human capital theories and asked for attention towards the significance of human factors, although the report did not particularly mention social capital theories. The Executive Summary of the Report says:

> Education reform is top of the agenda of almost every country in the world. Yet despite massive increases in spending (last year, the world's governments spent $2 trillion on education) and ambitious attempts at reform, the performance of many school systems has barely improved in decades. (p. 1)

Then the Report turned to the significance of the human factors:

> To find out why some schools succeed where others do not, we studied twenty-five of the world's school systems. . .. We examined what these high-performing school systems have in common and what tools they use to improve student outcomes. The experiences of these top school systems suggests that three things matter most: 1) getting the right people to become teachers; 2) developing them into effective instructors and, 3) ensuring that the system is able to deliver the best possible instruction for every child. (p. 1)

The Report went on to say:

- It was naive to assume that classroom quality would improve just because we changed our structure;
- Get the right people to become teachers (the quality of an education system cannot exceed the quality of its teachers);
- Develop these people into effective instructors (the only way to improve outcomes is to improve instruction);

- Put in place systems and targeted support to ensure that every child is able to benefit from excellent instruction (the only way for the system to reach the highest performance is to raise the standard of every student). (p. 13)

The rest of the Report elaborated on these points, and the Report puts up a significant statement: "The quality of an education system cannot exceed the quality of its teachers" (p. 16). The McKinsey Report 2010 (Mourshed et al., 2010) takes a different approach to analysing education development, trying to identify factors for development from 'fair to good', 'good to great', and 'great to excellent'. However, the human factors continue to be the main line of thought. The 'good to great' journey is characterised by "shaping the teaching profession" (p. 48); and the 'great to excellent' journey is characterised by "improving through peer-led support and teaching innovation" (p. 50). Another human factor that the 2010 Report has identified is the presence of 'strategic leaders' in all high performing countries: "New strategic leaders were found in all reforms we studied, while new political leaders were present in half of them" (p. 97).

Since the McKinsey reports, teachers continue to be the focal point in the examination of success factors. For example, the International Summit convened by the US Secretary of Education Arne Duncan in 2011 was about "Improving Teacher Quality around the World" (Asia Society, 2011). The Grattan Report in 2012 attributed East Asian success to teaching and teachers, such as initial teacher education, induction and mentoring, research and lesson preparation, classroom observation and the teacher career structures in these East Asian countries (Jensen et al., 2012). Particularly mentioned in this report is the significance of group work and peer support among teachers, including master teacher, mentorship and role modelling, group lesson preparation, classroom observations, and a progressive career ladder to reward good teaching. The Grattan Report is almost single-mindedly focusing on the analysis of the significance of teachers in high performing East Asian countries. It notes, in particular, that "the role of teachers is essential: they are partners in reform...The four systems are not afraid to make difficult trade-offs to achieve their goals" (p. 2). Further, in Steward's *A World-class Education* (2012), the success factors are identified as "developing effective teachers and school leaders" and "modernising curriculum, instruction and assessment."

How HPES See Themselves: Common Emphasis on the Significance of the Teaching Professional

While organising this volume and inviting scholars from HPES to do a self-analysis of possible reasons and factors that might explain their own success, in order to know what is regarded as the most pertinent reasons and factors, we deliberately did not provide a template or prompt a range of reasons, unlike what we would do most of the time when developing a book. We simply requested our authors to share with us what should be the most important reasons and factors that might be explainable factors for the success in their own systems. Despite different historical and cultural contexts across HPES, we were surprised with two main threads of thought. First, instead of answering our questions directly, most of our authors wrote to criticise their own systems. Treating this as answers, it implies that continuous self-critique could be a most important factor for success, and this is definitely a necessary pre-requisite for continuous progress of any system. Other common themes standing out from the contributors of this book is a very strong focus on teaching as a profession and on teacher education for strengthening the teaching profession. Our authors in this book invariably regard teachers as an important factor in the course of pursuit for a competent system in their respective jurisdictions. Interestingly, when we asked Professor A. Lin Goodwin to offer her observation about possible explainable factors of success in the countries included in this book, out of the three lessons she managed to draw from these countries, two are related to teachers and teaching:

- Lesson One: Teaching as a high quality profession – Attracting, retaining and sustaining quality
- Lesson Two: Teachers as professionals at the centre of education reform, improvement and accountability (Goodwin, Chap. 11 in this volume)

Below are some of the explanations by our authors in this volume.

Finland

Referring to Finland, Niemi (Chap. 7 in this volume) points out that teacher education is a key player in the Finnish education system. The focus of Finnish teacher education is to develop research-based knowledge, skills and professional culture. The teacher education programmes particularly stress on research training, and to internalise a research-oriented attitude towards their work. Research is seen as central or foundational to teachers' independent thinking, inquiring, scientific literacy, questioning phenomena and knowledge. More importantly, teacher education itself is a research target, so that the system can become a self-generative improvement mechanism. Research is thus fundamental to developing teachers as professionals. As professionals, Niemi says,

> Teachers have to take an active role in raising serious questions about what they teach, how they teach it, and the larger goals towards which they are striving. Teachers need to view themselves as public intellectuals who combine conception and implementation, thinking and practice in the struggle for a culture of democratic values and justice. Teachers have a right and an obligation to articulate educational needs and challenges in the society they serve. They also have to be active in public debates and decisions affecting the development of schools and education. As professionals, teachers cannot only be implementers of decisions, but also partners in their development. Teachers are expected to be able to take an active role in evaluating and improving schools and their learning environments. They are also expected to refresh their professional skills, to cooperate with parents and other stakeholders, and to be active citizens.

South Korea

The significance of teachers in the South Korean education system is almost unparalleled. Cho (Chap. 8 in this volume) states that

> in South Korea, teachers are supposed to supervise students' intellectual, academic, and social development, while parents are to respect teachers as trained professionals.

Cho regards that a teacher is a highly respected and acknowledged professional in South Korea, and a teacher or school principal is ranked first by South Koreans as a preferred job for its job security. Thus, there are far more people who wish to become teachers than the system can absorb, and as a result, only the top 5 % of senior high school graduates can be admitted to a college of education. The teacher–student relationship in South Korea is interesting; as teachers no doubt enjoy high authority in students' mind, teachers also see students as their prime concern, thus creating a "warm authoritarianism" phenomenon in South Korea. This provides a specific balance between teachers' authority and their love towards their students, which together blend a specific meaning of respect towards teachers.

Shanghai

The Shanghai chapter in this book almost exclusively attributes their success to teacher and teacher education, and this theme dominates the whole chapter. Zhang, Xu and Sun (Chap. 9 in this volume) suggest that there are four features that can be accountable for the strengths of the Shanghai education system, namely:

- strong in-service professional development system;
- cooperation among teachers, schools, government and universities;
- admiration of school-based professional activities and teachers' practical knowledge and innovation; and
- the government's encouragement and financial support for teacher professional development.

The Shanghai chapter provides details of school-based training and professional activities, including mentorship for new teachers, teaching and research groups, lesson preparation groups, grade groups, classroom observation and classroom evaluation, task-driven training, and vacation training and school visits. The Chinese education system has a strong belief in the role modelling of the master teacher, thus mentorship is penetrating through the whole school system. Beginning teachers typically have two mentors, one for classroom management and another one for subject-specific guidance. A significant part of mentorship is mutual classroom observation, based on which pedagogical issues are discussed.

There is a strong research culture in Chinese schools. Zhang et al. cite a national survey in 2010 that 87.6 % teachers were engaged in teaching and research group

(TRG) activities once a week over the past 2 years, and 54.4 % participated in these activities more than once a week. Collective lesson preparation is another distinctive feature in the Chinese school system, and Lesson Learning Groups (LPG) are established generally in schools. Lesson planning has consumed a significant amount of teachers' time in school, because it is done in groups. But it shows how significant lesson planning is for teaching in China, and the group planning is itself a venue for professional interaction between teachers to look for better pedagogical approaches or models to teach certain subjects and topics. Zhang et al. regard that LPG is an important form of professional development for teachers. TRG and LPG together pay a role in enhancing lesson planning capability and classroom teaching skills of teachers, and thus also contribute to the sustainable development of teachers' professional standards.

Hong Kong

To Esther Ho (Chap. 10 in this volume), Hong Kong's education success is attributable to a high degree of teacher participation in decision-making in several significant areas related to the school curriculum and students' learning. These areas are:

- instruction, which includes deciding on the courses to offer, course contents and textbooks;
- student affairs, which includes admission, assessment and discipline; and
- budgeting, which includes allocation of resources and budgeting.

The example Ho particularly cited is the curriculum reform in mathematics. According to a study by Fok, Wong, Tang, Ngan, and Wong (2009), the Education Bureau in Hong Kong had adopted various effective decentralised strategies in curriculum reform while the reform was driven centrally. From the examination of the math curriculum reform in Hong Kong, they suggest that a reform using centralised top–down approaches must accept voices from the bottom–up, especially those from professional associations so as to close the gap between policy and implementation. Overall, researchers attribute the success of Hong Kong's basic education to the balance between various decentralised strategies under the government's centrally driven educational development.

Singapore

Very much like the Shanghai chapter, but in a different manner, Lee and Low (Chap. 4 in this volume) view teacher training in the Singapore mainly from the perspective of how the National Institute of Education (NIE), NTU – the only teacher education institution in Singapore – prepares teachers for the national need, particularly for Singapore's national agenda of developing twenty-first century skills for students. This is a serious agenda of NIE; and because of this, NIE has set up a Programme Review and Enhancement initiative in 2008 to plot the future direction of teacher preparation, and published a report in 2009, entitled *TE21: A Teacher Education Model for the 21st Century* (NIE, 2009). The Report sets the teacher education direction for Singapore in preparing twenty-first century teachers. Very much like the statement of the McKinsey Report 2007 that "The quality of an education system cannot exceed the quality of its teachers" (Barber & Mourshed, 2007, p. 16), Singapore's TE21 Report says: "21st century learners call for 21st century teachers" (NIE, 2009, p. 22) and the Singapore teachers have to become twenty-first century teaching professionals. The vision for twenty-first century teachers go beyond knowledge, it requires teachers to nurture the whole child, and requires teachers to acquire new knowledge, skills and dispositions to ensure the child's survival and success as individuals, as members of the community, and as citizens of the nation.

Singapore's 21st century competence (21CC) agenda penetrates the education system, and students' learning outcomes are clearly shaped and stipulated in MOE's official website (see Fig. 4.1 in this volume). Most important among the 21CC attributes are self-directed learner, active contributor, confident person and concerned citizen. NIE's teacher education model aligns with the national goal to develop 21CC teachers and the TE21 Report also develops a set of Graduand Teacher Competencies (GTCs), so that twenty-first century students are to be taught by twenty-first century teachers. These attributes are contained in a framework that covers the three major dimensions of teacher capacity, namely professional practice, leadership and management and personal effectiveness (see Table 4.4 in this volume). Other emphases in the TE21 Report include a values-driven underpinning philosophy, learner-centredness with a belief that all students can learn, developing a strong sense of teacher identity, and contribution to the profession and the community. In addition, all NIE student teachers are required to develop a reflective tool and culture by enrolling in the Institute's Teaching and Learning e-Portfolio which they will share during teaching practice, so that there will be objective information for each teacher to see their teacher learning trajectories for further self-improvement as they embark on their journey as professional teachers. Lee and Low emphasise that Singapore's education success is an outcome of its insistence on a tripartite collaborative operation model that will ensure alignment and coherence between MOE, NIE and schools. MOE ensures coherence between policy and practice; NIE ensures a theory–practice linkage that will lead to coherence between research and practice; and schools closely work with MOE and NIE to feed baseline data for them to understand the realities in school, ensure access to classrooms for pedagogical research, and to help develop a research culture in school and to share their findings with other schools in the communities of practice (CoP).

Teacher, Teaching and Teacher Education: Common Factors, Different Practices

Attributing teacher, teaching and teacher education as common factors notwithstanding, how these factors are deployed within each system varies. How different authors in this volume describe the way they look at teachers, prepare teachers and their function in contributing to high performance or success are also remarkably different. The Shanghai and Singapore chapters (Chaps. 9 and 4 in this volume) are closer to each other in explaining how the teacher education programme prepares high performing teachers, how the teachers' career ladder system produces master teachers and mentors, and how the lesson preparation and lesson studies provide research to produce high quality teaching. They focus on ensuring good training, good system and good practices that will ensure high quality teaching and learning outcomes. The South Korea chapter (Chap. 8 in this volume) focuses on the prestige of the teachers, the respect accorded to teachers, and the job security of teachers, all of which help attract top talents to aspire for teaching. The major line of thought is also that with good teachers, there ought to be good teaching, and as a result these should give rise to good learning outcomes.

However, the Finnish and Hong Kong chapters describe the role of teachers quite differently. For example, Niemi's (Chap. 7 in this volume) focus is on Finnish teacher research and to internalise research in the process of teacher education as a significant expectation for the teachers to function effectively in the teaching profession. To Niemi, the core of the teaching profession relies on teachers' research ability. While I assume all teachers teach, Niemi's message is teacher's research abilities precede or determine how well teachers will improve their future teaching through research that feeds back into their practice. Goodwin (Chap. 11 in this volume) offers an interesting observation about the Finnish teachers:

> It would surprise most Americans to know that teachers in Finland not only teach about half the time required of American teachers, they "do not need to be present at school if they do not have classes." However, Sahlberg is quick to point out that this does not mean Finnish teachers work less hard than elsewhere, but instead that part of their work is "devoted to school improvement and work with community".

Obviously, how Finnish teachers contribute to the country's high performance might not be reflected in their direct teaching performance, but their improvement to the learning environment and the research quality that will further their understanding of what they teach and how they teach. Goodwin further elaborates on how Finnish teachers may function differently from teachers in Singapore and Hong Kong, citing OECD's observation that the Finnish teachers "are encouraged to contribute to the knowledge based on effective teaching practices throughout their career" (OECD, 2011, p. 237) while the Chinese "methods for improving their education system over time relies on research performed by teachers" (p. 237).

Ho's (Chap. 10 in this volume) interpretation of the success factors is similar to those of Niemi and Goodwin in that she did not particularly examine the teaching ability of teachers, whether there would be a career path for teachers or whether the school environment was encourage teachers to improve their lesson plan and teaching practices. Instead, she espoused about whether the education system provides teachers with the autonomy to make judgments and to allow teachers to develop school-based solutions about which more important aspects of teachers' contribution if teachers are regarded as a factor of success. To quote:

> In search of the success factors beyond the current education reform, the present chapter argues that the dynamic interaction between decentralisation of SBM [School-based Management] and centralisation policy of multilevel assessment might be the key contributor. Decentralisation policy provides flexibility for schools to make decisions in allocating resources and top diversify and innovate teaching and learning process. This allows the government to decrease its involvement in direct policy implementation but to increase the autonomy of school leaders and teachers and involvement of parents to make changes at the school level to better serve the students.

Ho further elaborated that in the 10 years after the Hong Kong government has introduced School-based Management (SBM) from the School Management Initiatives (SMI), teacher participation was gradually enhanced as reflected in PISA 2009, especially in the areas of instruction and assessment. She found that the SBM evolved into different forms – shared, teacher-driven, principal-driven or centralised forms, and among these various forms, the 'shared' form showed the strongest association with students' learning outcomes, followed by 'teacher-driven' and 'principal-driven' forms.

Conclusion

The value of this book, as aforementioned, lies in the insider's effort to seek the perspectives of other insiders to respond to the international quests for success factors that might explain high student performance in various international assessment exercises in the case studies focused on in this book. As there are many efforts organised to look into success factors internationally, we feel a call to initiate a self-analysis as well. When we organised this book, we also tried not to develop a template or guide the authors in identifying what could compose a macro map of factors. In order to tap what lies in the hearts of our authors as the most authentic and pertinent questions of concern or explainable success factors, we welcomed the authors sharing whatever was considered important to them. This approach does bring up two major findings. As mentioned above, most of our authors record debates, controversies, issues and criticism, rather than celebrating success. As a comparativist, I have had the opportunity of participating in many academic and teacher meetings in most of the jurisdictions involved in this book project, and my experience has been quite alarming. Instead of celebration, they mostly criticise how unsatisfactory their situations are, where they felt they have lagged behind, where the gaps of achievements are, and where the inequalities lie. The insider picture is not one of celebration, but of self-criticism. The first finding in organising this book is that this invariable self-criticism could be the most significant drive for these HPES to perform better, not really better than other countries, but more often the discussion was about how to out-perform what they are currently able to perform. I witness this strong drive among HPES whenever I participate in their internal discussions.

The second amazing finding in organising this book is the emergence of the common themes: teachers, teaching and teacher education. HPES are paying overwhelming attention to strengthening their teachers as professionals, and seeking to improve teacher performance. The focus of attention though is quite different, for example:

- Shanghai focuses on the teacher education system and professional practice: the teacher's career ladder in schools, the master teacher and mentorship scheme, peer observation, and group lesson planning.
- Singapore emphasises the tripartite alignment between MOE, NIE and schools, and how GTCs are designed to prepare Singapore teachers to become twenty-first century teachers, and the strong belief in the development of twenty-first century skills for twenty-first century teachers.
- South Korea emphasises how respect towards teachers can become a foundation of the whole society that would attract the best talents to aspire to become teachers and to empower teachers to exercise their authorities, yet, their love towards students forms a unique phenomenon of 'warm authoritarianism'.
- Finland focuses on the research ability of teachers as a foundation for the development of the teaching profession, and how the internalisation of research is pertinent to facilitate teaching in order to foster an inquisitive mind and how the research mind can become a driver for teachers to aspire to make teaching a self-improving profession. Finland's respect for teachers may not lie in their authority, but in the autonomy where the society gives them a high degree of trust, rather than scrutinising them with a stringent accountability system.
- Likewise, Hong Kong's finding is that Hong Kong's high performance may be more attributable to the decentralisation of the school system, which provides autonomy to teachers for school-based developed instruction and assessment.

The summary of findings from the selected HPES participating in this book project shows how teacher, teaching and teacher education are unanimously seen as factors of success, yet they serve a different kind of factors in each jurisdiction. The limitation of our approach to soliciting factors accounting for success is typical of that of qualitative research – we cannot find representative factors, but instead, we have found typological ones. If we treat the above summary of findings for each jurisdiction as a typology developed from each of them, they form a pretty macro picture about how we can construct a system of teacher, teaching and teacher education that could form an overall productive success factor for our readers to consider. We need a rigorous teacher education system and strong peer-supported teaching practice (Shanghai), an alignment of policy and implementation as well as theory and practice (Singapore), a respectful system to ensure the best talents would want to become teachers (South Korea), an internalised research mind for teachers, and trust towards teachers in exercising their professional autonomy (Finland), and a decentralised school system to allow teachers to make school-based judgements and decisions on instruction and assessment (Hong Kong).

References

Asia Society. (2011). *Improving teacher quality around the world: The international summit on the teaching profession*. New York: Authors.

Barber, M., & Mourshed, M. (2007). *How the world's best performing schools come out on top*. London: McKinsey & Company.

Fok, P. K., Wong, N. Y., Tang, K. C., Ngan, M. Y., & Wong, K. L. (2009). 鑑古識今:從課程發展策略的視角看課程改革 [Learning from the past: To review curriculum reform from the perspective of curriculum development strategies]. *Hong Kong Teachers' Centre Journal, 8*, 73–85.

Heffron, J. M. (1997). Defining values. In J. D. Montgomery (Ed.), *Values in education: Social capital formation in Asia and the Pacific* (pp. 3–23). Middlesex, UK: Hollis Publishing.

Jensen, B., Hunter, A., Sonnermann, J., & Burns, T. (2012). *Catching up: Learning from the best school systems in East Asia*. Melbourne, Australia: Grattan Institute.

Ministry of Education (MOE), Singapore. (2009). *Inaugural international education roundtable shares insights on expectations and challenges for top performing education systems for the future*. Retrieved from http://www.moe.gov.sg/media/press/2009/07/inaugural-international-educat.php

Montgomery, J. D. (1997). Are Asian values different? In J. D. Montgomery (Ed.), *Values in education: Social capital formation in Asia and the Pacific* (pp. 29–47). Middlesex, UK: Hollis Publishing.

Mourshed, M., Chijioke, C., & Barber, M. (2010). *How the world's most improved school systems keep getting better*. London: McKinsey & Company.

National Institute of Education (NIE). (2009). *TE21: A teacher education model for the 21st century*. Singapore: National Institute of Education, NTU. Retrieved from http://www.nie.edu.sg/files/spcs/Te21_online_ver.pdf

National Commission on Excellence in Education. (1983). *A nation at risk: The imperative for education reform*. Washington, DC: U.S. Department of Education.

OECD. (2011). *Strong performers and successful performers in education: Lessons from PISA for the United States*. Paris: Author.

Putnam, R. D. (1995). Bowling alone: America's declining social capital. *Journal of Democracy, 6*(1), 65–78.

Schultz, W., Ainley, J., Fraillon, J., Kerr, D., & Losito, B. (2010). *ICCS 2009 international report: Civic knowledge, attitudes and engagement among lower secondary school students in 38 countries*. Amsterdam: International Association for the Evaluation of Educational Achievement (IEA).

Stewart, V. (2012). *A world-class education: Learning from international models of excellence and innovation*. Alexandria, VA: ASCD.

Tucker, M. (2011). *Surpassing Shanghai: An agenda for American education built on the world's leading systems*. Cambridge, MA: Harvard Education Press.

Biographies

Andreas Schleicher is Education Policy Advisor to the Secretary-General of OECD. As Division Head of the Indicators and Analysis Division of the OECD Directorate since 2002, he is responsible for the development and analysis of benchmarks on the performance of education systems and the impact of knowledge and skills on economic and social outcomes, including the Programme for International Student Assessment (PISA), the Programme for the International Assessment of Adult Competencies (PIAAC), the Programme for Measurement on Teachers, Teaching and Learning and the Education Indicators Programme (INES). Before joining the OECD in 1994, he was Director for Analysis at the International Association for Educational Achievement (IEA). Professor Schleicher studied Physics in Germany and received a degree in Mathematics and Statistics in Australia. He is the recipient of numerous honours and awards, including the *Theodor Heuss* prize, awarded in the name of the first president of the Federal Republic of Germany for *exemplary democratic engagement*. He holds an honorary professorship at the University of Heidelberg.

Anne Lin Goodwin is Professor of Education and Vice Dean at Teachers College, Columbia University, New York. Her research and writing focus on the connections between teachers' identities and their development; between multicultural understandings and curriculum enactments; and on the particular issues facing Asian American teachers and students in U.S. schools. She has published widely in key education journals and is the editor of several books. Recent articles include: Curriculum as colonizer: (Asian) American education in the current U.S. context, Teachers College Record, and *Globalization and the preparation of quality teachers: Rethinking knowledge domains for teaching*, in Teaching Education. She has a chapter forthcoming in a volume edited by Linda Darling-Hammond and Ann Lieberman entitled, *Quality Teachers, Singapore Style*. Professor Goodwin has served as a consultant to a wide variety of organizations around issues of teacher education, diversity, and assessment. She has been privileged to collaborate with educators in the Middle East, Europe and Asia to bring about school, teaching and curriculum reform.

S.K. Lee et al. (eds.), *Educational Policy Innovations: Levelling Up and Sustaining Educational Achievement*, Springer Education Innovation Book Series 1,
DOI 10.1007/978-981-4560-08-5, © Springer Science+Business Media Singapore 2014

Ben Levin is a Professor at the Ontario Institute for Studies in Education, University of Toronto, where he is Canada Research Chair in Education Leadership and Policy. He has served as Deputy Minister for Education for the Province of Ontario and as Deputy Minister of Advanced Education and Deputy Minister of Education, Training and Youth for Manitoba. Dr. Levin is widely known for his work in educational reform, educational change, educational policy and politics. He holds a B.A. (Honours) from the University of Manitoba, an Ed. M. from Harvard University and a Ph.d. from OISE.

Chuangyuan Sun obtained his Ph.d. from Shanghai Normal University and is currently lecturing courses on teacher professional development at Shanghai Open University.

Ee Ling Low is Associate Dean for Programme and Student Development at the Office of Teacher Education, National Institute of Education, Singapore and is concurrently an Associate Professor of English Language and Literature. Previously, she was Sub-dean for Degree Programmes (2004–2009). She obtained her Ph.d. in Linguistics from the University of Cambridge, UK under a Nanyang Technological University–National Institute of Education Overseas Graduate Scholarship. In 2008, she won the Fulbright Advanced Research Scholarship which she spent at the Lynch School of Education at Boston College. She was a visiting professor at the Department of Linguistics at Chulalongkorn University in June 2008. She has published several books on English linguistics and phonetics, and many journal articles and book chapters on speech rhythm, stress and intonation and initial teacher education. In 2008–2010, she served as the Executive Director of the Asia-Pacific Educational Research Association (APERA), a role for which she was awarded fellowship of APERA in recognition of her dedication and commitment to her service in 2010. In 2012, she was awarded a Public Service Administration (Bronze) medal by the President of the Republic of Singapore in recognition of her dedication and commitment to the cause of Education in Singapore.

Esther Sui Chu Ho is a faculty member at the Department of Educational Administration and Policy, and Director of the Hong Kong Centre for International Student Assessment within the Faculty of Education at the Chinese University of Hong Kong. With her extensive experience and expertise in teaching in Hong Kong primary and secondary schools, Professor Ho's contributions extend to policy-making in the Hong Kong education system. Professor Ho has been involved in a number of award-winning research projects on Home– School Collaboration and International Studies in Education and was awarded the Fulbright Scholarship to Pennsylvania State University (2004) and Johns Hopkins University (2010). She served as a research and teaching consultant to the World Bank in the national project "District Primary Educational Programme, India" and was Principal Investigator of Home–School Collaboration Projects (1999–2001 and 2001–2004) and Hong Kong PISA Projects (PISA 2000+ to PISA 2012). Her research interests include sociology of education, parental involvement, home–school community collaboration, school effectiveness and school reform, decentralisation and school-based management, research methodology in education, multilevel analysis in educational research.

Hannele Niemi is Professor of Education at the Faculty of Behavioural Sciences, University of Helsinki, Finland. She also Chair of the CICERO Learning Network for multi-disciplinary research on learning. She has contributed in many EU and OECD projects as an expert or researcher and served as a keynote lecturer in several international forums, for example, in Hungary, Slovenia, Spain, Portugal, German, Norway, Sweden, Scotland, England, France, and Estonia. Her main research interest areas are teachers' professional development, moral education, and technology-based learning environments. She has published several articles and books on education in Finland and Finnish teacher education (e.g., Research-Based Teacher Education in Finland, 2006 and Education as a Societal Contributor, 2007) and contributed in many international education research publications (e.g., Evidence in Education, Linking Research and Policy, OECD/CERI, 2007). She has published in ten languages. During the past 20 years, she has been a chairperson or a researcher in many national and international evaluation projects for development of educational research and teacher education.

Jocelyn Shi Yah Tan is a Research Associate at the National Institute of Education, Nanyang Technological University, Singapore. She received her Bachelor in Information Systems Management from Singapore Management University, Post-graduate Diploma in Education from the National Institute of Education, Nanyang Technological University and a Masters in Teaching English to Young Learners from University of York. She was awarded the Ministry of Education (MOE) Overseas English Language Study Award in 2010. Her areas of interest include comparative studies, education governance, education policies, teacher education and educational leadership and administration.

Junjie Xu obtained her Ph.d. from East-China Normal University and is currently undertaking her post-doctoral studies at Shanghai Normal University. She is a team member of PISA-Shanghai.

Laik Woon Teh is Senior Fellow at the Office of Education Research, National Institute of Education, Singapore and Principal Research Specialist, Ministry of Education (MOE), Singapore. He graduated from Trinity Hall, University of Cambridge, UK with a Physics and Theoretical Physics Tripos as a Public Service Commission Scholar. He furthered his education by obtaining a Master's in Administration and Social Policy from the Graduate School of Education, Harvard University. He then obtained his Ph.d. on an MOE postgraduate scholarship from the Graduate School of Education, University of California, Berkeley, specialising in Quantitative Methods and Evaluation. Dr. Teh's research interest is the application of statistical and measurement models in policy analysis and programme evaluation. In his 10-year MOE career, he has completed numerous studies that apply multilevel models, structural equation models, Rasch models, propensity score matching and Heckman selection models to estimate the causal effects of policies and programmes. The findings of these studies have motivated new policies and programmes as well as their refinements in Singapore. Dr. Teh participates actively in the economics and social research network of the Singapore Public Service and is on the advisory panel of a research fund of MOE.

Minxuan Zhang is the Dean of the Shanghai Normal University and Deputy Director of the Shanghai Municipal Education Commission. Since joining the Shanghai Normal University in 1986, Dr. Zhang has continued to undertake research on educational finance, the economics of education and university student loan schemes. Because of his wide ranging experiences in academic studies and research in Hong Kong (Comparative Education Research Centre), the United Kingdom (College of Education, Oxford), the United States of America and Canada, Dr. Zhang has been involved in the launching of educational reforms in mainland China. In 2001 he received his Ph.d. from the University of Hong Kong. For several years, Dr. Zhang has undertaken research and provided policy advice nationally and overseas in more than ten different areas.

Sing Kong Lee is Director of the National Institute of Education (NIE), Singapore and Managing Director of NIE International. He led in the articulation of the 3:3:3 Roadmap, which outlines NIE's strategic directions from 2007 to 2012. In 2007, he served as the Inaugural Chair of the International Alliance of Leading Education Institutes, putting NIE firmly in the global league of teacher education providers. Among his many awards received are the Public Administration Medal (Bronze) (1981), Save Planet Earth Merit Award (1992), Asian Innovation Award (Bronze) (1998), Chevalier dans l'Ordre des Palmes Academiques (1999), National Technology Award 2000, Urban Agriculture Award (2000), Excellence for Singapore Award (2001), Singapore Innovation Award (2001), Public Administration Medal (Silver) (2004), Fellow of the Singapore Institute of Biology (2005), and the National University of Singapore Distinguished Alumni in Science Award (2009). Professor Lee was most recently awarded the Public Administration Medal (Gold) in 2011 by the President of the Republic of Singapore. In 2011, he was awarded the Medal of honour for the case of education in Vietnam by the Ministry of Education and Training of Vietnam. In 2012, he was conferred honorary professorship by Xinjiang Normal University and in 2013, he was another two awards, the Nanyang Award for Service by Nanyang Technological University and the Medal for Distinguished Service 2013, awarded by Teachers College, Columbia University.

Wing On Lee is Dean of Education Research at the National Institute of Education, Singapore. He is also President of the World Council of Comparative Education Societies and Honorary Professor of Education at the University of Sydney and University of Hong Kong. Professor Lee is a world-renowned scholar in the fields of comparative education, citizenship education, and moral and values education. He has published over 28 books and 140 journal articles and book chapters. He received the Medal of Honour from the Hong Kong Government in 2003 and the Hong Kong Soka Gakkai Association International Award in 2010. He has obtained research funding of over HK$34 million during his academic service in Hong Kong. Professor Lee has been Visiting/Honorary Professor at a number of universities in the UK, USA and Chinese Mainland. He has served as a consultant to the World Bank and Asian Development Bank, and is a member of the International Advisory Board of Mongolian Education Alliance.

Author Index

S.K. Lee et al. (eds.), *Educational Policy Innovations: Levelling Up and Sustaining Educational Achievement*, Springer Education Innovation Book Series 1,
DOI 10.1007/978-981-4560-08-5,

Subject Index

S.K. Lee et al. (eds.), *Educational Policy Innovations: Levelling Up and Sustaining Educational Achievement*, Springer Education Innovation Book Series 1,
DOI 10.1007/978-981-4560-08-5, © Springer Science+Business Media Singapore 2014

Lightning Source UK Ltd.
Milton Keynes UK
UKHW02n2307270318
320122UK00003B/84/P

9 789814 560078